Well-written, full of insights and drama, wisdom and penetrating truth. This book is anointed to deliver multitudes from the outpouring of darkness that has entered our society through pornography. I urge every pastor and counselor, everyone who truly loves the church and shares the hope of seeing God's people cleansed for Christ's return, to use the information in Laurie Hall's *An Affair of the Mind.*

Francis Frangipane,
Author, Senior Pastor of
River of Life Church, and
Director of Advancing Church Ministries

Many women will identify with Laurie Hall's pain, but I believe many others will find the strength to face their husbands' problems and be inspired with the knowledge that God can bring healing and hope to the most broken of families.

Len Munsil,
Executive Director and General Counsel,
National Family Legal Foundation

Never have I read such a realistic approach to the healing process of the spouse of a sex addict. Laurie Hall's thoughts will definitely enable other wives to look at themselves and their own recovery instead of their husbands' addiction.

Neal Clement, Director,
American Family Association

An Affair of the Mind generates a deeper understanding of the hidden devastation sex addicts bring to their families. It is must reading for every pastor and every couple caught in this snare.

The Rev. Vernon Stoop, Jr.,
Executive Director,
Focus Renewal Ministries

For all who wonder about the epidemic called "sexual addiction" sweeping across our land, *An Affair of the Mind* is a valuable source of information and insight. I recommend it highly.

Carolyn H. McKenzie,
Executive Director,
Citizens for Community Values,
Memphis, Tenn.

I strongly recommend this book to anyone either trapped in this addiction or living with someone who is trapped. This book is a "must" reading for pastors, counselors, youth leaders, and others who work with hurting individuals and families.

Ardyce A. Miller,
Executive Director,
Freedom Ministries Training
and Counseling Center

It's time that pornography is faced as the very real problem it is for many Christian families. . . . Every time I speak, women ask where they can get help . . . to understand the problem and how to win the battle for their husbands and families. Now, finally, I can recommend Laurie Hall's *An Affair of the Mind*.

Karen Holgate, Executive Director,
h.o.p.e. (help oppose pornography and
exploitation)

They say pornography is a victimless crime. As a former porn addict of 25 years, I know better. The truth revealed in Laurie Hall's *An Affair of the Mind* could change forever the way our society views pornography. . . . Not since Dr. James Dobson's film *A Winnable War* has there been a more important resource for counselors, pastors, and every man and woman.

Phil Burress, President,
Citizens for Community Values,
Cincinnati, Ohio

An Affair of the Mind should be read by everyone who could possibly ever be called upon to council or comfort a victim of pornography. . . . It is a powerful resource straight from a victim who received her comfort directly from God.

Bob Anderson, President,
Oklahomans for Children and Families

FOCUS ON THE FAMILY®

An Affair

OF THE MIND

BY LAURIE HALL

TYNDALE

Tyndale House Publishers, Wheaton, Illinois

AN AFFAIR OF THE MIND

Library of Congress Cataloging-in-Publication Data
Hall, Laurie, 1951–
    An affair of the mind : one woman's courageous battle to salvage her family
from the devastation of pornography / Laurie Hall.
    p.   cm.
    Includes bibliographical references.
    ISBN 1-56179-464-3
    1. Pornography—Religious aspects—Christianity. 2. Marriage—Religious
aspects—Christianity. 3. Men—Sexual behavior. I. Title.
BV4597.6.H35   1996
241'.667—dc20   96-10500
                                                                       CIP

A Focus on the Family Book Published by
Tyndale House Publishers, Wheaton, Illinois 60189

Unless otherwise identified, Scripture quotations are taken from *The Amplified Bible,* copyright © 1958, 1962, 1964 by The Lockman Foundation. Used by permission. All rights reserved.

Some names of case studies mentioned in this book have been changed to protect the privacy of the individuals involved.

Focus on the Family books are available at special quantity discounts when purchased in bulk by corporations, organizations, churches, or groups. Special imprints, messages, and excerpts can be produced to meet your needs. For more information, contact: Sales Dept., Focus on the Family, 8605 Explorer Dr., Colorado Springs, CO 80920; or phone (719) 531-3400.

Editors: Gwen Ellis and Michele A. Kendall
Cover Design: Praco, Ltd.

Printed in the United States of America

15 16 17 18 19 20 R 02

To Promise Keepers

Contents

Note from the Publisher

Pornography is not a pleasant subject. Every year Focus on the Family corresponds with thousands of families who have been impacted by porn's evil grip, sometimes to the point of devastation. Therefore, we have chosen to publish *An Affair of the Mind*. The author of this book attempts to honestly confront the evil realities of pornography addiction and its impact on families. She does so by sharing her personal experience and pain. In the process of sharing the hard truth, it has been necessary to include certain material that may be offensive to some readers due to its direct and graphic nature. It is not our goal to shock or embarrass readers, but to equip them to recognize and confront the symptoms of sexual addiction. For those who may wish to skip the most graphic portions of this book, we have included a cautionary statement at the beginning of several chapters.

Sadly, the realities described in this book are more pervasive than any of us wish to believe. But they must be faced. We wish to express our appreciation to the author for her candor and willingness to help others with her story. It is our hope that thousands of families will find hope and freedom through her message.

Acknowledgments

I've noticed that people often treat the acknowledgments in a book like they do the begats in the Old Testament—they yawn and skip right past them. That's a pity. The acknowledgments tell you the story behind the story.

For those of you who want to know how I ever survived, the first caring people God surrounded me with were my Gammie and Gampie Moison and my Aunt Muriel and Uncle Chan Ruckstuhl and Aunt Jeanne and Uncle Jim Tate. Their love for me has been steadfast throughout my life. They have always been there for me, even when they couldn't understand my pain, even when watching me struggle made their hearts hurt, too.

Then, there are my children, all four of them—the two I bore and the two who have come into my heart through marriage. They are the bright, shining moments that let me know God heard my cries and gave me wonderful gifts in the midst of a marriage that brought great pain. And I couldn't ask for any better neighbors than Ralph and Hazel Urie, who after welcoming this hurting family into their hearts and home, became my daughter's in-laws. Then, there are my husband's family. Even though this whole ordeal has been difficult for them, they have tried their best to understand and be supportive.

Friends can be closer than a brother and I've been privileged to have friends who truly are. There's Paul and Arlene Marquis. Arlene held me when I cried like a baby and sang lullabies to me. Paul kept my Mac II up and running and was also the brother who made my husband face his addiction (I'll always love you for that, Paul!). Jim and Teresa Quinn gave us the gift of our Marriage Encounter weekend and the very precious gift of sharing their hearts and lives with us over the last 17 years. Teresa taught me how to be honest with myself. She always believed in me, and she helped me to believe in myself.

Bonnie and Marty Betz have opened their hearts and home to us too many times to count. Bonnie helped me muddle through the outline of this book, and she also was a wonderful sounding board for some of the new (to me) truths

God was teaching me. Marty always has places to go and people to annoy. He's a great big marshmallow who keeps me laughing.

Then, there's Mark and Sharon Brook. Mark encouraged me to become a runner, which helped me rebuild my lungs after they turned to squash rot from having pneumonia three times. My running gave me the physical stamina to write this book. Sharon is my partner in learning more about the work and ministry of the Holy Spirit. She also graciously edited the rough copy of this book in record time, and she sure found out how often I *loose* my *judgement* (this is a private joke).

Lyn Steriti and I have been through some tough times together. I can always call Lyn and tell her exactly how I'm feeling—I never need to pretend to be doing better than I am. Dianne Jungkman is one of the most courageous women I know. She has helped me become wise in places where I didn't have a clue.

Fred and Berta Saldana have been a quiet, safe place for my husband to go. Fred has been a real brother, and Berta always has thought-provoking conversation. Rich and Cynthia Larson graciously let us camp out on their farm during our five months of homelessness. Ed and Debbie Sprogis, Brian and Freddie Jones, Clayton Burnham, Alan and Ann Marie Stevens all reached out to my husband during our separation.

Richard Brannon, my husband's old army buddy, tracked us down and called one night when I really needed to hear from someone. Richard, you'll never know how much hope your call and flowers gave me. Jane George Shaw is a very special friend. Jane constantly encourages me to be all I can be. She's been a steady support during this book's labor.

Gail Sciara and Kathy Duncan, my midwifery friends, have given us the great gift of learning more about what it means to have a personal relationship with our heavenly Daddy.

Finally, I count it a great privilege to know some very loving, courageous women who have been willing to open hearts of pain and share with me the tremendous damage pornography has brought into their lives. Their sharing gave me a grid for interpreting my own pain and helped me see patterns of behavior. Neal Clement, of the American Family Association, has helped me verify these patterns of behavior. Neal's work with the sexually addicted is a wonderful gift to the body of Christ.

In the pages of this book, you will read about some clergy who were extremely helpful to us. How wonderful to be able to thank clergy that God used to bless us. Earl Sandifer came into my life only for one sermon, but his impact was lasting.

Earl taught me how to pray, and it changed my life. Stan Rockafellow reminded me that God loves me. Alan Scott kept reminding me that worship is the way out of bondage. Gary Durham graciously checked part of this manuscript for sound theology—for all you theologians out there, any unsound theology is not his fault!

Sir Craig the Bensen, our current pastor, has the unique gift of being able to cut to the chase. He understand what makes you tick, and you can be real with him and he's not shocked. He has brought out beautiful things in me that I didn't even know were there. He is also helping my husband rebuild his mind. Deb Bensen is my special prayer partner. She has unique gifts of encouragement and never fails to let me know about things that could help me grow and be all God wants me to be.

Mike Kriesel and Roland Ludlum opened their churches to us and allowed this hurting couple to come and worship and be prayed for week after week, even though we didn't belong to their congregations. Roland ministered great healing into my spirit through his personal prayers—even though he knew nothing about our situation, God always showed him exactly how to pray! Peter Anderson tried to understand. Father Roger, I can still remember the warmth of your hand on my head when you prayed for us at our Marriage Encounter weekend. You gave me the courage to believe that God does have good plans for us.

No work like this can be accomplished without prayer. Whenever I felt overwhelmed by the enormity of the task, the prayers of Marty Eels, Deb Murray, Chuck Martin, Gracie Brunelle, Steve and Lynne Smith, Sylvia Wilcox, Michael and Yami Morgan, the Cambridge United Church, and the women in my Bible study gave me the strength to go on and the wisdom to figure out how to get to where I needed to go. Gary and Leila Arleth have been dear prayer partners. They have loved us in ways that amaze me and I am very grateful for such good neighbors.

My writer friends have helped me hone my writing skills so I could dare to tackle this project. Ted Tedford, my editor during almost five years of newspaper work, used the slash-and-burn approach to help me learn how to get to the point and make it live. Ted's wife, Marie, as well as Rita Robinson and Ethel Paquin, kept encouraging me that someday I could rise above cub reporter to be a real writer.

"Doc" Saunders took me under his wing and gave me tremendous courage right when I needed it most. Doc, you're the greatest! Steve Laube knew a scared, radioactive chicken when he saw one and did what he could to see that this book got into the right hands. You're a very special guy, Steve!

Gwen Ellis and Al Janssen of Focus on the Family were tireless advocates for this book. They saw its potential and believed in its possibilities. They were willing to wait when the labor took longer than expected. Michele Kendall had the onerous task of doing the final editing work—thanks, Michele. And Kathi Allen provided the cheerful welcome that always made me feel glad I'd called.

Last, but surely not least, are those who've given us good counsel. I learned a lot under the gentle, skillful hands of Pam Kentish and Pam Milosevich. Both Pams understand how a broken heart can lead to a broken body. As they cared for my sick body, they ministered healing into my wounded spirit. Ron and Ardyce Miller were the first light at the end of a very long, dark tunnel. Without their words of life, we would have given up. Charlie Guest has the unique gift of ministering healing to broken hearts. Charlie has ministered life to places where we didn't even know we were dead. Charlie, we love you!

And, of course, there is our most Wonderful Counselor. Thank You, Lord, for forcing me to take You out of my theological boxes and put You in Your rightful place. Thank You that You are so much more loving and more powerful than I could ever have imagined. Thank You that it was an act worthy of You and fitting to Your divine nature that You, for whose sake and by whom all things have their existence, in bringing many sons into glory, should make the Pioneer of their salvation perfect through suffering. For because You Yourself, in Your humanity, have suffered in being tempted, tested, and tried, You were able to immediately run to my cries and assist and relieve me when I was being tempted, tested, and tried. Therefore, I say to the only wise God, my Savior, be blessing and glory and wisdom and power forever.

He drew a circle that shut me out,
Defiled, rejected, a thing to flout.
But love and I had the wit to win;
We drew a circle that took him in.

Victims
of a
Victimless
Crime

My Story

This Is Not a Fairy Tale

I sit huddled in my car, watching weeds tumble carelessly out of the cracks in the pavement in front of a community health clinic. Across the street, wadded papers, blown by a desperate wind, cling nervously to a chain-link fence. In the gutter below, a rat pokes its head out of a pile of cigarette butts.

"Well, you picked this neighborhood," I say to myself, pulling my coat tightly around me as I step out of the car. Anonymity. That was the thing. I glance around nervously. I am pretty sure I don't see anyone I know. More important—does anyone who knows me see *me*?

Inside the clinic, I am Mrs. Nobody. "Don't give your name," the receptionist told me when I'd called about coming in for testing. "Just come forward when your appointment time is announced."

Invisible, I sit flicking through the dog-eared pages of a *Time* magazine. Articles are interrupted by short bursts of nail gnawing. Despite repeated attempts, the nail on my right index finger stubbornly holds its ground. One final teeth-aching jerk rips it off.

"Ten-thirty blood drawing," the receptionist announces.

I stumble to the counter, unknown at a time when I desperately need to be known.

"That will be $20," she says, keeping her eyes on the paper in front of her.

Amazing! For $20 I can have my fortune read. I'd had more expensive meals at McDonald's. I shove a bill in her direction. No telltale check for me. My receipt is a piece of paper with only my personal identification number (PIN) on it.

A nurse motions for me to follow her to the examining room. Cases of condoms and latex gloves are piled high on the counter. I sink into the chair she offers me.

"You've come for AIDS testing?" she asks, handing me a questionnaire after checking to make sure the numbers across the top match the PINs on my receipt.

"Yes."

"I'll give you a few minutes to fill this out," she says, leaving the room.

I stare dully at the paper. The questions are humiliating. Have I been with another woman? Do I have multiple sexual partners? Do I use IV drugs? Do I practice "unusual" sex? No. No. No. No. My pencil gathers force as it goes down the page.

I come to the category labeled "Other." There is no line that reads, "Possibly exposed to sexually transmitted diseases after husband acted out with prostitutes the things he saw in pornographic magazines." It probably never occurred to the people who made up the questionnaire that pornography could be anything other than a victimless crime.

Inside, I'm drowning, swept away in a hurt so big and wide there's no way to reach the other side. *It's one thing to have to deal with the pain of having a husband mess around on you,* I tell myself, *but to face a possible death sentence imposed by the man who promised he'd love, honor, and cherish me and forsake all others, keeping himself only unto me until death due us part? Death! By AIDS?*

The questionnaire is sticking to my palms. I shake it off and bolt for the door.

Stop right now! I tell myself sharply. *This is taking care of you. You need to take care of you.*

I sit back down and grit my teeth.

The door opens. The cheerful nurse reenters and picks up my questionnaire.

"I see you haven't engaged in any high-risk behaviors," she says, glancing at my answers. "Why do you think you need an AIDS test?"

"None of your business," I desperately want to say. But I do the right thing. I give her the answer.

"My husband has a sexual addiction. He's been with other women." I stare straight ahead.

"Oh," she says, looking at me with pity.

I hate this. I really hate this.

"He's getting help now," I mumble lamely.

"That's good."

How can that be "good" if we're not supposed to make value judgments on people's lifestyle choices? I ask myself. *Society tells me I have no right to be upset about this. They tell me that pornography is a victimless crime. That nobody gets hurt when some-body looks at any body. I read somewhere that it's a First Amendment right. The pornographers have a right to make money, Jack has a right to look at it—and I have a right to be sitting here getting an AIDS test.*

I roll up my sleeve. *Let's get this over with.*

"Keep your receipt in a safe place," she says, neatly depositing the telltale vial in the lab tray. "Call in two weeks and read off your PIN so they can check to see if your results are in. Call right away because it can take up to five days to get an appointment."

"An appointment? Can't you just give me the results over the phone?"

"No, we want the social worker to be with you when you find out."

"The social worker! Why?"

"So you don't do anything desperate, and so she can give you lifestyle counseling," she says with a kindness that drips with condescension.

I go back out and sit in the waiting room. It is a little charade we play. When I had called to make my appointment, they told me they couldn't schedule tests for other sexually transmitted diseases at the same time they scheduled an AIDS test. That's because you need a name for the STD tests. You're only a number for the AIDS test. "We don't want to breech confidentiality," the receptionist said after scheduling an appointment for my AIDS test early on the morning of the twenty-eighth.

"Well, what if I don't care if you know who I am?" I asked. "I really don't want to make two trips in. We live a long way out in the country."

"That's the policy."

I see. You're not interested in treating people, you're interested in operating on a series of protocols, I thought.

I hung up and redialed.

"I'd like to schedule a battery of tests for sexually transmitted diseases late on the morning of the twenty-eighth," I said to the receptionist.

"What name is this under?" she asked.

I panicked momentarily. I had intended to give her my real name, but on the first call she'd made it clear she doesn't want to know who I am. Who am I, anyway?

"Laurie Hall," I blurted out. Laurie Hall was my grandmother's name. Suddenly, I felt comforted that she was with me. Yes, Gammie could do this. Yes, I can do this.

So, now I am sitting here in the waiting room of the health clinic trying to pretend that I have changed from PIN 7834-6652-8943 to Laurie Hall. It's finally time for my appointment.

As she calls me back to the examining room, the nurse looks closely at me. "Didn't I see you here earlier?" she seems to say.

She knows. I know. But we pretend we don't know.

The doctor asks me why I need the tests and I tell him.

After the exam, I gather the shreds of my dignity about me and slink out of the clinic, back to the safety of my car.

"They don't even know my name," I cry, pounding the steering wheel.

Over the next two weeks, my thoughts bounce from subject to subject, never alighting long enough to make sense of anything. I think mostly of my children, and my heart twists around itself, squeezing the breath right out of me. If Jack has given me a sexually transmitted disease, I can be treated and go on, but what if I have AIDS? That can't happen to my children. It just can't.

Everything I've ever done since I first knew I was going to be a mother was so they could have a good start in life: writing down everything I ate when I was pregnant; not taking any medication in labor because what comforted me might hurt them; nursing them to build up their immune systems and make them feel secure; making sure they had their naps and their fruits and vegetables.

If I have AIDS, who will take care of my babies? And they'll always be ashamed. Who wants to tell someone their mother died of AIDS? How could I let this happen to them? What if Jack has it and he dies first, and I'm sick and all alone with the children? Who will take care of them? The bile of panic rises in my throat. I push it down. I go through the motions.

I'm dealing with this, I tell myself. *Besides, it's stupid to worry. I might not have AIDS. I might not have anything. Jack might not have picked up anything. I'm blowing it all out of proportion.*

But when my daughter knocks a bottle of ginger ale off the counter, I scream at her; and every time the phone rings, I jump.

I'm not dealing with this, I think. *This is too much to carry alone.*

Locked in his own world of guilt and fear, Jack is unable to share my pain. I'm not sure I want him to. Who to call? It's so risky. Only a few people know. Drowning in fear, I dial my pastor's number. When everything came out, Jack had called Pastor for advice about a counselor.

"I'm waiting for the results of my AIDS test and I'm afraid," I blurt out as Pastor answers the phone. "I need someone to pray with me,"

A mumbled apology. He has a deadline and he will call me back at 4:30.

I understand. I deal in deadlines. I wait.

At 5:00, the phone rings.

"Can we set up an appointment?" he asks. "Of course, it will be hard to find time," he adds quickly. "Things are busy. They really are."

But I don't want an appointment. I just want him to say, "I'm sorry you're hurting." I just want him to say, "This is so unfair." I just want him to pray for me.

I just want him to understand, but it's safer for him to pretend this isn't really happening. Such a disrespectable thing to happen in such a respectable congregation. I understand. I really do. AIDS happens to other people—people we can be neutral about because they deserve what they get. Or, maybe, people we can appear to be sympathetic with. As long as they aren't in our congregation.

Frantic, I call a friend.

"The Bible says it's a sin to be afraid," she lectures.

"The Bible also says to weep with those who weep," I retort.

"You're not surrendered enough to Christ. You need to trust that He will bring good out of this," she says.

My courage used up, I mumble, "Good-bye."

I stumble through the next few days. The results from the sexually transmitted diseases come in. I'm clean. I want to share my relief with someone, anyone. "I made it. I'm safe!" I want to shout. But who would understand? They didn't comprehend the pain, so there's no way they could understand the joy. So, I share with the only One who really knows. "Thank You, God. I don't know how You did it, but thank You."

Now I have to find a way to use up the time until the AIDS results come in. I visit my favorite store. I go to church. I talk with friends. Just like everything is okay. Just like my world isn't tumbling down around me.

"Hey, good to see you. How're you doing?" people ask.

"Scared to death," I want to say hysterically.

But I've learned my lesson. People either want you to be "great, great!" or neutral. Nobody really wants to know how you are—it makes them too uncomfortable. So, just shut up and play the game.

"Fine, how are you?" I say and smile.

Finally, the two weeks are up. It takes two calls: one to find out if the results are back, another to a different number to set up a time and place to meet because, they tell me, they can't give me the results at the clinic. It's not private enough. Any other test I've ever had I could get the results right in the office. What's the matter? Am I unclean or something? Or, are they afraid I'm going to freak out and scare the other patients? I dial the second number.

"We want a neutral location, like a store parking lot, where we can be anonymous," the social worker says.

She describes her car and what she will be wearing. I describe mine and what I will be wearing. Real cloak-and-dagger stuff. Just like I'm Bob Woodward and she's Deep Throat or something.

It's all so absurd. I'm not a number, I'm a person. How can I drive to a parking lot and let some anonymous social worker climb into my anonymous car and give me my anonymous results, then drive anonymously home? Alone—all alone.

My courage falters. I cancel the appointment. If I've been exposed to AIDS, I've been exposed to AIDS. If I haven't, I haven't. Yes, I want to know, but I can't be a nonperson for the most important test of my life. I just can't.

Up Close and Personal

Pornography and spirituality do not coexist. If a person is spiritually aware, he has respect for himself and others. Pornography sells and feeds off of disrespect for self and others.

⸢Ann[1]⸥

The lips of a seductive woman are oh so sweet, her soft words are oh so smooth. But it won't be long before she's gravel in your mouth, a pain in your gut, a wound in your heart. She's dancing down the primrose path to Death; she's headed straight for Hell and taking you with her.

⸢Proverbs 5:3–5⸥

The story in the first chapter happened five years ago. And I finally did get the results of that test—they were negative. Two years later, Jack also went for an AIDS test, and his results were negative, too. Jack's test occurred five years after the last time he was with a prostitute. That five-year window of vulnerability is important for our peace of mind. Although much is still unknown about HIV (human immunodeficiency virus—which causes AIDS), health professionals think that it can take up to five years after exposure for HIV to show up in the testing. Jack and I can now be fairly confident that we are safe from this dreaded disease.

The Facts, Ma'am, Just the Facts

It is difficult to tell you the story of how I happened to be in a community health clinic going through an AIDS test. Originally, I had thought to tell you through a

9

cold, analytical discussion of the facts, ma'am, just the facts. I had wanted to present to you an intellectual approach to the problems pornography introduces into a marriage. For, you see, that was our problem. Twenty-seven years ago, my husband, Jack, met the devil and she was dressed in black lace and red garters. For most of his adult life, she kept him enthralled, slowly sucking out his vital essences so that, in the end, he scarcely resembled the man I'd married. In the retelling, I had no desire to marinate in the misery we'd been through. And so, I crafted a book proposal and an opening chapter that were carefully sterilized of the pain.

"We'll publish it," said Gwen Ellis, then managing editor for Focus on the Family book publishing, "but we want you to tell your own story."

"My *own* story?"

Surely, that was not to be required of me. Actually, I had planned to tell it, but carefully disguised among the stories of other women I knew who'd gone through the same ordeal.

"I want the readers to feel what you've been through. I want them to know what pornography does to a marriage," Gwen told me.

Ah, but that was the problem. How to put the feelings into words? How could I convey the loneliness, the desperation, the devastation, the shame, the outrage, and the betrayal of trust without betraying trust? Because my story isn't my story alone. There are others who have entered at tangential points—some of whom have been key players, many of whom have wounded me deeply. How could I tell you my story without telling you their stories as well? Then, there was the problem of exposing our family to the scrutiny I knew would follow such an approach.

God Cannot Heal That Which Is Covered

Every family has issues, and most of those issues should properly remain within the family. Love is never eager to expose the failings of others. But when those failings threaten to destroy the person engaged in them, then they have become a rottenness that has the potential to disintegrate the family.

Rottenness thrives on the darkness secrecy provides, and it feeds on the shame family members fear will follow exposure. The only way to excise the rot in our lives is to slice open the denial and expose the shame to the light. But this excision must be carefully done. Just as one would never do surgery without properly sterilized instruments or allow the unmasked to peer into the wound, so one is wise not to invite those who have no sense of their own baggage to view yours. Viewing the baggage of others has become something of a fetish in our society.

We've become a nation of voyeurs who feed off the offal of ruined lives. Our feeding troughs are the talk shows, books, and magazines that tell shocking story after shocking story about how people have consumed themselves and others. We become consumers ourselves by feeding off the misery these people have wrought, and having eaten, we wipe our mouths and move on.

We have not become better people because none of the shocking stories are weighed against any standard of righteousness. Indeed, we are told there is none. We have not become wiser people because we have not learned to understand cause and effect in the choices these people made. Indeed, we are told that people are victims, helpless in the face of whatever cruel thing life brings their way. They must always react, never act.

I have no desire to contribute to the feeding frenzy. I will tell you a shocking story—my own—but I will weigh it against a standard of righteousness. I will explain the cause and effect of choices made both by my husband and me that either contributed to continuing misery or brought light into darkness. I will tell you how God changed me by forcing me to take Him out of the theological boxes I had put Him in.

I will tell you because pornography is a wretched thing. It destroys lives, and the only way I can prove that to you is to document how it almost destroyed mine. I will tell you because there is hope for those whose lives have been ravaged by pornography, and the only way I can prove there is hope is to document how *my* life was healed.

Coming Soon to a Neighborhood Near You

Perhaps you think you don't know anyone who uses pornography; but I can say with a fair amount of certainty that whether it's a secret use, as in Jack's case, or an admitted use where pornographic magazines and videos are openly displayed in the home, people you know are struggling to make sense of the damage pornography has brought into their lives. I can make that statement with confidence, because pornography is a $12–13 billion a year industry. That's more money than if you combined the annual revenues of the Coca-Cola and the McDonnell Douglas corporations.[3]

No longer hidden in back alleys, porn outlets are more numerous than McDonald's restaurants—and convenience is the name of the game. In most towns, you can fill up your car, pick up a candy bar and soft drink, and grab a copy of the latest issue of more than 450 hard- and soft-core pornographic magazines all in one stop.

As of April 1, 1990, the population of the United States was 248,709,873. That same year, over 300 million X-rated videos were distributed in our neighborhoods—more than one sexually explicit video for every man, woman, and child living in our country! The sad fact is that in the intervening years, sales and rentals of adult videos, most of which are taped in the San Fernando Valley of California, rose 75 percent—topping $2.1 billion in 1993 alone.[4]

Nor does it look as if things are going to change in the immediate future. According to Keith Stone of the Los Angeles Daily News, the Clinton administration has taken a hands-off approach to the prosecution of pornography.

> Although the Clinton Administration insist that they are continuing to investigate and prosecute obscenity with the same fervor as the Bush and Reagan Administrations, the siege has been scaled back. Before Clinton took office, Los Angeles police were deputized by the federal government so they could help prosecutors conduct monthly raids on Valley pornographers. According to Lt. Ken Seibert, head of the Los Angeles police department's administrative vice unit, under Clinton, there have been no raids. Gone, too, are the monthly meetings with federal prosecutors to chart strategy.
>
> "Adult obscenity enforcement by the federal government is practically non-existent since the administration changed," Seibert said.
>
> Patrick Trueman, who served under President Bush as chief of the U.S. Justice Department's Child Exploitation and Obscenity Section, says, "I maintain the war is over; the pornographer has won."[5]

Because of this hands-off approach, many more families will become victims of a "victimless" crime.

So, after careful consideration, I've decided to tell my story and the stories of some other women I've been privileged to know who have been through the same thing. To protect them and my extended family, I'm using fictitious names. Those are the only changes I'm making in the stories. What you read here is all true. Every word. I know, because I lived it.

CHAPTER 3

Pinched from the Waiting

Women are often told they love too much or love the wrong kind of man. Love is now a diagnostic criterion for measuring mental health. If you love the unlovable, let another person's desires take precedence over your own, or even worse, love someone who has hurt you, then (women are told) you are likely love addicted, codependent, and emotionally unhealthy.

Dan Allender and Tremper Longman III[1]

Hope deferred maketh the heart sick . . .

Proverbs 13:12 (KJV)

"I'm going to be home for dinner tonight," Jack said at the breakfast table.

"*Really?*"

"Yeah, I need to spend more time around here."

After he left, I flew around the house, dusting, polishing, singing. "Daddy's going to be home for dinner tonight!"

The kids joined in, laughing and playing "Here's-what-we'll-do-with-Daddy-tonight."

By late afternoon, the house sparkled, and a coconut cream pie, Jack's favorite, was chilling in the refrigerator. I made sure to leave enough time to wash and curl my hair. After the table was set, I went upstairs and laid a fire in the fireplace in our bedroom. I put on my makeup and laid my best negligee on our bed. Then I dashed downstairs and lit the kerosene lamp in the bay window because I knew

Jack liked to see the lamp burning when he pulled into the driveway.

"Mommy, when is Daddy going to be home? I'm hungry!" Ian stood next to the oven, watching me check the roast an hour after Jack was supposed to arrive. It was getting dry.

"How about I feed you and Sandy? Daddy and I can eat when he gets here," I said.

Dinner was punctuated by Ian hopping up and down from the table. Pulling the curtain back and pressing his nose against the window, he would look wistfully into the driveway.

"I want to give Daddy a big kiss right when he comes through the door," he said.

He seemed so small, his little back half hidden by the wine-colored curtain. I felt a tightness gathering in my throat.

"Hop back up to the table, forward observer," I said. "You have to eat your dinner so you can grow up big and strong like your daddy."

Funny how the words just barely squeaked out of my mouth. There seemed to be no air behind them—no air at all.

Sandy played with the food on her plate, pushing it first to one side and then another.

"My tummy feels kind of ouchy," she said, her mouth sagging as listlessly as the bright-pink ribbons she had asked me to put in her hair "'cause I want to be pretty for Daddy."

I squirmed in my chair. "Well," I said, "why don't you and Ian get into your jammies? You can eat your dessert while I read you a story."

"I don't want any pie, Mommy." Ian thumped to the floor. His thin shoulders sagged as he slowly climbed the stairs. Sandy dragged behind him.

I cleared the table with brisk efficiency. *Well,* I thought, vigorously scraping the untouched plates into the trash, *they can have their pie for a snack tomorrow.*

As I read to them, Ian would suddenly say, "Shhh!" and cock his ear toward the driveway. "I thought I heard Daddy's car." But there was only silence to echo the silence.

The story went on and on. Sandy's head drooped on my chest. Ian's body seemed rigid against my side. Somehow, my lips kept moving. Somehow, there was enough air to give sound to the words. Somehow, the kids said their "Now I lay me down to sleep." Somehow, I thought of a tickle chase up the stairs to their bedrooms.

"Oh, Mommy!" Sandy said, collapsing in giggles on her bed. "I love you so much!"

Throwing her arms around my neck, she drew me down for a wet kiss. I buried my face in the sweetness of her hair.

"You sleep tight and don't let the bedbugs bite," I said, tucking the cool sheets in snugly.

Ian was already in bed, the sheets pulled up to his chin, when I came into his room. He was staring at the ceiling.

"I'm going to stay awake until Daddy comes home," he whispered. "I want to give him a kiss."

"I promise I'll send him right up," I said, lightly kissing him on the forehead. He seemed so lost in the bed. Just a small face on a white pillow.

"Love you," I said into the darkened room as I flicked off the switch.

"Love you," came the reply.

There it was again—that gasping for air. I made it down the stairs and groped my way into the family room. The couch was still warm from story time.

I stared at the fire, watching it dance and flicker. A thought peeked out from behind the curtain of my mind. I turned my head. The thought gathered force and stood in front of me. I pulled the curtains shut. The thought came roaring back, yanking them open. *Look at me!* it demanded.

And I looked. Because now the thought filled the whole stage of my mind. Playing before me in scene after scene was an endless review of other nights, just like this one: nights when Jack said he would be home, nights that followed days of getting ready—cooking his favorite things, dressing up, laughing with the children about what we would do when Daddy got home; and nights when dinners turned cold, and hard, and colorless, and pinched from the waiting; and when children's faces turned cold, and hard, and colorless, and pinched from the waiting. And then his breathless arrival at 10:30, 12:30, 2:00 A.M.

"Sorry. Had to work late," he would say, holding his palms up and shrugging his shoulders. "It will be different next time," he would tell me. But it never was. "This time I'll make it, you'll see," he would say. But the next time it was just like before and there was always an excuse.

Now the thought was screaming at me. *Do you see a pattern here?* it demanded.

I squeezed my eyes shut and clapped my hands tightly over my ears.

"Oh, God," I gasped. "Something's wrong! Something's *very* wrong and I don't know what it is!"

For Jack, it started the summer he was 18. His parents, missionaries in Africa, had just gone back after a year of furlough. Jack stayed in the States because he was going to start college in the fall. Raised in Africa, he felt disoriented and alone in this strange new country.

That summer, he worked building Harvestore silos. The guys in the work crew had a couple of soft-core pornographic magazines in the truck's toolbox. Jack had never seen anything like them before, and he found the magazines to be an anesthetic for the lost and lonely feelings he had inside.

By the time we met, three years later, Jack had been drafted into the army and was in the presidential honor guard. He had a White House security clearance and often did jobs involving heads of state. At this point, he was a casual user of pornography, which he didn't have to go far to find. Since his unit was required to get haircuts every three days, he went regularly to the barber shop, where he was confronted with centerfolds plastered all over the walls. This whetted his appetite for more, and he began to buy pornographic magazines.

Because the other guys in his unit knew he was a Christian, Jack bought and used his magazines secretly. He told himself he didn't want to wreck his testimony. He reasoned that it was okay for him to do something in private that, if done publicly, would instantly be recognized as an out-of-character action for a Christian. This convoluted reasoning led him to craft a public persona that fit the general expectations others have of Christians, and a private persona that was in direct conflict to his public life. He was so good at separating his two lives that he effectively disassociated himself from himself for more than 20 years. One of the greatest struggles in his recovery has been to "pull himself together" again.

After about four years of secretly consuming pornographic magazines, Jack began to attend R-rated movies. "That's nothing," you say. "Lots of people go to R-rated movies." Yes, lots of people do, and that can be where it starts. A nice guy doesn't go into XXX-movie theaters or strip shows in the beginning. They're too far out of character for him. But let him get started with soft-core pornographic magazines and a few explicit sex scenes as seen in many R-rated movies—making sure that everything is done secretly so there's extra denial and extra shame—and soon the line between what a nice guy finds acceptable and unacceptable are softened; until, at last, he risks the wrath of his conscience and goes where he never would have imagined himself going.

Jack followed the path studies show other sex addicts follow. These studies about the pornography addicted tell us that not only are R-rated movies a hook leading to harder stuff—as in Jack's case—but initially soft-core pornography causes more damage to the value system of the viewer than does hard-core porn. This is especially true in movies where sex is consensual.[2]

This is the point at which I met Jack, on a blind date while I was a student at a college about 50 miles from Washington, D.C. During our courtship, Jack had a fun-loving personality and would sing songs and crack jokes while he worked. People enjoyed being around him.

For me, the fact that he was a "missionary kid" helped vouch for his character. His service in the White House also gave him credibility. During our courtship, we taught Sunday school together, and when we talked about our hopes and dreams, we seemed to have the same values. Nothing he did led me to believe Jack had another side to him that was totally different from the one he was presenting to me. Jack never talked about his addiction when we were dating. He never used crude or off-color language, and I never saw pornography around when we were together. He was *very good* at his public persona. I totally believed in him.

My family and friends also thought he was a squeaky clean, super-nice guy. My college roommate thought so, too. "Jack?" she said when I told her about his addiction. "He was the last person I would ever have imagined would have that kind of problem. He always seemed so wholesome."

We married after I finished college, and we both became staff members of a large church in the South. During this time, Jack began to work long hours, but there was always a good reason. And although I longed to have Jack home more, the fact that he was gone so much didn't seem to be out of the ordinary. My own father had also worked many long hours, building a successful business. I frequently told Jack about my desire to spend more time with him, but I never thought that part of the long hours he was away were being spent at movie theaters taking in R-rated films or holed up some place devouring the latest pornographic magazines. I thought he was out "serving the Lord."

We stayed at the church for six years, and then Jack took a job in New England as the regional service manager for a heavy-lift equipment company. The long hours continued. When I asked him why he was gone so much, his explanation that machine breakdowns and personnel issues meant long days made sense to me. Sixty-hour weeks seemed to be part of the American way of doing business. However, just before I discovered his addiction, he was often gone for 80 hours, leading me to suspect that there was something more going on than just an unusually long workday. But up until that time, I believed, as I think many American wives believe, that a good woman stands behind her husband and helps him be successful in his chosen profession by taking care of things at home and not hassling him too much about how many hours he works.

Spiraling Down

In the beginning, Jack's casual use of pornography and R-rated movies had no outward effect on his personality. As yet, his addiction had not caused him to take actions that would trample on the things he held most dear. But the thoughts and images porn presented became seeds lurking deep in his mind. Several years of repeated exposure to it watered those seeds. The fact that he was doing everything secretly provided the warm, dark place for the seeds to germinate. And once they began to sprout, they took on a life of their own and began to choke out his.

Then, shortly after we moved to New England, one of his coworkers took him to a club that featured "exotic dancers." He was hooked and began to attend strip shows several times a week. Now the influence of pornography was beginning to compel him into lifestyle choices that deeply violated the things his public persona said he believed. Eventually, rationalizing that since what he was doing was private so he wasn't hurting anyone, Jack began picking up women who hung around these clubs and paying them for sex. Again, this was done secretly. No one, not even a good friend who was a coworker, knew.

Soon, the tension between Jack's public and private lives began to create incredible guilt. He knew he wasn't living the way he said he wanted to, the way he represented himself to family and friends, yet he was reluctant to give up his secret life. He wanted his loving family and he wanted his women. He kept telling himself he could have both. But his gut knew differently, and the guilt generated began to eat at him. Since he wouldn't stop doing the thing that caused the guilt, he began looking for a scapegoat. As his wife, I was convenient, and soon his guilt came spilling out as anger and abuse.

Hey, Someone Turned Up the Heat!

These things didn't happen suddenly. Jack's deterioration was gradual. The light in his eyes didn't go out all at once, and his laughter didn't turn into sullenness overnight. The guy with the easy, open ways didn't evaporate into a pathological liar in the blink of an eye. If the changes had been sudden, they would have screamed, *Pay attention! Something very wrong is going on here!*

Because the changes were gradual, they became invisible in the busyness every young couple experiences. Jack was developing his career; I was raising children. For a long time, I chalked up the changes to the everyday pressures of life. I mourned what was happening to him, but I wasn't suspicious. Suspicion is such an ugly thing. It's so opposite of all that love is about, which is believing the best in each other, going the extra mile, giving the benefit of the doubt. I was like that old frog who starts out in a pot of cold water that's been placed on a burner that's being slowly turned up. I had a gut-level sense that things were changing for the worse, but I wasn't really aware of the danger until the pain reached boiling point.

As unsettling as it may be, this is not an uncommon scenario for couples where the husband is secretly involved in pornography. Over the years, I've talked with a number of wives whose husbands' public faces were those of your average nice guy while "in their other lives" they were violating all that they said they held dear. Often these men participated in some ministry aspect of their church, either singing in the choir, doing an outreach ministry, being an elder, or even being the pastor himself. To those looking on, their marriages seemed strong; but, in the hidden places, there was rot. The wives could feel this decay with their spirits, but they kept telling their spirits to be quiet because everything they could see with their eyes and hear with their ears said things were fine.

Waking Up and Smelling the Coffee

Once I knew Jack was in some type of bondage, he steadfastly continued to deny there was a problem. And how was I to tell for sure? Sexual addiction is unlike drug and alcohol addiction. There are no needle marks. There is no tell-tale breath. There is no stagger or slurred speech. Sexual addiction is a private thing. You can shoot up in the secret places of your mind while you're sitting in a roomful of people.

If Jack had brought pornography into the house, I might have caught on faster. But only once in the 24 years we've been married have I seen pornography in our home. Because Jack was so clever with his lying, and because he was so skillful with his "nice guy" public persona, I couldn't get anyone else to agree that something was terribly wrong. I was all alone in my conviction that things weren't as they appeared, and it almost drove me insane. In fact, I'm not sure it didn't. I can remember crawling into bed one day, pulling the covers over my head and running my forefinger rapidly up and down my lips, babbling just like the folks who are certifiable do. It was a wake-up call that I was going to totally lose it if I didn't start acting based on what I knew was true rather than on what others told me was true.

So, how did I go from drooling under the covers to restoring my sanity and my marriage? My denial started to break down the night I fixed a special dinner for

Jack and once again he failed to show up. This is the story that opens this chapter. But because everything was so secret, I didn't have a clue how to get us out of the mess I didn't know we were in.

The real journey to healing began several months later, when Jack didn't come home in time to baby-sit our kids so I could go to a childbirth class I was teaching. At breakfast that morning, I told Jack that I'd hired a baby-sitter to watch the children while I was at class.

"Why don't you call and cancel?" he said. "I'll be home in time to watch the kids."

A baby-sitter had been a smart solution to my problem of making sure the kids were well cared for. I'd decided to hire a baby-sitter after regularly being stranded with the kids when Jack didn't show up in time for me to get to the class. By hiring a sitter, I didn't have reason to resent him, and the children weren't put in the position of having to be "good" in the hospital waiting room. I could just go and teach my class. It had worked well for a number of years. Now I was being asked to risk frustration again.

"I don't want you to go to any trouble," I said.

"No trouble. I'd like to do it for you."

It sounded so wonderful, I could hardly believe my ears. *Maybe he's wanting to spend time with the kids after all,* I thought.

"Well, I don't know. What if you don't make it home on time?"

"I'll make being on time a priority."

"Well, okay. Just one thing. Call by 4:30 if you can't make it. That gives me a couple of hours to get a baby-sitter so I'm not stranded."

"I wouldn't strand you," he said innocently.

You have before, I thought. But since I felt he was finally trying to get it right, I just said, "Sure."

When the phone rang at 6:45, I doubled over in cramps. Jack wasn't home and I knew it had to be him. That could mean only one thing.

"Um . . . have to work late," he said.

"You mean you've known for better than two hours that you weren't going to make it home and you didn't call me?"

"Uh, yeah."

"*That* was a very unloving thing to do!" I said loudly and hung up. All right, it wasn't exactly telling him off, but it was the first time I'd ever said anything besides "I understand and I'll figure something out." And it felt good.

I bundled the kids into the car, bribed them with a milkshake, and ran between the maternity ward and the waiting room all night so I could keep an eye on them. When I finally got home, Jack was in bed—asleep. After I got the kids into bed, I decided I'd had enough. I was leaving. Of course, it was a totally irrational act. I didn't have a plan; I didn't have any money. I knew I couldn't leave the kids with Jack, and I certainly couldn't take them with me to nowhere. But desperation doesn't need a plan.

Bags packed, I marched to the door. Left. Right. Left. Right. I was out of here. Left. Right. Left. Right. Suddenly, out of the corner of my eye, I saw my Bible on the coffee table.

"Who put that there?" I asked myself, knowing it wasn't in its usual place.

Dropping my suitcases, I walked over to the table. A suffocating sense of dread settled on me. I stood riveted, unable to tear my eyes off my Bible. The longer I looked at it, the more I squirmed inside. Finally, I picked it up, its spine carefully balanced in my hand.

"Have you got anything to say about all this, God?" I asked out loud, not really believing that anyone was listening.

The weight of the book grew heavier and heavier in my hand, until at last I could balance it no more, and it fell open to 1 Peter, chapter 1. My eyes fell on verse 3: "Praised, honored, blessed be the God and Father of our Lord Jesus Christ, the Messiah! By His boundless mercy we have been born again to an ever-living hope through the resurrection of Jesus Christ from the dead."

An ever-living hope. I saw instantly that my problem was that I had no hope. I had used up my options. There was nothing left inside but a growing despair. Funny, I'd never thought of it as hopelessness.

I looked at the verse again—my hope is ever living because of Christ's resurrection from the dead? The verse was breathing on the cold ember of hope in my heart, and I could feel the tiniest bit of warmth stirring.

"But, God, I've done everything I could to keep the marriage vows I made to Jack. I just can't do this anymore!"

And then, in a quiet place carved out of the confusion in my spirit, I heard these words: *You didn't make your marriage vows to Jack, Laurie. You made your vows to Me, and I will show you how to keep them.*

CHAPTER 4

The Great Adventure Begins

When your life is threatened, survival is the question.
Once survival is assured, healing is a possibility.

The Rev. Dr. Craig Bensen[1]

Long enough, God—
    you've ignored me long enough.
I've looked at the back of your head
    long enough.
Long enough
I've carried this ton of trouble,
    lived with a stomach full of pain.
Long enough my arrogant enemies
    have looked down their noses at me.

Take a good look at me, God, my God;
    I want to look life in the eye,
so no enemy can get the best of me
    or laugh when I fall on my face.

I've thrown myself headlong into your arms—
    I'm celebrating your rescue.
I'm singing at the top of my lungs,
    I'm so full of answered prayers.

Psalm 13[2]

The morning after Jack failed to show up in time to baby-sit so I could go to my childbirth class, I stood in the door, looking dumbly at the delivery girl.

"Flowers? For me?" I gasped.

"Says here they're for Laurie Hall—that you?"

I nodded.

"Then enjoy," she said, handing me a huge plastic bag covered with rainbows.

Inside the bag, a large coffee mug overflowed with bright spring flowers. Perched among the riot of carnations, irises, and tulips was a tiny envelope. *Who would have sent me flowers?* I wondered, as I fumbled to get the card out.

> Dear Laurie,
>
> I was wrong not to call. Sorry I put you in a bind.
>
> Love,
>
> Jack

I was dumbfounded. It was the first time in 13 years of marriage that Jack had sent me flowers! And it was because he was feeling guilty. I'd never known him to feel guilty or express any kind of regret for the times he'd left me in the lurch. Over the years, there'd been lots of other special dinners and special plans when he'd failed to show up or even to call. What was different about last night?

"You said something, that's what's different," I said to myself. "You told him it was not very loving. You didn't let him off the hook by trying to be understanding and pretending it didn't really matter."

The realization was cold comfort. I'd rather have him send me flowers for the first time because he loves me, not because he's feeling guilty. It just doesn't feel the same.

I set the mug down. It was lovely, and when the flowers were gone, I'd have a nice big cup for my tea. Turning the mug around, I caught my breath. Splashed across the front was a bright rainbow. Our church was against anything with a rainbow on it, since it is a major symbol of the New Age movement. Could I use something with a rainbow on it?

I had it first.

It was the same still, small voice that had confronted me about my decision to leave Jack. The same quiet voice that had promised He would teach me how to keep my marriage vows. It was the Lord.

"That's true, Lord, you did!" I remembered the Bible story of the terrible 40-day storm that wiped out almost every living creature. God had kept Noah and his family safe in an ark. When the storm was over, He had planted a rainbow in the sky as a sign that He would never destroy the earth by water again.

And then I heard His voice again.

You are coming into a time of great storms, Laurie. It will be difficult, but there will be no destruction.

My Theology Is All Made Up

I'd been taught that God didn't speak directly to people in this age. I'd been told that He speaks *through* the people above you, your authority figures. Especially, I was told, God wouldn't speak to women because, as one elder told me, "women are not created in the image of God. They are created in the image of men; therefore, women are to be subject to men." But now, in less than 24 hours, I'd had two encounters that seemed to blow my theology right out of the water. What was happening to me?

Don't confuse me with the experience, God, I thought. *My theology is all made up.*

Grabbing my Bible, I looked up Noah's story in Genesis. I wanted to know about the rainbow. I read:

> And the bow shall be in the cloud; and I (God) will look upon it, that I may remember the everlasting covenant between God and every living creature of all flesh that is upon the earth. And God said unto Noah, This is the token of the covenant, which I have established between me and all flesh that is upon the earth. (Gen. 9:16,17, KJV)

The rainbow is the sign of a *covenant?* What's a *covenant?* I'd heard the word only once, when a preacher had said you could call the Old and New Testaments the Old and New Covenants. He didn't explain the meaning of the word; he simply mentioned it as he gave his sermon.

My stomach clutched as understanding of an awesome truth came to me. I'd been in church all my life. I'd taught and attended many Sunday schools and Bible studies. I'd been out soul winning. But what did I really know about the God of the Bible? What did I know about covenant?

When All Else Fails, Read the Instruction Book

After I'd read the account of the flood, I turned to the Book of Acts to see what the New Covenant had to say. *Our church prides itself on being a New Testament church,* I thought. *Better look there and see what I can find out about what the early Christians believed.*

In the past, I'd looked up chapters and verses here and there in Acts, but I'd never read the book all the way through. What I found as I read were men and women whose lives were totally transformed by their encounters with God. Here were people whose fear of man was swallowed up in their hunger to know God and to make Him known. Here were men and women whose zeal to share what they had discovered compelled them to encounter their cultures and literally blow their worlds apart.

Two hours later, after reading all the way through the book of Acts, I was on my face beside the couch.

"God, I don't have what these people had. And I can't figure out what's missing. I don't have any question that I'm one of your children; I know I'm born again. But I don't know what I've been saved *from* or what I've been saved *to*. Salvation's got to be more than just fire insurance."

I paused to blow my nose. Tears! This was a first. I'd always been sincere when I prayed—but I'd never been broken. I remembered seeing a "Jesus Is the Answer" bumper sticker on a car the week before. *If Jesus is the answer, what's the question?* I thought, wiping away fresh tears.

"Here's the truth, Lord, I've been faking it. I've been doing church and trying to live by all the rules, but I'm miserable. Christianity is a nice idea and it's kept me out of trouble, but I don't have anything to offer a lost and dying world except zippy platitudes. I haven't even really found anything for myself."

Did I dare go on and say what I was thinking? Hands covering my head, I cowered on the floor and blurted out the terrible truth.

"If this is all there is to the Christian life, God, it's not worth having!"

I waited for the thunderbolts to strike me dead. None came.

"All right, God, if you're not going to kill me for not wanting the Christian experience I now have, then give me what they had. I'd rather die than keep living this way. I want it! I want it! I want it!" The floor shook as I pounded it with my fist. "Whatever it takes, Lord, I want it."

In the silence that followed, I distinctly sensed a sigh of relief. Then a heavenly *Yes!* And then . . . a chuckle.

• A Light Shining in the Very Great Darkness

Isaiah 60:1,2 says, "Arise, shine; for thy light is come, and the glory of the Lord is risen upon thee. For, behold, the darkness shall cover the earth, and gross darkness the people: but the Lord shall arise upon thee, and His glory shall be seen upon thee" (KJV).

There are two kinds of darkness in this passage: a darkness that covers the earth and a gross darkness that covers the people. The Hebrew word used in this verse for the darkness that's covering the earth is *chôshek*. It means falsehood, ignorance, and blindness. The Hebrew word for the gross darkness that is covering the people is *'arâphel*, and it refers to the misery and gloom that settle on people who are blinded by falsehood and ignorance. It's a miserable state that makes your soul feel like it's drooping inside you.

Scripture says this is the common condition of all people. Blinded by the darkness of our false beliefs, we stumble along the best we can, vaguely feeling like something's missing. Our minds say we're on the verge of discovering the answer to our dilemma—but our guts know we still haven't got a clue. This conflict between our minds and our guts causes tremendous tension. Outwardly, we may act as if we've got it all together, but inwardly we know the truth. We are hopelessly lost in a place we can't see. Up comes a little anxiety to let us know we're not operating with integrity. Unable to stumble out of the darkness, we gradually pull away from life and its relationships, until our shivering souls are huddled deep inside us.

Scripture says there's only one condition that's more desperate than being in the darkness of ignorance and false beliefs. And that's thinking that we know what's going on when we haven't got a clue.

Jesus said in Matthew 6:22–23, "The eye is the lamp of the body. So, if your eye is sound, your entire body will be full of light; but if your eye is unsound, your whole body will be full of darkness. If then, the very light in you is darkened, how dense is that darkness!"

That was my condition as I sat looking at that rainbow mug 11 years ago. I had a firm belief that I knew what truth was, and that belief kept me from dealing with the realities of my life. I was operating on what I *thought* was true rather than on what *was* true. When I painfully crashed into reality, I told myself it was because I hadn't gotten it right. I told myself that if I would just try harder, do better, be better, it would all turn out the way I knew it should.

After all, this is what I had been taught. I had been told that God doesn't care nearly as much about what we are going through as He does about how we respond to what we are going through. The prescribed response to any unhappy circumstance was to deny self and jump through a series of hoops. This formula was guaranteed to get the "right" results. If I hadn't gotten the "right" results yet, I was assured, it was because I wasn't jumping high enough. The darkness of my deception was great.

These beliefs about God rendered me powerless to deal with the realities of my life. Because I felt powerless, blindness to those realities was the only option. Psychologists call it denial. I sat in the sweltering room of my pain and repeated my formula for coping over and over. "It's not hot, and I'm not here," I kept telling myself, until I almost believed it. Almost.

But then God had mercy on me. He began to break down my denial the night I made that special dinner for Jack. A tiny crack let in enough light for me to say, "Something's wrong here." Next, God showed me the passage in 1 Peter on the night I made up my mind to leave and He helped me understand that my basic problem was hopelessness. And, finally, God shook me up with a rainbow mug and showed me I knew little about what Christian faith really is.

❧ Falling in Love Again

I began rising at 4:30 every morning to spend one to two hours with the Lord. I was filled with a hunger and thirst for the Bible, and I read it through, cover to cover, over and over again. I was completely amazed at what I saw. It didn't matter what class, race, or gender I belonged to, or what I did or didn't do—in God's eyes I was precious and worthy of love simply because I was His child. This love came wrapped in a package called forgiveness, and there was nothing I could do to earn it or even make God glad He had given it to me. It was totally free. All I could do was receive it.

But God said I had a basic problem in receiving His love. I had an inborn condition that caused me to gravitate away from Him and toward that which would destroy me. This inborn condition generated darkness and thrived on lies, and I was helpless to deliver myself from its power. Because of His great love for me, He was not willing to allow me to continue to perish, so He sent His Son to redeem me from the power of darkness and lies and bring me into the kingdom of light and truth (John 3:16 and Col. 1:13). My redemption would come about as I entered into a right relationship with God.

Here was the Creator of the universe longing to have fellowship with me. If I agreed to know Him, He would become my Daddy and I would become His heir (Rom. 8:17). All that He is and has would be available to me (2 Cor. 8:9). Jesus looks at me not as His slave to subjugate but as His friend and sister (John 15:15 and Matt. 12:50). One other truth grabbed my attention—one I could scarcely believe. God wanted to give me power and strength. He wanted to be my *Immanuel*. My God with me.

In Hebrew, *Immanuel* is a compound word. In their separate pieces, the words that make up *Immanuel* mean "strength alongside, strength within" or "mighty power accompanying." Imagine that! God wanted to give me strength alongside, strength within; God wanted to accompany me with mighty power. I saw that Scripture had much to say about power and authority. I read repeatedly that Jesus has authority over every principality and power and that He has made me a joint heir of that authority. These things were good news to someone who felt powerless. These words were life-giving to someone who had no strength.

Trying to Bring Order to the Inner Chaos

Of course, I had heard a hollow outline of these truths in the churches we had attended. I had known the facts of them in my head for years. But now they took on a depth of meaning that stood in sharp contrast to the way I felt my life was going. I was terribly confused about how to apply them. All I knew was that the tension was mounting between my feeling that something was terribly wrong with my marriage and what appeared to be reality—that Jack was a devoted family man and church member. At that point, if someone had told me he was leading a double life, and had been for our entire marriage, I would not have believed it, and neither would a lot of other people. I just knew that Jack had totally withdrawn from us. Not only was he gone 14 to 16 hours a day, but when he was at home, he sat impassive and silent. I knew that something was wrong, and with my original theological underpinnings still intertwined with the new things I was learning, I assumed it was me.

Many times I would get down on my knees and beg Jack to tell me what I had done wrong. But he wouldn't speak. In the rare times when he did speak, he would lie. I would relate to him something that had happened, and he would say, "Oh, that's not what happened at all." I would act on instructions he had given me, and he would say, "I didn't say that, I said something different." I was constantly confused about what really had happened. Was I imagining things? Or was it really the way I thought it was? This mind control left me feeling powerless. Because of my church's teaching on the submission of women, I didn't know what to do with my gut feeling that things were not right. I didn't know how to confront Jack. I felt utterly beaten down, crushed, and thoroughly ravaged. There were many times I despaired even of life itself.

Then came the good news. God wanted to deliver me from fear. There was a way out of my darkness! I was being terrorized, and He wanted to give me inner peace. I was despairing, and He wanted to give me an ever-living hope.

These times with the Lord were sweet. After devouring whole books of the Bible, I'd pray through a psalm or passage of Scripture and tell Him I wasn't happy with my life. In the beginning, I would quiver with fear, thinking that such revelations would bring nothing but divine wrath. But the answer I'd hear was, *Yes, life can be tough sometimes. I don't blame you for being upset.*

Gradually, fearful and wounded though I was, I learned to creep onto my Daddy's lap and relax in the freedom and joy that come from not feeling condemned. There's only one feeling that comes from a heart set free of condemnation and that's the desire to worship the One who has freed you.

A Great Adventure of Faith

That was the beginning of my great adventure of faith. Do you know what makes a story an adventure? It's the cliffhangers—the times when you're not sure the hero and heroine are going to make it. It's the times when the good guys stumble into the bad guys' trap and there's no way out, and the train is coming or the rope is fraying, and disaster is seconds away. Then, in the distance, just when your heart is about to pound right out of your chest, you hear the trumpet sound of help on the way. That's an adventure. We love to read them. It's a little harder (sometimes a lot harder) to live them.

An adventure comes as the result of a quest. In order to be a true adventure, the quest has to be desperate and all-consuming. Being desperate for and consumed by something can be pretty uncomfortable—make that miserable, *real* miserable.

For the first 13 years of my marriage, my quest was to be the best wife that ever was and have the best marriage that ever could be. I spent a lot of time trying to figure out why things weren't turning out the way I wanted them to, but I still didn't get it. The alarm was ringing, but I was too deeply asleep to know what was going on. I was aroused just enough to realize there was an annoyance, but my eyes were still so blinded by the darkness that I didn't have a clue what was causing the noise or how to turn it off. But now, in the fourteenth year of my marriage, God had a plan and He was going to show me.

Learning the Power of Fasting

After a time, I began to fast regularly. I didn't know anything about it and I'd never known anyone who'd done it. I was just vaguely aware that it had been done by Christians in the past, and every now and then I saw references to it in the Bible. I went to a Christian bookstore and found a thin volume on fasting.

"Ha-ha, Lord!" I said, enjoying a private joke with Him. "Wouldn't you know that a book on fasting would be thin?"

I began fasting once a week, bringing the concerns of my life before God. I found these times of fasting opened my eyes to many things I'd been blinded to before. After one period of fasting, a friend shared with me 2 Corinthians 10:3–6:

> For though we walk and live in the flesh, we are not carrying on our warfare according to the flesh, using mere human weapons. For the weapons of our warfare are not physical weapons of flesh and blood, but they are mighty before God for the overthrow and destruction of strongholds, inasmuch as we refute arguments and theories and reasoning and every proud and lofty thing that sets itself up against the true knowledge of God; and we lead every thought and purpose away captive into the obedience of Christ, being in readiness to punish every disobedience when your own submission and obedience are fully secured and complete.

I meditated on the passage for quite a while. I'd thought for years that if Jack could just understand the situation, he'd see his way clear to come home to us. Now I began to recognize that Jack's problem wasn't simply lack of information about what was involved in being a good husband and father; rather, there was a battle going on for his mind. He had internal arguments, theories, and reasonings that over the years had locked him into a spiritual prison cell. Only God knew the lies that had been woven together to make this stronghold. This passage said that God specializes in rooting out false reasoning so He can cast down strongholds and set the prisoner free. It said that God wasn't going to use the human weapons of reasoning, anger, blame, or arguing to accomplish the overthrow and destruction of things that were binding Jack, so I shouldn't either.

Verse 6 caught my attention: God would punish Jack's disobedience when my own submission and obedience were fully secured. But I was already trying to be obedient! I'd also trained the children to respect and obey Jack. In the early days of our marriage, taking to heart the command that wives should be submissive to their husbands, I'd even called Jack "sir." Eventually, I stopped doing that because he told me it bugged him. I had always been quick to do what Jack asked me to do, and I had worked hard to honor him. What was wrong?

I began to pray 1 Peter 3:1–11—that dreadful passage that talks about wives submitting to their husbands. I had submitted in the past without allowing myself the luxury of assessing whether I wanted to or not. So, how come God hadn't acted? Could it be that I misunderstood submission? I began to wrestle with God about it. I was beginning to feel how empty my marriage was, I was beginning to feel used, and I was beginning to feel quite resentful that I should have to do *anything* for my tormentor.

My prayers went something like this: "Dear Lord, help me learn what You really mean when You say wives are to be submissive to their husbands. This passage says I'm supposed to adapt myself to him so that even if he doesn't obey Your Word, he may be won over not by discussion but by my godly life. Help me to reverence him, honor him, esteem him, appreciate him, and prize him. My heart is feeling hard and dark about this. I am so angry with Jack that I don't want to do anything for him anymore. He doesn't deserve it. But I don't deserve Your love and grace for me and You give it to me anyway. So, help me to find *one thing* I can do today to show him I adore him, admire him, praise him, and am devoted to him."

Then, I would do that thing that God showed me, whether it was fixing Jack a cup of tea when he got home or mending his work shirt.

These simple acts of obedience were all I knew to do to remedy my situation. I didn't understand how or why, just that God said He would fix things if I would do what He showed me to do. As I began to be obedient to God, understanding came. That is the way of the Lord—first obedience, then understanding. We want to understand first so we can decide whether or not we will obey. But He says we are to act on faith, believing that all He has said He will do.

I also prayed daily that God would work in Jack's heart according to what Ⅱ Peter 3:7 says: "In the same way, you married men should live considerately with your wives, with an intelligent recognition of the marriage relation, honoring the woman as the weaker but realizing that you are joint heirs of the grace of life, in order that your prayers may not be hindered and cut off. Otherwise you can not pray effectively."

I like that passage. It shows that God is deeply concerned about the way a husband treats his wife—so concerned that it affects the way He hears a man's prayers.

‣ Faint Hints of Dawn in the Midst of the Darkness

Gradually, the Lord began to open my eyes. I saw what I was doing or had done in the past that Jack used as excuses for the way he was behaving. It was incredibly painful to have these things revealed. I felt as if we were straining at my gnats but swallowing Jack's camels. Nevertheless, the Lord assured me it was important for me to remove anything that Jack could use as an accusation. Worst of all, I was to confess these things to Jack and ask his forgiveness. That was a bitter pill, especially when he would laugh at me. But as I followed through, I became freer and freer inside. Jack, however, felt ever more miserable because it was harder and harder to blame me.

After several months, I decided to try a three-day fast. The time I normally would have spent eating was spent worshiping God and praying 2 Corinthians 10:3–6, asking God to cast down the strongholds in both Jack and me. On the third day of the fast, a strong impression came into my mind: *Jack has three problems. He's taken $350 that doesn't belong to him, he's committed adultery, and he has a lot of pride. I am going to deal with things in that order.*

I couldn't believe it. I was sure I was deluded, maybe even hallucinating because I was hungry. I knew my Jack wasn't a thief, and let's just forget about the other two issues. Still, it seemed strange to me that I would know this. Where would it have come from?

"These are pretty serious charges, God," I said. "I'm going to need some confirmation that they're true."

Within a few days, I had confirmation that the first charge was true. (However, it was going to be awhile before I knew that Jack was addicted to pornography.) A friend, Larry, stopped by and asked me for $900 he had lent Jack to buy a car. Jack had told me about the original transaction at the time he'd bought the car, but he told me he had paid for the car all by himself. He specifically told me, rather proudly, that he hadn't had to borrow any money to get it. And now, here was Larry, saying that not only had Jack borrowed money from him, but also the repayment was past due.

I couldn't understand why Jack thought it necessary to lie to me. I hadn't questioned him about the purchase in the first place. It was information he had volunteered. I really didn't care if he'd had to borrow money to get the car. I *did* care that he hadn't repaid it as promised, and I was devastated to realize he'd lied to me about it. Still, I was able to handle the whole conversation with grace. I knew the Lord was showing me Jack had taken money that didn't belong to him. He was also showing me Jack had a problem with lying.

Going Back into the Darkness

That night, when I told Jack about my conversation with Larry, Jack tried to confuse me by saying I hadn't understood. He said he *had* told me he'd borrowed the money. This time I was not confused. This time I didn't back down. Instead, I took a deep breath and said, "I don't think the real problem is the $900 that you owe Larry. I think the real problem is the $350 you took that doesn't belong to you."

Jack's face registered shock and then relief. "I'm *so* ready to deal with this," he said, and then he told me that the summer he was 19, he'd borrowed $350 from one of his dad's financial supporters to buy a car. He'd never repaid it. He was angry with his dad for leaving him in the States and going back to "serve the Lord." In Jack's twisted thinking, not repaying the money was a way to get back at his dad for abandoning him in a strange country. The longer he went without repaying, the harder it was to call the man and figure out a way to deal with the issue.

I was relieved and excited. We were making headway. Although, at this point, I had no idea if the other two revelations were true, I felt the Lord was casting down at least one stronghold in Jack's life. Things were going to be better soon, I just knew it. But I was wrong.³ Jack couldn't bring himself to contact the man. It had been so long—18 years—he just didn't know what he would say. So he let it slide. And I sank deeper into despair.

You Want Me to Receive Help from a Samaritan, Lord?

Several months later, I went on another three-day fast. I was desperate! Jack's behavior was getting more bizarre: more wild-eyed staring, more smoldering anger, more withdrawal. On the third day of my fast, my best friend gave me a registration form for a Marriage Encounter weekend. Clipped to the inside of the form was $20 for the registration fee.

"Jim and I want you guys to go on this," she told me. "We went and got a lot out of it."

I gulped. Marriage Encounter was a Catholic weekend. I had grown up in a home where Catholics were regularly condemned, and I had attended churches where they were regularly attacked from the pulpits. Although I didn't think they were evil, I certainly didn't think they could be saved. And I knew that I shouldn't be unequally yoked together with unbelievers, not even in a weekend encounter! Yet, I had fasted and prayed for an answer and this was what had come. I could almost hear God chuckling.

I was amazed when Jack agreed to go. The weekend wasn't scheduled until January—a full six weeks away. Plenty of time to tell the Lord He didn't know what He was doing.

That Christmas, I received another rainbow as a gift. This one was on a trivet. "Look for the rainbow" was written in flowing script across the bottom. I knew God was reminding me of His promise that there would be no destruction in the midst of my storms. And, somehow, I knew He was encouraging me to antici-pate what He would do on the Marriage Encounter weekend.

Being Loved to a New Perspective

When we drove onto the grounds where the Marriage Encounter was being held, I felt a lot of fear and trepidation, mingled with tremendous anticipation. I was hoping for answers to our marriage problems. What I didn't know until later was that the gift of the weekend wasn't for our marriage, it was for me. (At this point, our marriage couldn't be helped because the Marriage Encounter seeks to show couples how to share their hearts with each other. Since Jack was living a double life, he couldn't risk opening up for fear of revealing something that would explode his duplicity. But God had a lot to teach me about sharing my heart.)

From the beginning, the weekend blew me away. We were greeted with hugs, our luggage was carried to our room, and our every need was anticipated. I wasn't used to such unconditional love. It made me feel uncomfortable.

Then the talks began. *Can these people teach* me *anything?* I wondered. I sat there with my arms crossed, waiting for some blasphemous thing to be uttered. My heresy detectors were extended full length.

Put those stupid things down. I'll let you know if there's anything going on that isn't right! the Lord said to me.

When the priest said relationships were more important to God than accomplishments, I knew I had heard the first "heresy." Although the churches I had attended were fundamental in their doctrine about salvation by grace, they taught that God had a long list of expectations for us. These expectations had to do with a series of rules about what I should do and shouldn't do. I had experienced a lot of inner turmoil over the years because I never quite believed that God required those things of me, but I couldn't defend my position from Scripture. So, I was both shocked and delighted to hear the priest say that my willingness to play by the rules didn't matter to God as much as how much I loved Him and others.

I thought I heard the second "heresy" when the priest said that feelings were neither right nor wrong; they were just feelings. Once again, while we were encouraged, even commanded, to have good feelings, some of the churches we had attended had taught that "bad" feelings were right up there next to questioning authority, for the things that could get you into serious trouble with God. These acts of rebelliousness were to be avoided at all costs.

I had to go back to our room and think about this. The priest was saying things that I had always thought were true of God, but had gotten confused about because I had been taught the opposite viewpoint. By now, I'd spent many months searching Scripture for truth, and I sat there pondering what the priest had said. I remembered the many things I'd learned in Romans about how Paul had encouraged the baby Christians not to go back into a slavery to rules because salvation is by grace through faith, not by works. I remembered many places where Jesus had expressed feelings, particularly "bad" feelings like anger and frustration and even depression.

I remembered a passage in Hebrews 1–2 that I'd been meditating on. That passage says the suffering Jesus went through qualifies Him to be my High Priest. Because He knows what it is to suffer, the passage continues, Jesus uses the office of High Priest to comfort us in our afflictions, not to judge us for being weak and foolish. I thought about the fact that Jesus had been considered a renegade by the religious leaders of His day because He hadn't conformed to their expectations of what a Messiah should or shouldn't do. I thought about how, rather than building monuments to Himself, He had invested His life in building loving friendships with a small band of men and women.

As these truths settled into my heart, a major paradigm shift occurred. What a relief it was to realize that God didn't require me to live up to some incredible standard of perfection! How awesome to think that there was a possibility of truly intimate relationships with God and others, based not on what was expected of me, but on the honesty of who I really was. Even before the Marriage Encounter weekend, I was beginning to experience the freedom of being honest with God in prayer; but now that I knew that it was really okay with God for me to just be myself, I began to experience a truly intimate relationship with Him. I stopped holding back what was in my troubled heart and began to pour everything out to Him.

Having Life Spoken Over Us

Father Roger blessed us at the Marriage Encounter weekend. Putting his hands on both our heads, he looked us right in the eyes and spoke life over us: "Jack and Laurie, a couple very precious in the sight of God, whom God believes in and for whom God has great plans."

Eight years later, I can still feel the warmth of Father Roger's hand on my head. His words blew a breath of encouragement on the embers of hope stirring in my heart.

I went into the weekend hoping for our marriage to be healed. But God was going to answer my prayers in a much bigger way than I'd ever dreamed possible. Through an encounter with unconditional love, God healed me of my spiritual pride. Through an encounter with the meaning of marriage, He released me to enter into greater intimacy with Him as His bride. Through an encounter with feelings, He released me to know myself and to permit myself to be totally known by Him.

Shortly after this weekend, we sold our house and moved to Vermont. And that's when the *real* trouble started.

The Uncovering

The progressive work of sanctification is only fully effective when the radical, inner transformation of justification is realized and appropriated by faith.

(Neal Anderson)

I will not in any way fail you nor give you up, nor leave you without support. I will not. I will not. I will not in any degree leave you helpless, nor forsake you, nor let you down, nor relax my hold on you—Assuredly not!

(Hebrews 13:5b)

F reshly buoyed from our Marriage Encounter weekend, we began our move to Vermont with much hope. We had some tools for communication. We got hooked up with a Marriage Encounter support group that met every two weeks, and I loved being with other couples who wanted their marriages to work.

Jack was trying to start a business out of our home, so he was around every day. I was delighted and so hopeful that we could finally become a family. But, soon, serious difficulties became part of our everyday reality. For one thing, Jack had no real plan for how he was going to make his business work. If work came in, fine. If it didn't, well, things would be better tomorrow. Our financial situation was precarious, to say the least. But this did not seem to bother Jack. He kept saying he would "get it together." (This approach to life is called "magic thinking" and is typical of an addict. But remember, at this point, I didn't know Jack was an addict. Everything was still a "secret.")

Because I wanted Jack to be successful, I worked hard at making a dollar stretch and I tried not to focus on our financial problems. But as time went on and the business never really got off the ground, I became concerned that Jack seemed so unaware of the real financial danger we were in. There were many calls from creditors, and soon I realized that Jack was lying to them and to me about what bills were getting paid.

Then, there was strange behavior, like sitting frozen with his fork to his mouth for 20 minutes. Sometimes, he would open his mouth to say something and nothing would come out. He could sit in his chair with his mouth wide open for many minutes. The times that he did speak, it was usually in sentence fragments that made little sense. If I asked for clarification, he would become angry. Later, when he was in recovery, I asked him what was happening inside him during these episodes. He said he would suddenly be paralyzed with fear and his mind would go totally blank.

Until the move to Vermont, I had enjoyed a good relationship with my children. There was, of course, their sadness over their dad's lack of involvement in their lives. Still, we were able to talk about most things. They generally obeyed me, and when they didn't, things were resolved with discipline, talk, and hugs all around.

Now Jack began to play games with the children, and things changed dramatically. He would tell me to have them do something, and then when they were doing it, he would tell them I was being unreasonable for expecting them to do it. He almost seemed to get enjoyment out of the chaos this game caused.

When I finally decided I would disengage from the game by asking him to deal with the children directly, he began to tear me down in front of them. Every time I talked with him about it, he told me he knew it was wrong and he wouldn't do it anymore, but he continued. This all came at a crucial time in the children's lives. They were entering their teen years, and they had just had to leave their friends and the home they had grown up in. They were confused and fearful about what was happening. Our home, which had been relatively peaceful up to that point, became a war zone.

I realized that part of the problem was that Jack's long hours had obscured his changed behavior. Before the move, he hadn't been around enough for me to know that his condition had really gotten this bad. Now he was with us every day, all day, and we were shocked at how little he resembled the person we thought we knew.

Some of Jack's behavior was a result of going through a type of withdrawal. At the time we moved to Vermont, there were no strip shows in our area. When he was working in Boston, Jack had attended these shows several times a week. Although he was still buying pornographic magazines and acting out with those, now there was no place for him to get his "fix." He didn't know how to cope.

Some of the behavior was a desperate blame-shifting. Jack could see that his life wasn't working and he was looking for someone he could make look as foolish and guilty as he felt. All these things are behavior characteristics that accompany an addiction. But there was absolutely no sign of any addictive agent in our home—no alcohol, no drugs, and no sign of pornographic magazines or videos. The enemy was unseen, but her presence permeated every aspect of our lives.

A Confrontation with Self

I was not coping well. I was mad at God because I didn't understand why He wasn't coming through on the promise He had given me so many years earlier. One day, while I was out walking, I was complaining to Him.

"I'm submitting to you in every way I know how, God; but no matter what I do, it's wrong," I grumbled.

Then I heard that still, small voice again. *I want you to stop submitting to Me and start abandoning yourself to Me, Laurie.*

I literally stopped in the middle of the road with my left foot held suspended in the air and shouted, "No!"

I shocked myself. No matter how difficult the task, I had never before refused to do what I felt God calling me to do. Suddenly, the Lord revealed my heart to me. He showed me that my submission to Him had been based on fear and guilt—fear that I wouldn't please Him, and guilt that maybe I had offended Him. Abandonment, I saw, would be based on love and trust. Abandonment would move me out of the place of safety into the place of risking it all. I would have to believe, all the way to my feet, that while God is not safe, He is good and completely worthy of my confidence, *no matter what the outcome.*

"It's too hard, Lord! I can't do it," I cried. Then I walked home, beaten.

But He wouldn't let me go. I struggled for a whole year, searching Scripture for some assurance that abandoning myself to God would provide a measure of safety. I found none. Instead, I found Jesus saying things like, "If you try to save your life, you will lose it. But if you are willing to lose your life, you will find it" (paraphrase of Mark 8:35) and "Fear is useless. What's needed here is trust" (paraphrase of Luke 8:50).

On my thirty-ninth birthday, I finally arrived at a point where the pain on the inside was so great that I knew that no matter what abandonment to God meant, it couldn't produce any greater pain than I was already feeling. Ready to surrender, I wanted to do something that would symbolize this important transaction. The church we came from baptized by immersion, teaching that baptism pictured death to our old way of living and resurrection to new life in Christ. I had been baptized years earlier. At the time, I had truly meant my commitment to live the Christian life, but I hadn't understood the cost. While Scripture makes it clear that we only need to be baptized once, the symbolism behind the act spoke exactly to what I was getting ready to do. So, I drove to a nearby river and walked in as deep as I could get.

"This is it, Lord. I'm giving You myself for a birthday present," I said, reenacting my baptism. "I feel like I'm hurling myself into the abyss, but I won't try to catch myself on the way down. I'll wait for You to catch me. Whatever it takes, however long it takes, I choose to trust that You are good and that Your love is all I will ever need to get through this life."

It was the first time I had ever totally accepted my own inability to earn God's approval, and it was the first time I totally rested in His unconditional acceptance of me. Salvation, I now knew in a way I'd never known before, was truly by grace through faith. I had opened the way for God to take the next step.

The Covering Comes Off

Remember I told you that after I'd fasted and prayed for three days, the Lord strongly impressed on my mind that Jack had taken $350 that didn't belong to him, had committed adultery, and had a lot of pride? Not long after that, I'd found out that he had taken the money, so I knew that part was true. And every time I would approach him about getting psychological help or some financial counseling, he would say, "I don't need help. Besides, I have a lot of pride, you know." So, I was beginning to accept that pride was an issue. But adultery?

It was like a sandwich. The $350 dollars was one slab of bread. The pride was the other slab. That left the adultery as the unsavory filling. Several times, I tentatively broached the subject with Jack. Each time, he steadfastly denied that he was being unfaithful.

I kept feeling an urgency to face the adultery, but I was absolutely mystified about how I could face it if there was no proof and Jack was denying it. It's a terrible arrogance to falsely accuse someone of committing adultery. I didn't want to do that to Jack. But there was something else stopping me: I hadn't completely settled the matter in my own mind. Jack's denials were what I wanted to hear because I didn't want to believe he was being unfaithful.

I began to say to myself, "Hey, you got two out of three." So I stopped praying because God might bring it up again. I kept my mind too busy to think about it. At night, I would lie awake because I was afraid if I went to sleep, something might slip past my carefully constructed mental blocks. This went on for many months. Meanwhile, my marriage continued to fall apart.

I was certainly in a dance of denial, but inside I was crying out for truth. I'm so glad that God looks past the surface, to the innermost part of our beings, sifting and analyzing the thoughts and intents of our hearts. Then, when the groanings of our pain are too terrifying for us to bring them into the light of day, the Holy Spirit intercedes for us before God's throne and says, "Look, she says she doesn't want to know, but she needs to know."

One night, as I lay there rigidly defying sleep, I felt the Lord comforting me. *You need to go to sleep now. There are some things I want to show you. Don't be afraid. I won't leave you alone.*

For the first time in months, I felt safe, and so I rested. That night, it all came out in my dreams. The prostitutes were there and they talked to me, and I felt the anger and shame that I'd never been able to express when my guard was up. When I woke up the next morning, I had come to accept that Jack's adultery was real.

"I still don't see any physical proof that anything in that dream could be true, Lord," I said. "But I abandon myself to what You want to do here."

I began that morning to journal my feelings about the adultery. I wrote about my anguish and sense of betrayal. Day after day, I wrote. Sometimes, when the feelings were too intense to own, I wrote short stories and allowed the characters to experience feelings I felt were unsafe to have.

After several weeks, I got to the point at which I knew I needed to totally abandon the outcome of Jack's adultery to God. I didn't know what actions I might have to take. Would I be able to stay in the marriage? Would I have to divorce him? It all looked so terrifying. This was a big step for me because it meant I had to be willing to risk the outcome.

On my thirty-ninth birthday, I had agreed to abandon myself to the "whatever." Now that commitment was being put to the test. I'd been praying for many years for Jack to be healed. What if it meant that something truly terrible had to be revealed in order for him to be healed? Was I willing?

Journaling this step was terrifying, but finally I came to the point of decision. I knelt at a chair in my living room and imagined it to be an altar. Carefully, I put my family and my marriage on that altar. Then I prayed: "They're yours, God. I never really owned them. I only thought I did. Do what you have to do. Just, *please*, be careful with my children."

The next morning when I was praying, I felt the Lord telling me, *I'm going to deal with the adultery now.*

I never cease to amaze myself. I'd been working through to this very point for about six years, the Lord had comforted me with His presence, and I'd spent the last month or so actively working through to acceptance of this very thing, and do you know what my first reaction was? Stark terror. See, there was still that one little place in me that was still hoping that maybe I was really just delusional.

As I sat there with my heart racing and my forehead breaking out in a sweat, I felt that comforting Presence again.

My grace is sufficient for you. My grace is sufficient for you. My grace is sufficient for you.

The Lord said it three times, just to make sure I got the point. Immediately, I felt complete peace and rested deeply.

Later that morning, I got a call from a creditor. Jack was managing the money and there had been a lot of calls from creditors. When I would tell Jack about them, he would always assure me that he had made the payment but that somehow it hadn't been recorded in time to avoid a call.

This particular creditor was the holder of the charge account Jack had used for business and travel expenses when he had been in management. Those expenses had been reimbursed by his employer. When Jack left the company, the reimbursement stopped—the expenses should have stopped as well. I had seen the bills coming in, however, and wondered why we were still getting them. Jack told me he was making minimun payments on a plane ticket we had purchased.

In the three years we'd been in Vermont, Jack had been working only sporadically, so it made sense that that bill might not be paid off. Several months earlier, Jack had taken a job, and I knew that money had been set aside to make monthly payments on that bill. But now I learned that no payments had been made for many months. I also learned that the balance was in the thousands of dollars. Shaken, I hung up and called Jack at work.

"I'm going to call your father," I said, after telling him about the creditor. "I'm going to appeal to him because he married us. I know there's something wrong here, and I'm going to ask him to help me find out what it is."[2]

Just as I hung up from talking to Jack's dad, Jack pulled into the driveway. He had asked his boss for a few hours off and driven home.

"I don't have a problem with money," he said as he burst through the door. "I have a problem with lust."

There's No Pain Like Discovering
That Your Worst Nightmare Is True

In the next few hours, much of the story came out. It came out haltingly; it came out reluctantly; but it came out. Jack and I worked out a plan for each of us to go for counseling and begin to attend a Twelve Step Group. But over the next two years, it became increasingly apparent that Jack was unwilling to be honest. His counselor would give him an assignment, and Jack would go to his next appointment and lie about having completed it, even to the point of making up stories about going to different people to ask for forgiveness. Jack was also lying to his Twelve Step Group about the progress he was making.

His behavior continued to be bizarre and he was still involved in pornography. He kept promising that he was going to try to do better, but he wasn't willing to change his lifestyle. He seemed to think he could somehow continue in both worlds—the world where he worked hard to convince people he was a devoted family man, and the world where he was consumed with his sexual addiction.

I watched my children wither as the forgiveness they extended to their father was treated as something they owed him rather than a precious gift from childish hearts that wanted above all else to believe in their daddy. Jack told himself that our willingness to forgive him meant he hadn't really done anything that awful, so he felt he could continue in his addiction. Besides, he told me, he didn't have to live by the same rules other people did.

Addicts need to reach the end of themselves before they are ready to give up their addictions. After many difficult and dangerous days, it became clear that Jack was nowhere near the end of his rope. After intense struggle and much prayer, I decided a separation was the most loving thing I could do. I realized that I needed to care more about Jack's soul than I did about our relationship. Separation was the only thing left to help him face the reality of his choices. It was the hardest decision I've ever made, but it was part of the ongoing abandonment to "whatever it takes, Lord."

CHAPTER 6

Used Up and Wasted

Hope deferred makes the heart sick.

(Proverbs 13:12a)

A person's hope is deadened when nothing she does is good enough, or when all her choices, no matter what they are, are used to punish her.

(Dan Allender and Tremper Longman III)

T he letters in this chapter were written to Jack during our separation. Writing them was a way I could keep him close to my heart. It was also a way for me to come to grips with the pain inside. I never mailed the letters because it wasn't wise to do so. They are shared with you only to help you understand the devastation caused by behaviors associated with addictions. For all the people out there who claim pornography is a victimless crime, I hope these letters are a reality check. They show that real lives are destroyed and real hearts are broken when somebody looks at any body.

Dear Jack,
We've been separated for two whole days now. Funny. I've been counting the hours, just like we did when we first got married.
"Wow! We've been married 10 whole hours," I'd say.
"Can you believe it? We've been married 24 whole hours!" you'd say.
"We've been separated three whole hours." And the countdown started.

45

Right after I hung up, I bundled the kids into the car and headed for Aunt Mary and Uncle George's place. I didn't want to be there when you got home. I couldn't stand to watch you clean out your closet. And I knew I couldn't go through another tearful round of "I'm going to get it together, I really am. Trust me on this."

As we were driving down to Massachusetts, I said to the kids, "I asked Dad for a separation." It just came out of my mouth the way "I'll take a large decaf and one of those cranberry muffins" would. I couldn't believe it. Seems like "I asked Dad for a separation" ought to have a different feeling in my mouth. The words are from another language; one I never thought I'd speak. It should have been harder to wrap my lips around them.

"We love you, Mom." They said it right together, as if they'd rehearsed it.

They're good kids. They deserve better than this, I thought.

Then, "You deserve better, Mom."

Deserve. What's to deserve in love? Love is about giving. You're supposed to endure all things, hope all things. But I'm too tired to endure anymore, and my hope ran out when I discovered you lied to me once more. How come you're such a liar?

"Mom, you did everything you could." Sandy's voice sounded firm, calm.

Kids shouldn't have to be a cheering squad for their parents' separation. Parents are supposed to cheer their kids on—together.

"Are you guys okay with this?" I asked them.

"Yeah, Mom, you should have done it a long time ago," Ian said with resignation.

It's the wrong answer, but maybe this is going to be all right, I thought. *Maybe they're not going to be trashed like other kids whose parents break up. Oh, God, please, Please, PLEASE don't let my babies fall apart. Please keep them safe while their family is falling apart.*

Later you called to make sure we got there, and you wanted to talk to the kids. Why? You never had time for them before.

Sandy collapsed. Talking with you brought all her angers and fears to the fore. She was crying so hard, she couldn't get her breath, and I had to catch her as she fell. Ian spent three hours on the phone with Tess. He couldn't tell me how he was feeling, but he choked it out to her.

Dear God, it's already started. My babies are dying, and I can't do anything to save them. I don't even have the strength to save myself.

Dear Jack,

Monday, Uncle George told Aunt Mary to take me out and buy me a new outfit—from the skin out.

"I saw your underwear when you washed your clothes. You need something decent to wear," Aunt Mary said.

The outfit is beautiful—something I can wear while I look for work. Just thinking about going back to work makes my insides feel all jumbled together with the most curious mixture of shame and gratitude. I feel like Cinderella, but I'm ashamed that my fairy godmother knows I need her.

Then yesterday, Uncle George told me to dress up in my new clothes; he was going to take me out to lunch to meet some of his business associates. One of them specializes in helping small companies start up. Uncle George thought I might get some helpful advice.

"Networking is everything," he told me.

My insides were in an uproar all the way into Boston. I felt like I was all dressed up in someone else's clothes. Just yesterday, I had been a wife and a mother, a home-school teacher and a childbirth educator. How I loved all those roles! Now I have to be something new—a businesswoman. It doesn't fit right.

"Her husband has a serious illness and he's not able to provide for his family right now, so Laurie is starting her own business," Uncle George explained to his associates over lunch. "Serious illness"—nice euphemism for sexual addiction.

After I got back from the lunch date with Uncle George, Ann called and asked me to stop by. I cried when she gave me a check to buy myself a new coat. My old one was so ratty, I was embarrassed to wear it, but I had nothing else, so I just wore it and hoped no one noticed. I'm so ashamed that Ann could see how poorly I have been taking care of myself. I went to the coat outlet and bought a full-length purple wool coat—purple for the color of suffering. When I slipped it on, it hung heavy all around me, enveloping me like a warm hug, and I felt loved. Whenever I have a bad day, I'm going to put it on.

Today, Aunt Mary and Aunt Sarah took me to a food warehouse and told me to load up several carts. I wept with joy that I would be able to feed the children. I bought lots of basic ingredients so I could cook nutritious meals from scratch, but I did get two box mixes—one of brownies and one of blueberry muffins—and a big bag of chocolate chips. It meant so much to get something special, something that would be a real treat for the kids in the hard days ahead. I comfort myself thinking about how the tempting aroma of freshly baked muffins or warm chocolate chip cookies will help them on those days when we will feel your absence so much.

Mary and Sarah paid for the groceries out of the rent money from Gammie's house. "She would want us to do this for you," they said. And I knew they were right. But still, I'm so glad Gammie doesn't know how our marriage turned out. She was family to the core, and giving up was an option she didn't understand. I feel that I've failed her.

Finally, when I got back from the warehouse, Uncle George handed me a large check to help me get some things to start a writing business. "You can use some of this for basic expenses, if you need to," he said.

I was overwhelmed and told him I'd make him my major stockholder. How did I get into this position of having to let others do for me? This is humiliation with a capital "H."

All this generosity is putting the 20 years with you in a stark new light—it was like living off corn husks and never having enough to fill the gnawing emptiness. Now, without you, good things are starting to happen. I feel as if God has opened the floodgates of heaven and poured out blessings on the dry, weary ground of my heart. Why couldn't it have happened with you?

I'm going to find a way to pay them back—Uncle George, Aunt Mary, Aunt Sarah, and Ann. I will. It might take me a long time; but I'm going to pay them back. In the meantime, I'm eating humble pie with a grateful heart.

Dear Jack,

I drove home today. I've driven home from Mary and George's dozens of times in the last few years and with each rotation of the tires, I always felt myself getting more and more excited. I was going home! But not this time. This time, the tires seemed to be driving me irrevocably toward the thing I don't want the most—a home without you.

When we walked through the door, the silence of the empty house screamed at us. All evening my ears kept straining to hear the crunch of your tires as you pulled into the driveway. I dreaded looking into your closet. It was dumb, but part of me wanted to believe that your stuff was still here. I took a hurried peek and then my eyes blurred. I had to do something with that empty space, so I quickly filled up the shelves with the canned goods Mary and Sarah had bought us. *We'll make it into a pantry*, I thought. I noticed the kids peeked in, too. All of us were hoping, always hoping, that you'd come back and be the husband and father we need.

Then it was time for bed and that was the hardest of all. Ian and Sandy didn't want to have prayer time, not even after I tried to explain to them how good God had been to us through other people and that we should thank Him for all His help.

"Prayer doesn't work, Mom," Ian said. "You've prayed for Dad for years and he's still the same."

His words pierced my heart. I don't want the children to lose their faith in God. God is the only Daddy they have now. They went to bed without praying, and I lay in bed trying to voice my concerns to God.

"I'll just pray for them," I told myself. But the words wouldn't come. Ian was right. I have prayed for you for years—20 long years—and nothing's budged. Nothing's changed.

Finally, I just cried out, "Are you up there, God? Do you care?"

There was no answer.

P.S. I forgot to tell you something. Once I knew I needed to pull out of your life, finding someone to care about you was extremely important to me. So, I called Promise Keepers and Focus on the Family and asked them if they would try to reach you at your new home to help you get on your feet. Both promised they would.

When I told Ian, he shook his head and said, "You never stop believing in him, do you, Mom?"

"Oh, no, Ian!" I replied. "I *don't* believe in your dad, I believe in God. He gave me a promise a long time ago that He would heal your dad. For a long time, I thought that meant He was going to heal our marriage. I'm not so sure now, but I know He'll heal your dad."

Ian just looked angry and walked away. It broke my heart.

Dear Jack,

Here I am, three weeks into our separation. I didn't sleep much last night. The bed seemed so cold without you in it. Finally, somewhere in the wee hours, I dozed off fitfully. When I woke up this morning, I thought back to that first morning when I awakened in your arms, so happy, so hopeful of all the bright tomorrows we were going to have. Yet, here I am 20 years later, thinking about how I might never again lie in your arms.

Besides loneliness, I feel sick—like I'm going to throw up—and I tell myself I have to be strong for the children. But that's not all I feel. What I feel mostly is anger. *I'm mad.* I don't understand why you won't let go of the pornography and the hookers. How could you choose them over the children? How could you choose them over me? You were all I ever wanted. *How come I wasn't enough for you?*

Today, I called some of our friends to tell them what was happening in our lives. Betty and Sam have always admired us so much. I had never asked to be their hero, but how I hated to be part of murdering their vision of our family.

"You've struggled with this a long time, Laurie. No one blames you. You've given it your best shot." That's what Betty told me as I was blowing my nose and sobbing into the phone.

Great! I gave it my best shot. But my best shot wasn't good enough—not for the thing I wanted most. How come my best shot couldn't get me the marriage I wanted so much? How come my best shot wasn't good enough for you?

After I got off the phone with Betty, I thought back to all the times I had to "go it alone" because you were out there doing your thing. Of course, you told me you were working, and I tried so hard to be on your team instead of on your back about the long hours you kept. Even though I tried to be a good sport, I hated it when I had to take childbirth classes all alone before the birth of our own children. (I kept playing with my wedding ring so the other couples in the class would know I was married.) I tried not to mind when you didn't come see me in the hospital after the babies were born. I tried not to mind the times when they were sick, or I was sick, and you weren't there to help me. Sometimes I'd cry and ask you why you were gone so many hours, and you'd tell me it was all for a good cause. You were out "serving the Lord," you told me, and then you'd say that next week we'd have more time together. But next week never came, and I kept trying to have a good attitude.

I kept the house clean and the children happy and baked bread and made cookies and kept myself attractive, but you were never there and when you were, you'd sit glassy-eyed and stare off into the distance. And when I'd ask your opinion on something, like what did you want me to do about sending the kids to school, you'd sit rigid in your chair and wouldn't say a thing.

So I'd get down on my knees and beg: "Please, Jack, time is running out, the decision about school has to be made by next week." But you'd keep sitting there and wouldn't say a thing. I'd do my best to try to figure out what you wanted me to do and I'd do that.

Then, when we'd go out somewhere, like church, you'd rally and be your charming self, and everyone thought you were just wonderful. "I want people to think I'm a nice guy," you'd say. Well, they did. With your sterling background and your likable personality, I thought I must be the problem, so I just kept trying harder. But inside, I felt like I was falling and falling, tumbling endlessly into an abyss. And there was no one to catch me.

Dear Jack,

You'll never guess what arrived today—an anniversary card with a bunch of $5's and a few $10's tucked inside. All together it added up to $50. The card was anonymous and said, "From all of us to help celebrate your Twentieth Anniversary." Can you believe it? They must not have gotten the word about our separation, so they can't be very close friends, but who would do such a thing if they weren't close friends?

Our twentieth anniversary a month ago was an awful day, and I hope never to live through another like it. It was like all the other anniversaries. You didn't have any plans to do anything special. You didn't have a gift. You didn't even have a card. Somehow the fact that it was our twentieth made the neglect harder to take. You said, "I'll get it together, I promise," just like you always do. This time I didn't pretend that I understood. This time I cried and cried.

I meant every word I said to you that day 20 years ago, all that stuff about loving, honoring, cherishing, and forsaking all others. Did you mean it, too, or did you just mouth the words? How could you mean them when from day one, for you this marriage has been about lust, not love?

Ironic isn't it, how lust destroys the very thing it lusts after until, at the end, the thing being consumed has no beauty that anyone would desire? Lust never has enough. When the magazines weren't enough, you went to the strip shows; and when they weren't enough, you bought the girls and took them back to your hotel room. And it didn't matter how many of them you had, it was never enough.

Now I've had enough. Enough hurting. Enough crying. Enough hoping. Still, I didn't spend the money in the anniversary card. I put it away in my bureau drawer. *Maybe, just maybe, it's a sign,* I thought. *Maybe Jack will get help after all.*

Dear Jack,

I put away the last of the Christmas things today. Oh, how it hurt! The kids couldn't stand to see the stuff, especially the stockings that said "Daddy," "Mommy," "Ian," and "Sandy." So, I took them down right after the separation, even before we left. But the rest of the stuff, I couldn't make myself put away until now. Christmas is about family and dreams of family. Putting everything away meant all the years of longing for a family that was whole were over. Saying

Christmas was over meant all my dreams of our life together were as dead as the needles that fell to the carpet under our tree.

Maybe it's part of accepting what is true instead of what I so desperately want to be true. Christmas was always a difficult time for me because you never gave me anything. I know, now, your inability to give was a natural outgrowth of your addiction to pornography. Lust is selfish. It gives nothing unless it can use that gift to get what it wants from the receiver. You were always wondering, "What's in it for me?"

Your lack of effort to get me a gift was always a bit awkward to explain to the kids. They were great tree inspectors, crawling in and out among the gifts, shaking, poking, guessing what might be there. They would always notice there was nothing for me.

"Mommy, how come there isn't anything under the tree for you?"

"When's Daddy going to take us shopping so we can get something for you?"

"I don't need anything. I have you and you're the best gift I could ever get," I'd say and give them a hug.

It doesn't matter, I'd think, because it was true—the children were the best gift I had.

But having my stocking hang empty when everyone else's was bulging on Christmas morning was somehow harder than not having anything under the tree, because you know tree gifts are from people, but we pretend the stocking is from Santa, who knows if you've been naughty or nice. And so I'd choke down the lump of coal in my throat and force back the tears. I must have been very naughty to never get anything.

As they got older, the kids caught on that Santa didn't visit Mommy. So, on Christmas morning, they'd jump up and down shouting, "Check your stocking, Mommy, check your stocking!" And so I'd take the emaciated thing down from the mantle and I'd find a stick of gum, a pretty picture, a smooth rock, or one of their treasures.

How can you be sad about this? The children love you. It doesn't matter if Jack doesn't, I'd think.

And I lived quite successfully that way for a number of years, until one Christmas morning, I looked at that pathetic stocking and said, "It does matter, and it hurts like hell." (At the time, such a strong word would never have come out of my mouth. But I know today that saying something "hurts like hell" is an appropriate way to describe what it feels like to be robbed of your personhood— only hell does that to us.)

So, what made me change? It was getting God's perspective on this marriage. It happened in a funny way. A few weeks before Christmas, I was reading in John 13 the time when Jesus went around the room washing His disciples' feet.

When He came to Peter, Peter said, "Lord, are my feet to be washed by You?"

Then Jesus told Peter that he didn't yet understand what this was all about, but he would someday.

Peter said, "You're *never* going to wash my feet!"

Jesus replied, "Unless I wash you, you have no part in Me—no share in companionship with Me."

I thought about that passage for a long time. I tried to imagine what it must have been like to be Peter. He was seeing the Man who told him he was "right on" when he'd said, "This is Jesus, the Christ, the Son of the Living God." He was seeing the Christ put a towel around His waist and do a menial servant's task of washing his friends' feet. Peter was probably boiling inside over the whole thing. "How can they let Him do that?" he probably asked himself. It just seemed so inappropriate to Jesus' true station in life.

When Jesus got to Peter, Peter refused. Yes, his feet were dirty, and yes, they needed to be washed; but Jesus shouldn't do such a thing. He, Peter, was unworthy of that kind of daily-care attention from the Lord. "Save it for the bigger stuff, Jesus. This piddly stuff like dirty feet doesn't matter. It's beneath your dignity." Peter's motives seemed so noble, so humble. But Jesus' rebuke was telling. "Unless I wash you, you have no companionship with Me."

I saw how what was masquerading as humility was really an inverted form of pride. Peter judged his true needs as not worthy of being met by Jesus. He was saying, "I don't need you in the minutiae of life, Lord. I can take care of things myself."

Do you see, Jack? It was the "I can take care of things myself" and not letting Christ be involved in the daily stuff, and only bringing Him out for the noble ventures, that was Peter's problem. He couldn't admit he was needy, especially in an area he told himself he shouldn't bother anyone else with because he could take care of it himself. That's pride.

Jesus was saying that it's when we learn we can't meet our own needs that we have true companionship with Him. Then we can giggle together as we splash our feet in the warm, soapy water. We can feel soothed as the soft towel rubs our tired feet dry. We can hug at the end of the gift and say, "Thanks, Friend, I needed that."

Needing someone to fill my Christmas stocking is the same thing. It's a piddly minutia in everyday life. It's about needing. It's about saying, "I can't do it myself."

It's about letting others into my life. So, that Christmas I went to our room and cried, "I do *need*, Lord. Fill my stocking. Fill it all the way up."

I couldn't see it then, but now I can see that in some ways we have a similar problem. I love to give, but I can't receive. You gobble everything up, but can't give out. Deep inside, in the hidden places where motivations arise, our brokenness is the same—neither of us can relax into the companionship that comes from embracing our neediness.

Make that "*could* relax." I'm learning, and it feels good. It's terrifying to trust in the goodness of others. It opens me to crushing vulnerability. But I'm coming to see that there's no other way to truly belong to life. Relaxing—learning to trust— is a new skill and I'm clumsy at it. Before this whole thing is over, I imagine I'll have lots of chances to practice.

Dear Jack,

I got the Monitor heater installed today. I wanted the house warm for the kids. I wanted them to know that life is better than living for five years in northern Vermont without heat. I can't figure out why you never put it in. It was here, ready to go. How could you let us be so cold?

It's so hard to get people to understand that your addiction to pornography has broader implications than just having you zoned out over Miss September. Lust made you selfish. You only took care of yourself. You wouldn't take care of us. Lust made you angry. When I'd decided the children had waited long enough to be warm, and I suggested getting someone to install the heater, you got furious and told me you were going to take care of it.

In hindsight, I can see I was the stupid one not to go ahead and risk your anger and put the thing in anyway, but I was trying so hard not usurp your place of leadership. The people at church told me if I would just trust you, you would rise to the occasion. They didn't understand how I'd been trusting you for years and years. They told me I would be controlling if I took over things that were your responsibility. So, our children were cold for no reason for five long years. I wonder if any of those church folk's children have been cold for no reason.

I figured I'd need about $525 to have the Monitor installed. That would get me a 265-gallon kerosene tank, pay to have the tank and the heater installed, and put 100 gallons of kerosene in the tank (that's the minimum order).

I started praying about it because I didn't know where the money was going to come from (it seemed like I was asking for the world). A few days later, a check arrived in the mail for the exact amount. So, in answer to prayer, the kids and I have received groceries, clothes, and heat. That's the kind of stuff I always read happened in someone else's life. My heart is so thankful that God would move others to help us, but my head says it's all too bizarre to think it's anything more than coincidence.

I think God is giving me plenty of opportunities to start feeling the goodness of receiving—to start accepting that I need others, that I can't do this life on my own. I also think He's being extra special to me because He knows how much I didn't want to separate from you. He knows how many years I cried out to Him for wisdom to know how to love you, when I was hurting so much inside.

I read Isaiah 54:4–6 in my devotions this morning. It explains how I feel:

> Fear not, for you shall not be ashamed; neither be confounded and depressed, for you shall not be put to shame; for you shall forget the shame of your youth, and you shall not remember the reproach of your widowhood anymore.
>
> For your Maker is your husband, the Lord of hosts is His name; and the Holy One of Israel is your Redeemer, the God of the whole earth He is called.
>
> For the Lord has called you like a woman forsaken, grieved in spirit and heartsore, even a wife wooed and won in youth, when she is later refused and scorned, says your God.

That's how I feel, like an ashamed, forsaken, heartsick, rejected wife. The Lord is now my husband, and He is taking good care of me.

So, anyway, after the check came, I called the oil company and had them put the Monitor in. And tonight, the house is gloriously, luxuriously, and exquisitely warm!

This place is under new management, I thought. *We take care of ourselves. We get things done.*

P.S. I forgot to tell you that when the money arrived, Ian said, "There are some really good people out there, aren't there, Mom?"

My heart has been so heavy as I watched his disappointment in you, because of your lying and manipulation, turn to bitter cynicism. I'm more grateful that someone restored Ian's faith in people than I am that we are warm.

Dear Jack,

Sam Matthews called today.

"I had an interesting conversation with Jack today," Sam said. "He said the reason you asked him for a separation is because he didn't pay the insurance bill." I wanted to throw up! I wanted to scream! You still didn't get it.

"Sam, it's true he didn't pay the insurance bill, just like he didn't pay a lot of bills he told me he'd paid. He kept using the bill money to fund his addiction."

I told Sam about all the times we'd had insurance canceled. I told him about my worries that the lights were going to be turned off and the phone disconnected. I told him we'd already lost our credit rating and how devastated I was to find out you had run up thousands of dollars in credit card bills to pay for your "good times."

I told him about the regular calls from creditors saying bills hadn't been paid and how when I would ask you about it, you'd tell me you'd paid the bills, that the payments just hadn't been recorded yet. I told him about the times you'd had enough money to make double payments and had not made them and how, scariest of all, you could lie to me about all of it with a perfectly straight face.

I told him how just a few weeks before our separation you had come into the kitchen, face flushed, eyes twinkling. "I just paid all the bills," you announced, "and it feels so good!" I gave you a hug and we did a little dance. But two weeks later, a notice arrived saying our insurance was being canceled for lack of payment. The next day, the phone and light company sent us shut-off notices.

That was the point at which I asked you for a separation. It wasn't because you didn't pay the bills. I asked you for a separation because you could lie so convincingly about not paying the bills. That's when I knew you were dangerously pathological. That's when I knew I'd crack if I stayed with you any longer.

It was so hard for me to tell Sam about all this because no one likes to reveal his failures and I especially didn't like to reveal yours. I spent so many years guarding your reputation, never saying anything about what was going on in our house, because I didn't want others to think less of you. I was pretty messed up in my understanding of what it means to honor your husband. I wasn't *honoring* you, I was *enabling* you.

"You know money's not the reason for the separation, Sam," I said.

"Yeah, I know," he answered. "I told Jack that junk about not paying bills was garbage and he knew it. I made him confess to me that the reason you asked for a separation was because he's an addict and he won't get help."

What a true friend Sam is, Jack. He loves you enough to tell you the truth and demand that you tell it to yourself.

Dear Jack,

I don't know which was harder—meeting you at Zachary's Pizza for supper or pulling out of the parking lot after dinner, each of us going to a separate home, a separate bed, a separate life. When you called to ask me out, I didn't know what to say. It's been four months since we separated and I did want to see how you were doing, but I didn't want to be manipulated by pleas of "I'll get it together." I wanted to see you in the process of coming together. So, I risked going. There were signs of progress, but I could see that you still aren't ready to deal with your addiction.

After dinner, I sat in the car for a long time, blinking back tears. I want so much for you to be whole and for us to be whole, but I know that can't happen until you're willing to tell yourself the truth about the choices you're making. I just couldn't understand where God was in all this. How come He wasn't keeping the promise He'd given me that night I'd wanted to leave you eight years earlier?

"Don't you care, God? Look, You gave me a promise. I'm not going to let You go until You show me what that means!" I cried. Then, because there was nothing more to be done, I started the car.

Before I could put the car into gear, I noticed a pickup truck pull into the restaurant's driveway. I felt a little creepy because the restaurant was closed and I was the only one in the lot.

"This is going to be okay. You don't have to be afraid," I said to myself as I eased the car out of the lot.

As I drove by the pickup, the Plexiglas bug screen on the hood caught my eye. Written on the bug screen were these words: Jesus Never Fails.

"Okay, Lord," I said, laughing out loud. "I don't see it, I don't feel it, but I'll believe it."

When I got home, Rick Brandon called. Jack, I don't even know how Rick found me. He didn't even know we'd moved to Vermont. Talking to him brought back so many memories about how we used to double-date and how he was your best man at our wedding. I told him all about what was going on, and he was shocked. He told me he was going to call you and tell you to put your pride aside and get the help you need. He told me he wasn't going to leave you alone until you agreed to do whatever it took to get well. "Then," he said, "I'm going to keep calling him back until I know he's really doing it."

When I hung up, I was so grateful. Who would have thought a friend from the distant past would track us down just when we needed him most? I know who: Jesus. He never fails. Okay, I'm getting it. And, somehow, I know, He'll make sure that you get it, too. Because Jesus Never Fails.

Healing Is a Process

Our separation lasted nine months, and the two and a half years that Jack's been back home have had some pretty big ups and downs. You were probably hoping I was going to say that the separation did the trick and we lived happily ever after. That would be a nice story, but it wouldn't be true, and I'm afraid it would raise totally unrealistic expectations. This is not a story about God's-Woman-of-the-Hour-with-Power-and-How-She-Solved-Her-Own-Problems.

This is not a story about "fixing things." "Fixing things" is usually just a way to manipulate behavior to give the appearance that things are "under control." The slickly packaged formula of the "fix-it" approach comes fully loaded with clichés that promise more than they can deliver. The end result of formulas and clichés is just more despair. God doesn't want to fix us. He wants to heal us. He wants to get down to the innermost part of our beings and breathe life on the deadness of our souls and spirits.

So, this is a story about a resurrection from the dead. I was dead. Jack was dead. As a result, our marriage was dead. A dead thing has no power to raise itself. Only God can raise the dead. We can choose to cooperate with the resurrection or we can hang on to the grave clothes and refuse to push past the pain that is a sign that life is returning to numbed limbs.

God raised me from the dead by breaking my heart. When your heart is broken open, the first thing that comes out is fear, with all its hatred and anger. (Fear is the slave master of dead souls.) To push past it, I had to own the anger and hatred that shackled me to the deadness within. You can't get past what you deny is there.

We push past the fear by learning how to love—not the wistful, starry-eyed love that lasts until the toast is burned or he forgets your birthday for the twentieth time; not the wimpy love that says, "It's all right. You didn't really hurt me." This is a love that says, "I will not cooperate with the evil that you are bringing into this house." This is a love that finds a way to reach past the pain of betrayal to roll up its sleeves and climb down into the ditch and get muddy and bruised while helping the one who has betrayed you get back on his feet. This love will overcome the natural revulsion the ditch arouses. This love will survive the heckling of spectators who accuse you of "needing" to get into the ditch to feel better about yourself.

Anger and hatred don't belong just to fear. Love also has its anger and hatred. God is love and in that love, His wrath burns like fire against the things that destroy those He loves. God is love and in that love, He hates it when things are wrong. As we learn how to love, we will discover that some things make us ferociously angry and some things arouse a depth of hatred we never knew was possible. But because our hearts are not pure like God's heart, we are often disappointed to discover that the anger and hatred that flow from love are frequently mingled together with the anger and hatred that come from fear. That's why 1 Peter 1:22 says, "Since by your obedience to the truth through the Holy Spirit you have purified your hearts for the sincere affection of the brethren, see that you love one another fervently from a pure heart."

I am continually realizing how impure my motives are. I want my marriage to be healed, and that can get in the way of really loving my husband. Love abandons the outcome to the process. Love is far more interested in genuine healing than it is in getting what it wants out of the deal. That's why, even though my heart cries for total healing of my marriage, I have learned that I have to abandon myself and my marriage to the process of healing and allow God to do the "whatever it takes" to bring each of us to the point at which we're willing to become whole.

For all the wives out there who've sat in empty parking lots wondering where God is in the midst of their sufferings; for all the mothers who watched their children's faces grow cold, hard, colorless, and pinched from waiting for fathers who never show up; for all the women who've wondered year after heartbreaking year when their husbands are ever going to hit bottom so they can push off in a new, life-giving direction—as you learn how to abandon yourself to God's love, you will discover that His gift back to you is an ever-living hope through resurrection from the dead.

That hope came to me when I found something greater than the answer to my problems. I found the Answer (it is more accurate to say He found me). And although I'd very much like to know what the outcome of this whole thing will be, I've learned that the most important thing for me to know is not *how* this is all going to turn out, but *Who* is going to turn it out. That's important, because Jesus Never Fails.

The continuation of my story is woven throughout this book. In the next chapter, we'll begin to look at how, when pornography is involved, the seeds of destruction are sown at the inception of a marriage.

PART TWO

An Affair
of the
Mind

How Pornography Destroys

the Spirit of a Marriage

What's the Big Deal?

The massive unleashing of sexuality which is occurring in Western civilization is a reflection of cultural decline. It is well-known that an inverse relationship exists between indiscriminate sexual expression and cultural excellence. It is cause, therefore, for extreme alarm when an industry flourishes to the extent of billions of dollars annually whose product for distribution are sexually explicit depictions of the vilest debasement of women, men, and children.

(*Harold M. Voth, M.D.*)[1]

Righteousness exalteth a nation, but sin is a reproach to any people.

(*Proverbs 14:34 (KJV)*)

The woman next to me on the plane was talkative. We discussed how many times we'd flown before and shared a bit about our families. Then she asked, "What do you do?"

"I'm a writer," I replied.

"How exciting! What do you write?" she asked, leaning toward me.

"Right now I'm working on a book about how pornography destroys marriages," I replied.

"Oh!" she gasped. "I know what you mean."

Turning away, she hid her face, but not before I saw tears in eyes that moments before had been bright with excitement.

Several weeks later, I was doing some research on a book about home schooling. I called a Christian home-schooling family we had known and admired for 10 years, to find out what they would like to see in such a book.

During the course of the conversation, I mentioned that I was working on a book about how pornography affects marriages.

My friend grew quiet.

"I know about that," she said softly. "Pornography almost destroyed our marriage."

A month later, a friend from church asked me how my book on pornography was going. I told her that I'd taken a break from it to do some research on home-schooling and found four more Christian families who'd been affected by porn.

"I'm amazed," I said. "Every time I turn around, I find out about more families who've been devastated by it."

Looking me in the eye, she said, "And you haven't even talked to me yet."

The First Shot in the Sexual Revolution

Before *Playboy* magazine hit the newsstands in 1954, sexually explicit pictures were not readily available to mainstream America. Sure, if he went to the sleazy part of town and knew where to look, a guy could find some "dirty" pictures. That's all they were, though—"dirty" pictures. No one pretended they were anything more. The pictures weren't surrounded by highbrow articles for young professionals: articles that made looking at naked women just one more perk on the corporate ladder, just one more ticket to be punched on the yuppies' road to CEO-dom.

And while they appealed to prurient interests, the "dirty" pictures from the seamy side of town were without context and didn't pretend relationship. There were no multipaged stories showing the centerfold of the month's academic and professional achievements or her close family relationships. *Playboy's* approach took porn to new levels of acceptability. Men came to believe that looking at the *Playboy* centerfolds wasn't the same as using a prostitute; it was just getting to know the girl next door, or maybe the one at the desk across the aisle. This wasn't using women. This was enjoying them.

The marketing strategy worked, too. *Playboy* magazines were put on regular newsstands with respected periodicals, and pretty soon, that respectability rubbed off. By 1970, a mere 16 years down the road, the President's Commission on

Obscenity and Pornography described the average consumers of pornography as predominately white, middle-class, middle-aged, married males dressed in business suits or neat casual attire.[2] Today, pornography is a $13 billion a year industry.

In the 40 years since *Playboy* first hit the stands, we've gone from a nation where a man's word was his bond to a nation where locked cars, locked doors, and locked hearts mean no one trusts anyone. One of the major factors in this cultural shift was our adoption of the *Playboy* philosophy of "use 'em and lose 'em." Believing that others are here for our use and enjoyment, we discard them when the momentary pleasure is over. We say whatever it takes to get what we want. We absolutely do not feel we have any responsibility to those we have used. Having eaten, we wipe our mouths and move on, searching for someone else to devour. Our paths are littered with pregnant girlfriends, rejected wives, and abandoned children.

The Corpus Delicti of a Victimless Crime

We'd like to believe that pornography is strictly an intellectual activity, that it has no behavioral repercussions or emotional implications. We have been told that it's a matter of free speech. We've been told that it's a "victimless" crime because we can't see any immediate victim. There is no corpus delicti to prove something has been killed. There is no empty shelf to show us what has been robbed. There is no pile of wreckage that can be parked outside the local high school to warn others of the consequences of dangerous activities.

Though there is no smoking gun, there is plenty of circumstantial evidence that a death has taken place. Those who want you to believe pornography is a First Amendment right won't talk about the silent devastation that occurs in the hearts of men, women, and children when someone in their family adopts the *Playboy* philosophy of disposable relationships. They just argue that pornography is "free speech" and try to persuade you that it has no effect other than the brief thrill of the moment. They want you to think that pornography is but a moment of time in an otherwise productive life.

They don't want you to know that the images of, and experiences produced by, pornography are permanently burned into your mind by a curious mixture of hormones that are released when sexually explicit materials are viewed. They don't want you to know that this mix of hormones becomes more potent when the sex portrayed involves violence or fear.[3] They *especially* don't want you to know that as a result of this "imprinting" process, sex for you will now be linked with fear, violence, and shame.

They also don't want you to believe that these permanently imbedded images recur at will, much like LSD flashbacks. These recurrences draw the pornography participant further and further into a world of fantasy. Over a period of time, the lines between what is fantasy and what is real become so blurred that the one affected slips into a form of insanity. His mind begins a process of dissolution as his thoughts track only one way. The unused part of the mind begins to wither and die, and he gradually loses his ability to think deeply about the issues of life.

Eventually, he becomes an empty shell of a man. Hollow to the core, he wanders aimlessly through life, seeking only one thing: fulfillment of the lust that has taken complete hold of him. Every other achievement becomes merely a means to that end. Until at last, instead of spending his time achieving, he spends most of his time fantasizing. He voraciously reads magazines, frequently views videos, regularly goes to strip shows, masturbates several times a day, and spends considerable energy trying to pick up women.[4]

No wonder Proverbs 6:26–27,32 says, "For by means of a whorish woman, a man is brought to a piece of bread: and the adulteress will hunt for the precious life. Can a man take fire in his bosom and his clothes not be burned? Can one go upon hot coals and his feet not be burned? But whoso committeth adultery with a woman lacketh understanding: he that doeth it destroyeth his own soul"(KJV).

One Bad Apple Spoils the Whole Barrel

Whether we want to believe it or not, who we are affects what our communities are. The way we live our lives affects the way our neighbors live theirs. The way we behave in private becomes the way we behave in public. We are salt and we are light, and if our salt has lost its savor and our light has been dimmed, everyone around us is affected.

In an article about the psychological and social effects of pornography, Dr. Harold Voth, a professor at the Karl Menninger School of Psychiatry, writes:

> By permitting the ever-expanding display of pornography, or sexually explicit material on the printed page, in theaters, on television (regular TV, cable, and satellite), our social structure is being bombarded continuously by powerful erosive stimuli. Sexuality in its mature form is a necessary aspect of the heterosexual bond and the stability of the family. The massive unleashing of sexuality which is occurring in Western civilization is a reflection of cultural decline. It is well-known that an inverse relationship exists between indiscriminate sexual expression and cultural excellence.[5]

Because of this, the ripple effects of the *Playboy* philosophy are broad based. In a society where using people is tolerated, more and more people will become "users" resulting in more and more "victims." Those who break trust on the most intimate matters will eventually begin to apply the same mind-set to business and civil-rights matters, saying and doing whatever it takes to get whatever they want.

Accustomed to one-night stands, "playboys" have no concept of having to work at something beyond the moment, so they feel put upon if they are asked to work through conflicts with bosses or family members. Used to immediate gratification, they have a low frustration level for the hard work of learning new job skills, and they are unwilling to wait until their pocketbooks can afford the things their hearts desire. Used to getting what they want by deception, they bilk consumers with shoddy merchandise and service. Used to a fantasy life where they call all the shots, they view those who don't fall into lockstep with what they want as uncooperative "jerks." Inhabitants of a world where there are no boundaries, they think nothing of invading the person and property of others and begin treating their employees, employers, friends, and neighbors with less and less respect.

In a society where using others is tolerated, the used find their security continually threatened as each day brings a new violation of trust. It doesn't take too many violations of trust for an individual to lose his ability to trust. When the number of untrusting individuals reaches critical mass, the society they live in loses its ability to trust. Losing our ability to trust is a grave matter. Without trust, our souls wither and die. Without trust, there can be no civilization.

The Way of Wisdom

Would it surprise you to know that the ancient Hebrews believed that wisdom is closely related to the things we look at? The Hebrew word for "wise"—*sakal*—gives us the understanding that the things we look at and think about affect our ability to be intelligent and prudent. Because of this, what we take in through our eyes is extremely important.

The eye is the window to the soul. Satan knew this, and because he desired access to their souls, he used Adam's and Eve's eyes when he tempted them to eat the forbidden fruit. First Satan told Adam and Eve that having wisdom would somehow affect their eyes, "for God knows that in the day ye eat thereof, then *your eyes shall be opened*, and ye shall be as gods knowing good and evil" (Gen. 3:5, KJV, emphasis added). Then, "the woman *saw* that the tree was good" (Gen. 3:6, KJV, emphasis added). Finally, immediately after they ate the fruit, "*their eyes were opened*, and they *knew* they were naked . . . and Adam and his wife *hid* themselves"(Gen. 3:7–8, KJV)

Opening our eyes to evil has relational consequences. Once their minds were awakened to evil, Adam and Eve immediately saw their nakedness in a new light. Where moments before they had viewed their bodies with no shame, suddenly they felt so much shame that they hid from themselves, from each other, and from God. By focusing the soul on nakedness in a way that produces shame and isolation from self, from others, and from God, looking at evil destroys both freedom (the ability to know oneself) and intimacy (the ability to share oneself with others).

See No Evil

Jesus also talked about how exposing our eyes to evil is related to our ability to be wise. In Matthew 6:22,23 He said, "The light of the body is the eye: If therefore thine eye be single, thy whole body shall be full of light. But if thine eye be *evil*, thy whole body shall be full of darkness. If therefore the light that is in thee be darkness, how great is that darkness!"(KJV). Once again, the ancients can help us get a better understanding of what's being said here. The Greek word for "evil"—*poneros*—means "that which is malicious and deliberately harmful of others." In other words, if our eyes are looking at things that are malicious and willfully harming others, we are putting out our own eyes. We are closing ourselves off to truth. The result will be a plunge into darkness.

Relate this to pornography. Whether it's a woman's rape that's carefully recorded and passed around for the "guys" to enjoy, or the defilement of a child that's made available for the appetites of the pedophile, or pictures of the attractive coed who titillates a corporate executive's fantasy, pornography is made by exploiting others for personal gain. Exploiting others for personal gain is evil in its rawest form. A man who feasts his eyes on pictures that have been made by exploiting others is plucking out his own eyes. He is plunging himself into darkness. He will lose his ability to be wise.

Today, we don't talk much about how what we see affects our ability to be wise. We just keep wondering why our society is losing its soul. Could it have anything to do with the window dressings we allow it to have? Could it have something to do with pornography?

I think that it does. I saw my husband lose his soul to pornography. I have held other women and listened to them weep as they told me how their husbands also lost their souls to pornography. Pornography kills the soul, steals the heart, and destroys the mind. Pornography is not a victimless crime.

CHAPTER 8

I Take This Woman

Yet you ask, Why does He reject it [your offering]? Because the Lord was witness to the covenant made at your marriage between you and the wife of your youth, against whom you have dealt treacherously and to whom you were faithless. Yet, she is your companion and the wife of your covenant.

Malachi 2:14

Covenant breaking or betrayal of trust is the greatest of all sins.

Keith Intrater

I t had come for no reason at all. That was the excitement of it. It wasn't Christmas or my birthday or an anniversary. It wasn't any particular day; but there it was—a present for me! My fingers fumbled with the wrappings, until at last a pile of paper lay at my feet and I held a thin rectangular box in my hands.

Lifting the lid, I saw the back of a picture frame. I turned the box over, shook it gently, and—plop!—the picture landed face up in my lap.

There before me was a slender slip of a girl in a beautiful wedding dress. A lace handkerchief that had been carried by generations of brides poked out from her diamond ring. Thick brown hair fell in cascades of curls behind a veil that framed a face alight with keen expectation. Her excited smile said, "This is my wedding day. Today, I will marry my friend, my beloved." The eyes were shining and eager.

My fingers traced the girl's outline. "Was that really me?" I whispered.

Then my eye caught a reflection in the glass in the corner. The dress was faded and one of the buttons was broken. A confused mass of lusterless hair hung here and there around a colorless face. Below the pale lips, a ragged chin line sagged. The eyes were dull and lifeless.

"My God!" I cried to the girl in the picture. "What have I done? How could I let this happen to you?"

What's a Covenant?

Like most young girls, I approached my wedding day with giddy anticipation. I was in love with a wonderful guy, and I just knew our marriage was going to be a great success, because I was prepared to work hard, make personal changes, and do whatever was necessary to make a happy home for Jack.

I was naive. Marriages don't happen by one party giving 110 percent. Marriage isn't a solo with one person belting out all the words. Marriage is written in two-part harmony. True, you should sing with all your heart. But one set of vibrating tonsils does not a duet make. It takes two to make a marriage. That's because marriage is a covenant.

Covenant is an ancient concept. Down through the centuries, civilized societies have used covenants as a way to make sure relationships between people are clearly understood. In his book *Covenant Relationships,* messianic Jew Keith Intrater said, "The covenant itself is actually a set of words that are spoken to define the nature of that relationship and set forth the principles of commitment to it. A covenant can be seen as an oath that seals the relationship between two people."[2]

According to Intrater, there are several parts to a covenant. The most important ones are:
- the personal relationship that the covenant is designed to confirm
- the specific covenant itself, or the oath taken to seal the relationship
- the signs of the covenant (elements that form a graphic impression as a reminder of the covenant)
- the blessings or positive rewards that ensue from keeping the covenant
- the curses or punishments that ensue from breaking the covenant[3]

Covenants are based on trust and accountability. When we trust, we are confident of something present or future. When the people and institutions we trust are held accountable for their promises to us, we can place our confidence in them because we can rely on them to be true to whatever understanding we have with them.

Your Place or Mine?

Covenants contain a list of blessings and curses. The blessings come when we keep the terms of the covenant; the curses come when we violate those terms. A mortgage is a good covenant to help us understand how this works. Under the covenant terms, you the borrower (covenantor) make a promise of specific payments over a set period of time to a lending institution (covenantee) in exchange for a sum of up-front money to buy a house. As long as you meet the terms of the covenant by making your monthly payments, you get to enjoy the covenant blessing of living in your home. But if you decide you don't have to make regular payments, the covenant curse holds you accountable for your arrogance. Your place is turned over to the bank.

Human Nature Being What It Is . . .

Knowing human nature is weak, God said that before someone could be held accountable for violating a covenant, his accuser needed to produce several people who could testify to what he had done.[4]

This is why there were usually at least two witnesses at a covenant ceremony. If one party of the covenant felt he wasn't getting a fair shake, the witnesses would be called upon to testify about the terms of the covenant they'd witnessed. This same type of accountability is practiced today when we make legal covenants such as loans or real estate transactions. You've probably noticed that there is a place at the end of these documents for the signature of two witnesses. Witnesses protect both parties in the covenant from misunderstanding and possible fraud.

Other people often have a vested interest in the covenants we make. Because covenants involving ownership of property and long-term relationships between people have social implications, covenants for exchanges of property and covenants for marriages are recorded by the town clerk. This protects the rights of those in covenant by announcing to anyone who needs to know that a covenant agreement took place.

Covenants Were a Little Messier in the Old Days

Today, we make covenants with pen and ink (or word processor) and things are generally tidy. It was a little different centuries ago. Ancient covenants were made using the carcass of an animal (usually a calf) that had been cut in two. The covenantal parties would walk between the halves as part of the covenant ceremony. Passing through the pieces of the calf, the covenant makers were in effect saying, "God do so to me as this dead animal if I do not honor my new life as a covenant partner unto death."

This is the type of covenant God made with Abraham in Genesis 15:1–21. Hundreds of years later, He renewed this covenant with Abraham's descendants, by having the Israelites pass between the pieces of a calf after He brought them out of slavery in Egypt (see Jer. 34:13,18). This was part of the covenantal process whereby God began referring to the nation of Israel as His wife. He even spoke of Israel's violations of their covenant as adultery (Jer. 3:8; Ez. 23:37). And that brings us to the covenant of marriage.

In both the Old and New Testaments, marriage is spoken of as a picture of the covenant between God and His people, so there are many covenantal customs in today's marriage ceremony. Because we're not familiar with the concept of covenant, we often miss both the beauty and true meaning of our wedding traditions. For example, when the ushers place the family and friends of the bride on one side of the sanctuary and the family and friends of the groom on the other, they are symbolically re-creating the two halves of the covenant sacrifice that Israel walked through on its way to becoming God's wife. As the bride walks down the aisle between the two families, she takes the place of Israel, symbolically reenacting this ancient covenant ceremony.

Waiting for the bride at the altar is her groom. The groom doesn't enter the church first so he can beat his bride to the altar. The timing of his entrance symbolizes his position as covenant initiator. The initiator assumes the greater responsibility for seeing that the covenant is kept. Because he is assuming greater responsibility, the groom takes his vows first.

So, it isn't just a cultural quirk that men have traditionally been the ones to "pop" the question; it's a reflection of the underlying symbolism that God was the covenant initiator in both the Old Testament, when He sought out Abraham, and in the New Testament, when Jesus, who is referred to as the Bridegroom (Matt. 9:15, 25:1–13; John 3:29; Rev. 21:2–9, 22:17) sought out a people for His name. In both the Old and New Testaments, God took His vows first and assumed the greater responsibility for ensuring that we kept His covenant with us.

. . . And Thereto I Plight Thee My Troth

That phrase comes from the marriage ceremony in the Book of Common Prayer. It's what the groom promises the bride right after he has given her his covenant vow. Taking her right hand, he says, "I, Jack, take thee, Laurie, to be my wedded wife, to have and to hold from this day forward, for better, for worse, for richer, for poorer, in sickness and in health, to love and to cherish, till death us do part, according to God's holy ordinance [here comes the tongue twister], and thereto I plight thee my troth."

In today's English, those strange-sounding words mean "You have my word that I'm going to keep my promises to you." What promises? The promises of the marriage covenant. Typically, these promises include the forsaking of all others and the sharing of wealth.

These promises of faithfulness and generosity are designed to protect the home that is being established through the marriage covenant. The home is where children, who are the fruit of the marriage covenant, are nurtured. Children are unable to protect and provide for themselves. They need someone older and stronger to look out for them. When wealth is shared between a mother and father, children can be cared for properly.

We provide for and protect best that which we know is ours. The promise to forsake all others ensures that the mother's offspring will definitely be the result of the covenant relationship. It also ensures that the father will not compromise his ability to provide for his children by having them scattered about among many different mothers. Forsaking all others also means the lines of inheritance are clear so that wealth and property can be passed down through the generations.[5]

One of the purposes of forsaking all others is so that children can have a secure home. Yet, "never in pornography, is there a hint that sexual intercourse produces children, whose rearing requires commitment and financial sacrifice on the part of the parents."[6]

As part of the exchange of their vows, the bride and groom are publicly asked if they will adhere to the terms of their marriage covenant. Their proper answer is "I will." This, again, is a picture of the covenant ceremony between God and the nation of Israel that took place in a desert so many years ago. Here Moses acted as God's spokesman. After he rehearsed the vows to the covenant, the Israelites replied, "All that the Lord has said *will we do*" (Exodus 24:7–11 KJV, emphasis added).

I Call These Witnesses

God held Himself accountable to the covenantal vows He made and He repeatedly held the nation of Israel accountable to the promises it had made. In marriage, God holds both covenant partners accountable to the promises they make at their wedding and this is the purpose of having so many witnesses to the wedding vows.

There are three layers of witnesses to the wedding vows. First, there is a congregation of family and friends who care that this marriage is happy. But, sometimes, the bride and groom may speak so softly that their voices can't be heard at the back of the church. Therefore, there is a second layer of witnesses: the wedding party.

The wedding party stands with the bridal couple. The bridesmaids and groomsmen are close friends and relatives of the bride and groom. Because of the love relationship they have with the bridal couple, they would care even more than the general congregation about the couple's happiness. Therefore, they are near witnesses to the covenant. But, again, due to emotion or natural timidity, the bridal couple may speak too softly to be heard by their attendants.

For this reason, there is a third layer of witnesses: a best man and maid of honor who stand next to the bride and groom. The bridal couple usually select those they feel closest to for this special honor. They should be people the couple feels comfortable approaching for help in keeping their wedding vows. Now there are at least three people (the best man, maid of honor, and the pastor) who hear the exact promises the bride and groom make to each other. The apostle Paul said, "In the mouth of two or three witnesses shall every word be established" (2 Cor. 13:1b, KJV).

At the conclusion of the wedding ceremony, the pastor usually says something like "In the presence of God and these witnesses, I pronounce you husband and wife." This statement is one more reminder that the couple have entered into a sacred covenant whose terms were witnessed by others. Imagine what would happen if you asked the witnesses of your wedding covenant to hold you and your spouse accountable for the things you promised each other. I believe if we truly understood the power behind the accountability these witnesses bring to the marriage relationship, there would be fewer divorces today.

Signs and Seals of the Covenant

The primary sign of the marriage covenant is a ring. This ring is given in two stages: the promise and the commitment. In the first stage, a promise is made to enter into a discussion of covenant relationship. This stage is called engagement and is signified by the engagement ring. The commitment stage occurs at the actual marriage ceremony. Here, wedding rings are exchanged as a sign to anyone the couple meet that they are in a covenant relationship.

The seal of the marriage covenant, sexual intercourse, is the one thing that distinguishes marriage from all other social relationships. Think about it.

Everything else that we do with our spouse, we can do with others. This is the reason we say the marriage has been "consummated" once the couple experience a sexual relationship. If no sexual union has taken place, the marriage has not really been sealed.

Because the sexual relationship seals the marriage covenant, it belongs exclusively to the married couple. Civilized societies have laws against using things that don't belong to you because they know that once you use something, you change its ability to be useful to the owner. If you use it long enough, you become its possessor and therefore its de facto owner.

Anyone who draws the sexual affections of a husband or wife away from his or her spouse, desecrates the seal of their covenant and will eventually "own" the husband or wife. Once someone else owns your spouse, your covenant is destroyed. This is the reason civilized societies have laws against the alienation of affections.

The Elastic Bed Syndrome

Running rampant in our society is one of the greatest causative agents of the alienation of affections ever devised—pornography. Pornography says the marriage bed is elastic enough to stretch to accommodate more than two people. The whole purpose of pornography is to elicit a sexual response. Whether it's a video, a magazine, or "adult" entertainment, the goal is to arouse the sexual passions of the viewers.

When our sexual passions are aroused by someone other than our spouse, it's only human nature to compare our spouse's "sexiness" to the "sexiness" of the one we're attracted to. So, what happens to our view of our spouse when we can "enjoy" a firm, beautifully made-up, air-brushed centerfold? Studies show the spouse loses.

A case in point is a study done by Dolf Zillman of the University of Indiana and Jennings Bryant of the University of Houston. For six weeks, Zillman and Bryant had college students spend one hour each week viewing either nonviolent pornography or inoffensive situation comedies. They found that exposure to pornography strongly impacted how the students felt about their sexual experiences. The study further revealed that repeated exposure to pornography results in a decreased satisfaction with one's sexual partner, with the partner's sexuality, and with the partner's sexual curiosity. There was a decrease in the valuation of faithfulness and a major increase in the importance of sex without attachment.[7]

The startling thing about Zillman and Bryant's study is that it shows that just six hours of exposure to soft-core pornography is enough to destroy the viewer's satisfaction with his or her spouse. Interesting, isn't it, how modern social scientists have confirmed by research what the ancients knew by common sense: The best way to destroy a marriage is to excite the sexual passions of one of the spouses.

In my own situation, although I was careful with my clothes and figure, I found that my husband was increasingly critical of the way I looked. Even when friends and acquaintances told me I was an attractive woman, I wasn't attractive enough to compete with eternally young, surgically altered models.

Jack also expressed irritation when I was uncomfortable with some of the sexual practices he'd seen in pornographic magazines. In the end, he lost all interest in me as a sexual partner. This had a devastating impact on my view of my worth as a woman. It created such despair in me that I began to let my appearance go. At last, I looked the way his rejection made me feel—totally unlovely. Then I received the picture of me in my wedding dress. Shocked at how far I had deteriorated, I promised myself I'd do whatever was necessary to reclaim the girl in the photograph.

Over the years, I've spoken with other women who have had similar experiences. They tried extra hard to be attractive to their husbands; but the year-after-year battering of constant comparisons with other women and the continual attack on their desirability as a sexual partner wounded their spirits to such a point that they gave up and became the exact opposite of the firm, gorgeous, beautifully made-up women their husbands kept trying to force them to become. Ironic, isn't it, how pornography creates the exact opposite in real life of what it promises in fantasy life?

Can't Get No Satisfaction

Nonviolent pornography focuses almost exclusively on chance encounters between strangers, who suddenly arouse themselves to heavy immediate sex, but without kindness, and without enduring emotional relationships.

(Pornography: A Human Tragedy)

And thus let the marriage bed be kept undefiled, for God will judge and punish all guilty of sexual vice and adultery.

Hebrews 13:4b

[Please be advised that, of necessity, this chapter contains graphic material.]

"Well," Joyce said, after I'd poured out my heart about Jack's addiction to pornography, "if he can take what he's learned and use it on you, some good might come of it."

From the grin on her face, I could tell she thought the information he'd gleaned from pornography had turned Jack into a great lover. She couldn't have been more wrong.

Learning About the Birds and the Bees from the Bunny

Our sources of information about sex have changed dramatically over the last 40 years. Before *Playboy* made its debut in 1954, sex education was catch-as-catch-can. Those who grew up in the country had a good sense of how things

77

went from watching the animals on the farm. The kids in the city learned about sex in back alleys. A lucky few learned about sex from their parents. Things are different today. James B. Check, a professor at the University of York in Ontario, Canada, found that more and more children are learning about the birds and the bees from pornography. In 1985, Check found that in Canada, youths between the ages of 12 and 17 had the highest interest in pornographic material and were its prime viewers.[2]

With today's multibillion-dollar market, it's clear that the pornographers have been successful in reaching young people, making pornography the primary sex educator for four generations of American men.

So, was Joyce right? Is pornography a good sex educator? Does it make men better lovers? Can the magazines and videos teach them how to please their wives in new and thrilling ways? What happens when men who read or view porn try out their new "skills" on their wives?

Is pornography harmless to the health of the marital bed? Does it only whet the appetite for normal sexual relations? What happens when pornography enters the bedroom?

Pornography Promotes Promiscuity, the Death Knell of Great Sex

Pornography portrays an endless round of thrilling sexual escapades with an endless bevy of breathless, hot-blooded babes. And the not-so-subtle message is that these babes are more breathless and more hot-blooded if you're not married to them. But an interesting thing happens when the *Playboy* philosophy meets real life—it destroys sexual satisfaction.

"Couples not involved before marriage and faithful during marriage are more satisfied with their current sex life and also with their marriage, compared [with] those who were involved sexually before marriage," said Dr. David Larson of the National Institutes of Health.[3]

Dr. Larson and his colleagues also found that women who feel secure and loved and who trust that their men are around to stay are twice as orgasmic as women who are promiscuous.

There's more. A major sex study commissioned by *Redbook* magazine during the mid-1970s also found that "strictly monogamous women experienced orgasm during sex more than twice as often as promiscuous women."[4]

Contrary to the endless orgasms pornography promises, "I can't get no satisfaction" could be the next rallying cry for the *Playboy* crowd.

✎ Porn Makes Him Think He's a Lady's Man

Men who are involved in pornography often have a false impression of their own sexual prowess. In his fantasies, his imaginary partner squeals with delight and he just knows it's because he's some kind of supreme sex machine. If he's buying sex, well, he's getting false information there, too. Prostitutes are paid to fake it.

When Mr. Stud Muffin climbs into bed with his wife, he expects the same kind of undying gratitude. Instead of "I really want to be with you," his attitude is "Aren't you lucky to have me in your bed?" If the wife can't respond to his clumsy approaches like the girl of his dreams or the woman he picked up down at the local strip joint, well, it's *her* problem—after all, he was more than adequate for other women.

This is a self-defeating cycle. The less adequate he feels with his wife, the more he wants (and thinks he needs) to be with other women. The more dissatisfying (or even outright degrading) a sexual experience is for the wife, the less likely she is to want to have anything to do with her husband.

The fact that our society tacitly applauds the stud muffin image as a sign of real manhood works as positive reinforcement for a guy who's trying to justify multiple sexual partners. "Hey, I can't help it. I'm just your average red-blooded American male," he says. "What I've got is too good to keep locked up."

But the lie is, instead of affirming his manhood, having multiple sexual partners actually destroys a man's masculinity. Karl Menninger stated in *Love Against Hate:*

> It is an axiom in psychiatry that a plurality of direct sexual outlets indicates the very opposite of what it is popularly assumed to indicate. Dividing the sexual interest into several objectives diminishes the total sexual gratification, and men whose need for love drives them to the risks and efforts necessary to maintain sexual relationships with more than one woman show a deficiency rather than an excess in their masculine capacities.[5]

Porn Shortens Foreplay and Contributes to Premature Ejaculation

"We don't make love, we have sex," Jill confided. "There's no tenderness and everything is over so fast. I feel so used."

Wives whose husbands are involved in pornography often find themselves rushed through their sexual relationships. He's interested in getting down to the "good stuff." She wonders, "What happened to foreplay?" He zeroes in on her breasts, her genitals, or her buttocks. She'd like him to explore the sensuality of other parts of her body. He ejaculates in a matter of minutes, and she's left feeling frustrated.

Granted, even without pornography, men are more eager to get to the finish line than women, but pornography exacerbates the situation by focusing on the sensuality of certain body parts. Men who've been on a steady diet of porn often want to get right to the body part they fantasize most about, and a woman ends up feeling like she's a banquet where the only dishes sampled are the appetizers.

The problem escalates when shortened foreplay climaxes with premature ejaculation. Most women require from 5 to 10 minutes of intravaginal stimulation to reach orgasm, and about 12 percent require 10 minutes or more.[6] With premature ejaculation, that time is shortened to anywhere between a few seconds and a few minutes.

Though there can be other physical or psychological causes of premature ejaculation, masturbation is a major cause of "learned" premature ejaculation. There is a strong link between pornography and masturbation. Aroused by what he sees in the magazine or on the video, the viewer will "relieve" himself through masturbation. According to sex therapists Clifford and Joyce Penner, "Because of the fear of discovery, masturbation is usually a hurry-up job and the man learns to bring himself to the point of ejaculation very quickly."[7]

Shortened foreplay? Premature ejaculation? Are these the tools of a great lover?

Porn Creates Sexual Isolation

Whether it's exploring a certain body part they were turned on to through pornography, or simply imagining they are "making it" with one of the centerfolds, those involved in pornography are sexually driven by their fantasies. "So what?" you might ask. "A little imagination goes a long way to making great sex." Not if sex is about intimacy.

Intimacy is about opening up and revealing ourselves to another. It's not about manipulating another to fulfill our fantasies. Intimacy is about caring for another's pleasure as much or more than we care about our own. It's not about seeing another as just a tool to bring us pleasure. Intimacy is about truly desiring to be with another. It's not about not pretending to want to be with one person while in our hearts we wish we were with someone else.

Intimacy is about cherishing another in ways that go far beyond sex. It's not about seeing that person as disposable when the demands of everyday life put a crimp on sexual escapades. When you're just someone's outlet for his fantasy life, you know that all you're doing is having sex with your body while your partner's mind and heart are far away with someone else. Fantasy is the ultimate user's game and the ultimate tool for sexual isolation.

Porn Stimulates Interest in Perversions

In 1986, Dr. C. Everett Koop, the U.S. Surgeon General, invited 22 social scientists and mental health professionals to a three-day workshop to discuss mental health aspects of pornography. They found that "prolonged use of pornography alters the beliefs about the frequency of certain uncommon sexual practices in the general public."[8] In times past, we called these uncommon practices "perversions."

Perversion is a word we are reluctant to use in today's enlightened society. We shrink at appearing judgmental. We're reluctant to appear insensitive to the preferences of others. So, we cringe at labeling actions perverse, preferring instead to say, "Well, it's not for me, but if it melts your butter, it's okay for you." Let me suggest a definition for *perversion* that takes some of the emotion out of it. *Perversion is using something in a way it was not intended to be used.*

One of the perverse practices touted by porn is anal sex. The muscles of the anus and rectum are designed to contract and expel, down and outward. They are not designed to receive penises, or other devices, in and upward. The cells lining the rectum do not have the lubricating qualities of the cells lining the vagina, so copious amounts of lubricant are required for rectal sex. Even so, anal fissures are common.

There is another downside to anal sex—infection. The rectum is live with bacteria, which is why women are advised to wipe from front to back. What do you think happens when a penis is withdrawn from a rectum and thrust into a vagina?

Anal fissures and vaginal infections do not great sex make, as Gail can testify. Gail's husband repeatedly pressed her for anal sex, and Gail repeatedly experienced vaginal infections, as well as a total deadening of sexual feeling.

A Christian, Gail thought she had to submit to anal sex. "Doesn't Scripture tell me not to withhold my body from my husband?" she asked me.

"Yes, it does. But it also says to keep the marriage bed undefiled. Anal sex is defiling because it's a perversion. God doesn't require you to submit to perversion," I told her.

After thinking it through and praying about it, Gail told her husband that she would no longer go along with anal sex.

"He was angry when I said I wouldn't do it anymore, but it's such a relief to know I don't have to put up with it again. I felt so violated," Gail told me.

And yet, Armand Coppins, in *Memoirs of an Erotic Bookseller,* said of the women featured in pornography, "Even though used by a chain of men in all available orifices, the erotic heroine remains fresh, desirable, and ever ready for more."[9] In real life, it ain't so, Armand.

Porn Encourages Sexual Practices That Destroy the Dignity and Worth of Participants

The U.S. Surgeon General's report also concluded that "pornography increases the acceptance of the use of coercion in sexual relationships."[10]

Bondage is a form of sexual coercion heavily promoted in pornography. Whether it's the hard-core portrayal of women restrained in deplorable conditions, or the sadomasochistic portrayal of a dominatrix raining pain and humiliation down on a powerless male, or the soft-core portrayals of "cute" ways to tie up women in charming bedroom scenes, the message is clear: Having power over your partner to humiliate or deny her freedom of motion is a real turn-on.

In the real world, we tie up or otherwise restrain animals, not valued human beings with whom we want a consensual relationship. Handcuffs, chains, and other restraints are designed to render powerless those whose lives have been judged to be "bad" or "dangerous." They are not for use on people we love and cherish. The *Redbook* survey on female sexuality found that "sexual responsiveness and satisfaction are significantly affected by the relational context in which lovemaking takes place."[11] What kind of relational context have we got going when power and coercion are used as turn-ons?

Far from creating the wildly erotic highs pornography portrays, bondage packs a one-two psychological and physiological punch that makes it a real sexual turn-off. According to Helen Singer Kaplan, sexual arousal is controlled by the parasympathetic nervous system (PNS). The PNS functions apart from our will, "building up" the body. It is active when we are relaxed and open to a situation. We can't force ourselves to become aroused: Arousal is a by-product of feeling trusting about what is happening to us.[12]

Clifford and Joyce Penner say that "arousal is a response our bodies make that can occur only as we are relaxed and allow our bodies to receive pleasurable sexual stimuli. Soaking in the positive stimulation will trigger our PNS and set our complicated brain-nervous system and vascular system in motion."[13]

On the other hand, if we become anxious or afraid, our sympathetic nervous system (SNS) is activated. The SNS is our "fight or flight" hot button. It acts as an inhibitor, shutting off the PNS and therefore stopping the growing sexual excitement. Because of the fear and anxiety created by the powerlessness it engenders, bondage activates the SNS, robbing those bound of genuine arousal. At the orgasmic phase, the muscular contractions that form the orgasmic response are regulated by the SNS. Since the SNS is dominant when we are active rather than passive, this means that in order to experience orgasm, we need the freedom to actively move our bodies.

In other words, arousal is closely connected with "letting go" and occurs when we feel safe, whereas orgasm is a function of "going for it" and occurs when we are free to make body movements. Yet, pornography says that being bound and unable to move stimulates sexual excitement. Clearly, bondage has been oversold as an aphrodisiac.

Porn Encourages Rape

Porn not only encourages a loss of respect for women and results in lousy sexual techniques, it also encourages rape. In a study of 120 college-aged men and women, James Weaver, a University of Kentucky communications professor, found that even a one-time exposure to portrayals of consensual sex in ordinary R-rated movies led men to lose respect for women and to trivialize the crime of rape. According to Weaver, the implication in those movies that women are "hypersexual, panting playthings that can't get enough, leads the male viewer to think: 'Isn't it possible that this woman over here is like that, too?'"[14]

That kind of thinking is the jumping-off point for rape.

Once men begin to trivialize rape, they are more likely to rape. So, it should come as no surprise that there's a strong connection between rape statistics and pornography readership statistics. In 1983, two University of New Hampshire sociologists, Murray Straus and Larry Baron, studied the correlation between rape and readership of pornography. What they discovered was chilling. Studying the FBI's annual Uniform Crime Report for rapes reported to and recorded by police, Straus and Baron found that Alaska and Nevada were number one and number two in the nation for occurrences of rape.

The researchers then turned their attention to the Audit Bureau of Circulation (ABC) and studied circulation rates for *Chic, Club, Gallery, Genesis, Hustler, Oui,* and *Playboy*. Next to *Penthouse* (not included in the study because it doesn't provide circulation data to the ABC), these are the most widely read sexually oriented magazines in the United States. After compiling the total circulation figures, Straus and Baron found that Alaska and Nevada once again led all other states in the nation, this time in readership of pornography.

The fact that Alaska and Nevada have the highest rape rates and highest pornography readership rates is no coincidence. The study found "an unusually high correlation between sex magazine readership and the rape rate."[15] And Straus and Baron found that states that had the lowest readership of pornographic magazines also had the lowest rape rates.

Porn Encourages Marital Violence

Linda was repeatedly raped by her husband, a consumer of one of the popular soft-core porn magazines. Sadly, Linda's situation is not an isolated one. A study at the University of Manitoba and Winnipeg found that there are connections between consumption of certain sexually explicit materials, sexual fantasies, and hostility.[16] One study even showed that men who view pornography are more likely to rape if they think they won't be found out.[17] And who is easier to rape than a wife? Who would believe her if she got up the nerve to tell?

Pornography not only stimulates fantasies about sexual coercion, it actually encourages rape and other forms of sexual violence by perpetuating the myth that women will eventually come to enjoy pain and beg for more. Rather than leading to great sex, in real life a man who uses coercion and violence in his sexual repertoire will destroy his relationship with his partner.

Soft-Core Porn Packs a Hard Wallop

"Okay," you say, "I can accept that hard-core, violent stuff might cause men to rape, but the soft-core stuff that you can get down at the corner quick-stop is pretty harmless. Isn't it?"

We often fool ourselves about the impact of so-called soft-core pornography. Most of the studies cited in this chapter involve viewers' responses to soft-core porn. The truth is that *since soft-core starts out with the realm of what is possible, it causes viewers to experience a greater change in values than hard-core porn does.*

James Check conducted an experiment of 436 males in which he compared the effects of three different sexual materials: "simple erotica (such as is used in sex education programs); nonviolent, dehumanizing material (such as a man sitting atop a woman ejaculating into her face); and violent pornography (such as a man forcing an oversized plastic penis into a woman while she is strapped to a table). He wanted to see the effects of violent versus nonviolent forms of pornography."[18]

The results were chilling. Check found that the nonviolent material "increased the likelihood that subjects would commit rape and other forced sexual acts to *the very same extent* that the violent pornography increased the tendency to commit rape and other forced sexual acts."[19]

Commenting on Check's study, Dolf Zillman, who did the study that showed porn caused a decrease in satisfaction with one's spouse, said, "The investigation by Check has obvious implications for public health. It shows that on the whole, common, nonviolent pornography has the strongest influence on men's willingness to force intimate partners into forms of sexuality that are not necessarily to their partners' liking, and on the propensity to force sexual access."[20]

A study by James Weaver confirmed the same thing. Weaver took 60 male and 60 female undergraduate students and asked them to categorize men and women using descriptions such as forceful or accommodating, independent, indiscriminate or innocent, permissive or virtuous. A week later, randomly selected groups of students were shown brief scenes from contemporary television programs or films.

One group viewed nonsexual material; another saw scenes of romantic, consenting sex from films including *Lady Chatterly's Lover*. A third group viewed scenes in which women instigated sex; a fourth watched scenes in which men forced women to submit to sex. A fifth group saw "eroticized violence," including the terrorizing of nude women without apparent sexual threat.

They were then again asked to describe the character and morality of various men and women, and were read summaries of rape cases and asked to assign penalties against the rapists. *Weaver found that men who watched sex scenes selected from ordinary R-rated movies—especially scenes between consenting adults or sex initiated by women—developed a loss of respect for women and believed women to be more sexually permissive or promiscuous than they had imagined before the viewings. Both women and men who watched the sex scenes from the movies favored lighter penalties against a convicted rapist.*[21]

A Missionary from Hell

In a recent interview, Hugh Hefner, founder of *Playboy* magazine, applauded pornography's roll as a sex educator. Comparing himself to Jesus Christ, Hefner said he was a "missionary" whose most important accomplishment was "liberating [people] from sexual hang-ups."[22]

If Hefner is right and pornography is a celebration of our sexuality, a way to free ourselves from restraints that would keep us from experiencing all that is good about sex, wouldn't it be true that those most intimately involved in it—the models and actresses featured in pornographic materials—would find themselves completely fulfilled, with a strong sense of personal identity? If pornography teaches us how to have great sex, wouldn't you think that the women involved in the pornography industry would feel they had been treated as they wanted to be treated and that the men working with them had a strong sense of what was mutually pleasing in a sexual relationship?

Here's what one porn model had to say about how she feels about herself and the amount of pleasure she's received from pornographic sexual relationships: "I lived the *Playboy* philosophy. I felt worthless and empty. Out of my despair, I attempted suicide on numerous occasions," said Brenda Mackillop, a former Playboy bunny who worked at the Los Angeles Playboy Club from 1973 to 1976 and who frequented Hefner's mansion.[23]

Here's another plug for the *Playboy* philosophy. "It took me close to 20 years to undo what was done to me in pornography. Pornography is not a crime against sex. Pornography is a crime against real women, like me, who suffer real injuries to their bodies and to their minds. The only sex I knew was coercive. Imprisonment was not uncommon. All women were systematically kept in (pornographic) prostitution in the same way prisoners of war have been starved into compliance by their captors," said Sara Winter, who spent five years as a pornographic model and prostitute.[24]

And yet, the magazines and videos give the impression that if you treat women this way, they're going to love it.

Victor Cline says that pornography is a lousy sex educator. "Pornography contains much scientifically inaccurate, false and misleading information about human sexuality, especially female sexual nature and response," Cline stated in his book *Pornography's Effects on Adults and Children*.[25]

So, no, Joyce, pornography didn't turn my husband into a great lover. Far from being the sexual liberator it purports to be, pornography enslaves participants in sexual activities that destroy their personhood. Far from being the ticket to endless rounds of sexual highs, pornography introduces a strain into relationships that squashes sexual enjoyment. As far as I'm concerned, pornography gets an "F" in sex education.

An Affair of the Mind

Being follows imagination.

⌐Thomas Moore¹⌐

As a [man] thinketh in his heart, so is he.

⌐Proverbs 23:7 (KJV)⌐

Jack sat gripping the arms of his chair. His glazed eyes stared straight ahead. He was rigid—silent. It was a look I'd seen many times before, but I didn't know what it meant.

"Please," I said, dropping to my knees in front of him. "Talk to me and tell me what's wrong. Have I done something to offend you?"

Jack blinked at me and then his eyes jerked back to the wall. All the lights were on, but nobody was home. Jack had gone somewhere I couldn't go; and if I couldn't go there, how was I ever to find him? And if I couldn't find him, how could I ever bring him home?

Just a Guy Thing?

Some people think that porn is just a guy thing. They say that it gives a guy a sexual buzz and then returns him safely to earth. They try to tell you that porn doesn't affect a guy anyplace but below the belt. They wonder what the big deal is and hint (or outright say) that any woman worth her estrogen wouldn't be fazed by her husband's interest in pornography.

Others will admit that porn might not be good for a guy. But they think that if a guy just stops looking at the porn, everything will be okay. They seem genuinely puzzled when you try to explain that there are a multitude of stresses in the marriage. Just like the first group, this second group naively assumes that pornography is an isolated event in an otherwise healthy life.

What neither group can grasp is that pornography has a multifaceted effect on a man and because of that, it has a multifaceted effect on a marriage. In fact, pornography is like the evil weed that springs up in our New England pastures. Evil weed has a beautiful purple flower, and it seems harmless enough; but let it go to seed and it slowly but surely spreads throughout a pasture, choking out the good grass.

Once evil weed is in your pasture, it's a constant battle to make sure it doesn't take over. To get rid of evil weed, you have to dig it out, being careful to wrap up any seed pods so they don't drop on the ground and reseed the pasture. Then you have to spread black plastic over the site to make sure any seeds that might have fallen don't get a chance to germinate.

Just like evil weed, pornography seems harmless enough at the start. There's even a certain beauty in some of it. But once it goes to seed, it slowly but surely spreads throughout a man's life, choking out his good qualities. Once established, there's no easy way to get rid of its pernicious effects. Recovery takes a long time and a lot of work. This is because of the way pornography gets its hooks into a man. Although porn has an immediate physical effect on a man, porn isn't interested in just grabbing a guy below the belt—porn goes straight past his body right into his soul through his imagination.

The Gateway to the Soul

Imagination is seeing with the eyes of the heart. It is the most godlike thing we do. Through imagination, we are able to create something out of nothing. We take the thoughts, hopes, and dreams of our hearts and clothe them in some form that will make them visible. Then we pull them forth, giving birth to a house, a garden, an invention, a book, a painting, a song, or some other useful or beautiful thing that will enrich our lives. We imagine it and then we make it happen, just as God imagined the world and then spoke it into existence.

Imagination is the gateway to the soul. The soul is the thinking, willing, and feeling part of us. Imagination exercises the mind, disciplines the will, and thrills the emotions. Imagination feeds the soul by driving it to create something out of nothing. What we imagine becomes what we do. The writer of Proverbs knew this. He said, "As a man thinketh in his heart, so is he."

Olympic athletes also know this, and one way they prepare themselves for competition is to imagine themselves competing in their sport. This technique is called "visualization." If they are bobsled racers, before competing, they will visualize every foot of the bobsled course. They see themselves careening down the steep, icy slope at speeds of up to 90 mph. They visualize their bodies responding to the demands of the course, now lying back, now raising up, keeping a smooth and steady cadence to give the sled extra momentum. They study when to break and when to let 'er rip. They plot their strategy for every twist and turn.

The more often they visualize their run, the more second nature it becomes to them. Until, when they pound down that course on race day, they respond to the course not so much from their minds but from the innermost depths of their beings. They no longer *think* about the course, they have *become* the course.

Because being follows imagination, the battle is always for the mind. If your mind dwells on things that are good, pure, lovely, just, and excellent, you develop a character and a personality that are good, pure, lovely, just, and excellent. If, however, your mind dwells on things that are cruel, defiled, tasteless, dishonest, and worthless, you develop a character and a personality that are cruel, defiled, tasteless, dishonest, and worthless. In other words, just like the Olympic athletes, you reap in your being what you sow in your imagination.

The Power of Imagination for Good

Imagination that is based on truth is tremendously powerful. It's the way we "ruminate" on a situation, looking at it from all its various angles. If you are designing a home, you start with basic truths—for example, you need bedrooms for your two children and your husband needs a workshop. Depending on your budget, you take the basic needs and add extras, like fireplaces or bay windows, and imagine the kind of house you could put on your lot for the kind of money you can afford to spend. Your imagination has been used to problem solve. It has taken into account the needs and desires of your heart and crafted a solution that will make your life better.

Most of the time, our imaginations aren't used for such big projects. Usually, it's the stuff that makes everyday life run better—like creating a cake to celebrate a child's birthday or figuring out how to move a big rock from the yard. We use our imaginations to create solutions to our problems. In our mind's eye, we "see" the solutions and make adjustments to them so they more accurately fit our particular needs. The solutions and the adjustments must all be based on truth.

It Has to Be True in Order to Become Real

Only imagination based on truth can become real. That is because real things have to obey certain unchangeable truths, such as like begets like (a bean seed will always bring forth a bean plant, not a squash, a chicken, or a rock); one season follows another (you can't go from summer to spring without passing through fall and winter—though some of us here in New England would like to try it sometime); and your cupboards will always go from a state of greater order to a state of lesser order—they will never go from being a mess to being tidy on their own. Unchangeable truths are the laws that operate the universe. They are the only true basis for reality.

Once imagination ceases to be based on truth, it slips into fantasy. A fantasy is a play of the mind. It is a delusion. Even though it will seem real to a deluded person, fantasy cannot be constructed into reality because it isn't based on truth.

Let me repeat that. *Even though we may strongly determine that we WILL accomplish our fantasy, it cannot become reality because only things that are true can become real.* In order for fantasy to be constructed into reality, the laws of nature would have to be suspended so that objects and people could be manipulated to meet the fantasy. That isn't going to happen. Even though your mind may be totally occupied with trying to find a way to force things to act in accordance with your fantasy, it will be unsuccessful in discovering a way to suspend natural law. Your emotions pay the price for your failure to get what you so desperately want. You feel frustration, anger, extreme disappointment, and probably rage.

For example, perhaps I have fantasized building a house that will float several feet above my building lot. If I try to make that fantasy a reality, I will experience much frustration, anger, and extreme disappointment because I'm trying to force the house to violate the law of gravity. Of course, it's possible that I could use my imagination to create some invention that would allow my house to break free of gravity, just like NASA scientists used their imaginations to create rockets that would allow spacecraft to break free of gravity. But the invention that allows my house to float, just like the invention of the rockets, will have to be based on true principles of gravity, thrust, Newton's laws of motion, the property of propellants, and some mind-boggling math. In other words, I can take a fantasy that is impossible and make it possible if I can imagine a solution based on things that are true.

Imploding the Soul

In a healthy soul, imagination is a creative force that flows outward, giving birth to expressions of beauty and solutions to problems that lead to more productive living. In a deluded soul, the imagination becomes a vacuum sucking into itself people and objects that can be used for self-gratification. In time the deluded soul implodes on itself.

Instead of using imagination to look for ways to overcome life's difficulties, fantasy becomes a way to make selfish desires become reality by controlling others. Instead of using imagination to make life better, imagination becomes a trap to ensnare others and force them to do what the fantasizer wants.

In a sense, fantasy is like witchcraft. Using illusions and delusions, fantasy seeks to make the deluded one believe he has found truth. Using manipulation and control, fantasy attempts to force others to behave in accordance with the deluded one's wishes. The one given to fantasy is enthralled—his mind captivated by an unreal world from which the only escape is truth. And truth is the last thing the fantasizer wants because it will destroy his make-believe world.

Make the World Go Away

For the deluded one, imagination is reduced to a magic carpet that will take him wherever he wants to go but never lets him land and experience the country. Instead of being a resource to solve problems, the imagination becomes a convenient escape from life's pressures. To get the world off his shoulders, the fantasizer will "shoot up" in the recesses of his mind. Thus the very power that allows us to imagine solutions to life's challenges becomes the power that we use to avoid life's pressures. Without the ability to problem solve, we become victims, helpless to deal with what life throws our way.

Victimization is a downward spiral. The more powerless you feel, the more likely you are to "check out" by fantasizing a world where you are able to obtain your heart's desires by creating people and responses that will give you a sense of mastery. The more you fantasize, the more deluded you become. The more deluded you become, the more powerless you are to leave your make-believe world by crafting solutions to your problems. It's a vicious cycle, and you can't get out of it by fantasizing. You can only get out of it by telling yourself the truth.

Truth is the foundation on which the power to craft solutions rests. Truth is unchangeable reality. It doesn't depend on circumstances. What is true is always true in every place, on every occasion. Truth systematically links facts together to create an understanding of life's situations. Line upon line, precept upon precept, truth builds its house.

When the imagination is deluded, there is no truth, and where there is no truth, there can be no linking together of facts, and without that linking of facts, there are no true solutions. Powerless to find true solutions to the difficulties he faces, the fantasizer is impelled to visit over and over the imaginary world he has created in his mind. Here all his problems go away because he can be anything he wants to be and he can make others do anything he wants them to do.

"Shooting Up" in the Recesses of His Mind

Fantasy can be addictive. Dr. Mark Laaser has said, "Fantasy by itself can be exciting enough for the addict's body to produce adrenaline, which is stimulating and alters mood. Fantasy can stimulate other chemical reactions in the pleasure centers of the brain that positively alter mood and even have a narcotic-like effect. The addict then uses these effects to escape other feelings, to change negative feelings to positive feelings, and even to reduce stress. For example, many sex addicts will fantasize when they go to bed to put themselves to sleep. Don't underestimate the power of fantasy. Given the chemical changes it creates, sex fantasy addicts are, in reality, drug addicts."[2]

Because fantasy packs a one-two wallop of "feel good now" and actual chemical addiction, it is an extremely difficult habit to break. The devastation of fantasy is sometimes poorly understood by those in the helping professions. They may hint or even outright say that the wife of a man who has given himself over to fantasy is herself imagining the changes in his personality. But even though she may find it difficult to put them into words, the changes are real. They reflect a reshaping of her husband's mind that has a destructive impact on the marriage. We'll look a bit more at that impact in the next chapter.

CHAPTER 11

The Girl of His Dreams

If you believe that a pornographic book or film cannot affect you, then you must also say that Karl Marx's Das Kapital, the Bible, the Koran [and] advertising have no effect on their readers or viewers.

(Dr. Victor B. Cline¹)

The eye is the lamp of the body. So, if your eye is sound, your entire body will be full of light; but if your eye is unsound, your whole body will be full of darkness. If then, the very light in you is darkened, how dense is that darkness!

Matthew 6:22,23

M att's heart raced. He and his pals were starting their party-animal night with a hot new video they'd picked up down at the local adult bookstore. The pictures on the VCR stirred appetites he didn't know he had. He could hardly wait for the video to be over: a vanload of girls with "good attitudes" had been brought in as part of the evening's fun. Soon he and the other guys would get to use those girls to act out the new "techniques" they'd seen on the video.

I Use You, You Use Me

The Christian community was shocked a few years ago when a prominent evangelist was arrested on charges of soliciting a prostitute. The police found pornographic magazines in his car when they arrested him.

Pornography is bold in its assertion that you can use others for sexual satisfaction without reaping any negative consequences. So, it's not unusual for guys who read pornographic magazines and watch pornographic videos to go to strip clubs to "hire entertainers" to act out the things they've witnessed. But pornography lies. The first lie is that the viewer is having an intimate relationship with the men or women portrayed. *Playboy,* in particular, is a master at creating the illusion that you know this month's centerfold. Pictures showing her everyday life, and stories crafted to make her look like the girl next door, create a sense of "knowing" her.

Often, the women who provide phone or computer sex will pretend to "care" about the caller so they can keep him on the phone longer, running up the high minute-by-minute fee that 900 numbers charge or the up to $20-per-hour computer chat-room charge. Some of these men call back repeatedly to talk with the same woman because they've been led to believe they have a relationship with her. Meanwhile, the cash register is ringing.

Pornographic rock lyrics do the same thing. Performers use sex to get into your wallet, and often they try to persuade you that you're personally acquainted. In Sheena Easton's major hit "Sugar Walls," she pretends that she and the listener are actually having sex. "Played sometimes as many as ten or twelve times a day on local radio stations across America, the lyrics, accompanied by moans, sighs, and orgasmic squeals, have to do with vaginal arousal."[2]

Of course, it's all a lie. You don't know the girl in the picture. The woman on the phone only wants your money. You aren't having sex with Sheena Easton. You can imagine all you want, but your imagination has no basis in reality. It's all an illusion.

Pornography also gives out false information about human sexuality. It features men who can perform repeated acts of sex and women who experience endless orgasms after being defiled in ways that, in reality, cause women pain, not pleasure. Finally, the desirable women portrayed in pornography are often pumped up, tucked up, and made up. They are also often filled with disease. And rather than being present and fully engaged in what's going on, many of them are on drugs to dull the pain of their shame.[3]

Having It Your Way

In porn, you can roll your own. You can "make" someone do exactly what you want her to do. Dream Machine, a CD-ROM put out by Interotica, "features a woman who adapts her personality to users based on their choice of sexual fantasy. The folks at Interotica have calculated that their programming allows for 1.3 million experiences without duplication. And they note that the game's female character, viewed on-screen in a series of interactive video clips, is non-judgmental and safe."[4] In other words, she has no opinions but your opinions, no needs but your needs. She is a woman with no soul who is totally under your control.

Furthermore, porn creates the impression that men who have a variety of enticing, casual sexual partners are more manly and whole than the stick-in-the-muds who prefer one woman. Nothing could be further from the truth. A 1982 report by the American Medical Association's Council on Scientific Affairs found that "any person of whatever sexual preference, who shows a dominant pattern of frequent sexual activity with many partners who are and will remain strangers, presents evidence of shallow, narcissistic, impersonal, often compulsively driven genital- rather than person-oriented sex and is almost always regarded as pathological."[5] In other words, people who have sex with a multitude of real or imagined partners become self-centered, superficial, souless, compulsive, and mentally unbalanced.

Last, and perhaps most dangerous, pornography creates a world where you can have your cake and eat it, too. There are no consequences for people with power. The people in control of a situation always get what they want and they never get sick, caught, emotionally destroyed, or psychologically dismantled.

Smoke Gets in Your Eyes

Pornography is all smoke and mirrors. There's just one problem. It appears quite real to the viewer. It engages his imagination in a way nothing else can. Porn warps the ability to tell what's real and what's not because there's a physical response to what the eye sees and the mind imagines. When a man's body experiences erection and ejaculation as a result of fantasizing to porn, it makes the porn seem more real. There is even a chemical response in the brain that locks the whole thing into his memory.

The physical senses are "proving" what the mind has conceived. Not only is the mind confused about what's real, the body is confused as well. That which is unreal (the object causing the arousal is merely paper and ink or celluloid, which has no true power to touch you in a physical way) seems more real than that which is real (sexual arousal). True delusion has occurred. Delusion has a way of trying to become reality. The results are often chilling.

In the FBI's most ambitious attempt to create a profile of a sex killer, they found that such men who kill—and kill again—often cannot tell the difference between reality and fantasy, even when they are committing murder.

FBI interviews with 36 convicted sex killers—including many serial murderers—reveal that virtually all of them have long-standing fantasies of murder that are "as real to them as their acts of murder." In addition, the report noted that 81% of the sex killers said they were users of pornography.[6]

The men who became sex killers believed the lies behind pornography and, in believing the lies, they allowed their imaginations to become deluded. As they embraced the lies pornography taught them about sexuality, they gave the evil behind those lies full access to their souls. In their imaginations, they repeatedly surrendered their wills to the acts of sexual conquest portrayed in pornography. Their emotions were thrilled as they "experienced" the delusion. Their emotions were depressed when the "experience" was over. Once their minds, wills, and emotions were surrendered to the delusion, their bodies screamed to act them out. The result was a bloody trail of women who had been sexually tortured. The power of their imaginations had been used to access their souls in order to get their bodies to do evil. Proverbs 23:7 says, "As a man thinketh in his heart, so is he."

When Miss September Meets the Wife

When a man's imagination has been turned to evil, it has serious implications for his marriage. His imagination has trained him to be a user, and he will attempt to use his wife. He can be very clever in the ways he manipulates her. He may try the "sweet" approach—buying her flowers, taking her out to dinner, picking up some little thing he thinks she'll like—to manipulate her emotions so she feels she "owes" him something. Then, at the right moment, he'll inform her that the payback is a sexual act. If subtlety fails to work, he may use more drastic measures, such as shaming or scaring her into compliance. The goal is to turn his wife into the type of woman he has fantasized about.

- If the women of his dreams are passive, he will want his wife to be passive. Therefore, if she has an opinion, she's being controlling.
- If the women of his dreams have no needs but his needs, he will want his wife to have no needs but his needs. Therefore, if she has a need, she is being demanding.
- If the women in his dreams have no dimension other than sexual, he will want his wife to have no dimension other than sexual. Therefore, if she has

goals and dreams for herself, she's being too independent.

• If the women of his dreams are aroused by acts of perverted sex, he will want his wife to be aroused by acts of perverted sex. Therefore, if she can't get turned on, she's frigid.

• If the women of his dreams are luscious young babes with endless breasts and legs, he will want his wife to be a luscious young babe with endless breasts and legs. Therefore, if she's just a normal woman who's had a couple of kids, she's going to be too flat, too fat, too old, or too average to suit his gourmet taste.

When the person you're living with looks at you through distorted eyes, it distorts your ability to know who you are. Are you controlling, demanding, too independent, frigid, and ugly? Or are you normal?

Looking for Downtime

Fantasy has another devastating effect on a marriage. Men who are into fantasizing will look for downtime to indulge their habit. This makes them passive and leaves the wife and children in the lurch. Downtime can start the moment he walks through the door at the end of the day. He may sit rigid and silent (with or without the TV on), or he may retreat to his shop or garage. The main thing he wants is to be left alone. His wife's presence is an unwelcome interruption. His children are an aggravating intrusion.

He's physically present, but his mind is a million miles away. Although he is totally withdrawn from the family, his presence controls the family dynamics. Do you pretend he's not there, or do you acknowledge his presence and try in some way to draw him into family activities?

Dinner is often an especially difficult time, as he has little or nothing to add to the conversation. In fact, he would prefer no conversation: It gets in the way of his fantasies. His glumness permeates the room and makes the food sit like a rock in your stomach. Do you accept defeat, or do you try to engage in some lighthearted, inconsequential conversation? Either way he wins, because all conversation is forced and lacks substance, warmth, and humor. You know it; the children know it. You leave the meal emptier than you were before you sat down to eat.

Driving can be great downtime, especially if you're a passenger. When we'd get ready to go places, Jack would walk out to the car and climb into the passenger seat without saying anything. I was left to figure out that he wanted me to drive. Later, I realized he wanted to use the downtime for fantasy. Driving was safer than being his passenger because when he'd fantasize, he'd be all over the road and completely oblivious to oncoming traffic.

Fantasy Is a Real Mindblower

Living with someone who constantly "checks out" on you to enter fantasyland can make you terribly insecure. The anecdote at the beginning of the preceding chapter, about Jack spending the evening staring straight ahead, was replayed over and over in our home. After a while, I realized Jack's spaciness had nothing to do with me, so I stopped taking the blame for it and I stopped asking him about it. But that didn't make it any easier for me to see a man I knew once had a fine mind sit and stare blankly.

After indulging in fantasy for more than 20 years, Jack lost his ability to think about anything else. Dwelling so much on that which wasn't true made him unable to think about that which was true. He lost his common sense and his ability to solve problems. (Common sense is a gift that comes to us when we accept that there are consequences to our actions. When we live in a fantasyland where we create the consequences we want to occur, apart from any respect for reality, we lose our ability to see connections between cause and effect.) My husband, once a brilliant engineer, couldn't even figure out how to turn a freezer so it would fit through the door into the cellar.

He was absentminded in the extreme. He'd turn on the stove to make tea, forget to put the kettle on, and just walk out of the kitchen with the burner glowing red. He'd put wood into the woodstove and leave the door open, causing chimney fires. In the morning, it wasn't unusual to find the outside door standing wide open. He'd have gone out for something the night before and forgotten to close it when he came in. Sometimes, when someone would ask him a question, he would start to answer, only to stop halfway into the reply and then freeze with his mouth open. His mind had gone completely blank.

Jack always said he wanted other people to think he "had it all together." So, for a long time, when other people were around, he'd manage the herculean effort of staying focused enough so that only the most alert could see that he wasn't tracking well. In the end, though, his "checking out" became apparent to people besides the children and me. Too much time fantasizing meant he also lost his ability to do his work well. Finally, the man who was recognized three times as an outstanding employee was fired for being incompetent and lying to his boss.

Once a regional manager for a large company, overseeing millions of dollars worth of equipment and managing half a dozen men, Jack had an expense account, a cellular phone, a company vehicle, and a comfortable middle-class salary. Today, he is doing production work, packing 12-ounce bags of chocolates at $7.25 an hour. He stands at an assembly line seven-and-a-half hours a day, catching bags that come off the machine at a rate of 71 a minute. Then he puts them into boxes—24 to a box. Sometimes, he scrapes chocolate off the factory floor. And every day when he leaves home, he carries his briefcase. If he forgets it, he comes back in to get it. He needs it to remember what he was before he was brought to a piece of bread by means of a whorish woman (Prov. 6:26).

One day, when I was agonizing in prayer, asking the Lord to show me what was going on, He gave me a picture of Jack's brain. It was completely smooth, except for one terribly deep trench that ran down one side. I knew instinctively that the trench was the fantasy track in his mind. The trench was so deep that there didn't seem to be any way out of it. The rest of his brain, I could see, was virtually unused. Jack had blown his mind on fantasy.

Between a Rock and a Hard Place

Fantasy has other negative consequences on a marriage. Dr. Dolf Zillman and his colleague Dr. Jennings Bryant discovered a profound attitude difference toward male dominance between a group of men and women who had seen six pornographic videos and a group that witnessed six hours of prime-time situation comedies. The group that had been exposed to pornography "accepted male dominance over females twenty times more than did the control group [that watched comedy]. (This applied to women as well as men, although women less so.)"[8]

A man who has surrendered his imagination to the fantasy of pornography will believe he has the right to control and dominate his wife. Trying to figure out how to live in a situation in which the head of the house is passive and "checked out" is impossible. If, at the same time, he is being extremely controlling and manipulative, trying to force his wife to become the women of his fantasies, his perverseness will control the whole dynamic of the family.

Men who have unbridled power, and women who either manipulate them or submit to their abuse in order to survive, create a pathological family system. This is not the kind of family a wise woman wants to create. A wise woman doesn't want to submit to evil and she also doesn't want to manipulate her husband. She wants to honor him and train her children to honor him as well. But when his behavior is this bizarre, it's difficult to know how to do it.

I went to four different Christian counselors and two different pastors trying to find someone to help me understand how to deal with the situation. None of these particular individuals could understand what I was talking about. They either said or implied that I was the one fantasizing about what was going on. I was told I needed to be more submissive—that Jack was so weak because I was so strong. I was told I was unrealistic in my expectations. I was told Jack's only problem was that he had low self-esteem, and if I would just be the right kind of wife, he would be fine.

I would come away from these sessions broken and wondering if maybe they were right. Maybe it was all in my mind. Maybe I was the problem.

But then something would happen, and I would see the truth in my children's faces. It wasn't all a figment of my imagination. I wasn't expecting too much; I wasn't beating him down. There really was a problem. Jack really was slipping away from us.

Perhaps I did a poor job of communicating with these pastors and counselors. It is difficult to know how to explain behavior that is so out of the ordinary without having it look as if you are expecting too much of someone. But I think part of the problem was that these counselors didn't have any experience with sexual addictions, and so they didn't really understand how devastating pornography is to the mind. (Maybe my story will help.)

It wasn't until after Jack and I were separated and we met Dr. Ron Miller that my observations were verified. After examining Jack, Dr. Miller looked at him and said, "You've destroyed your mind by fantasizing. You've dug a deep channel going in one direction. The rest of your mind has atrophied."

That was exactly the picture the Lord had given to me many years earlier! I wanted to fall at Ron's feet and weep. God had heard my cry. Maybe now my husband would finally get the help he needed.

Unfortunately, shortly after our third meeting with him, Ron's health began to fail. Within a year, cancer took him. We were never able to get back to see him. Once more, I was left feeling all alone in my conviction that something was wrong with Jack's mind. But I clung to Dr. Miller's diagnosis.

There has to be someone else out there who knows about these things, I thought. *And with God's help, I'm going to find him.*

Let Me Entertain Me

Masturbation physically is a self-bent thing. Its focus is inward. It doesn't share. It doesn't know the verb "to give." It is a fire that feeds itself.

(Randy)

Shun immorality and all sexual looseness—flee from impurity in thought, word or deed. Any other sin which a man commits is one outside the body, but he who commits sexual immorality sins against his own body.

(1 Corinthians 6:18)

[Please be advised that, of necessity, this chapter contains graphic material.]

Pete's hands shook on the steering wheel.

"Easy, boy," he muttered to himself. "Almost there. Almost there."

Without easing up on the accelerator, Pete wheeled the car onto the old logging road. The tires shuddered as they left the tarmac and hit the rough gravel.

There it was up ahead—his favorite place. The car lurched as he slammed on the brakes.

Pete squirmed with excitement as he picked up the magazine. "Hot off the press and I do mean *hot!*" he chortled.

First of the month, like clockwork, he was there scooping up the latest issue—always. Because he knew Miss September was going to be better than Miss August, who was better than Miss July. Had to be, just had to be.

Yeah, sometimes it bothered him that the girl at the checkout knew he was a regular. But, hey, it was a decent store. Regular folks went in there and got all kinds of stuff: a couple loaves of bread, a gallon of milk, a bag of cookies for the kids—*and* the latest and greatest issue. If you bought it from a decent store, it must be okay. Right?

"We're not talking about some sleazy magazine from the slimy part of town," he told himself, shoving aside the same doubt that nagged him every time he picked an issue up. "This is art—high-class art with lots of important articles about lots of important people and major issues of the day.

"Besides, it's a man's right to do man's stuff." He winked at himself in the rearview mirror and something about the look in his eyes troubled him—but only momentarily. His sweaty fingers stuck to the pages as he turned rapidly past the important articles about important people and major issues of the day.

"There!" he sighed as he feasted on the centerfold. "Yeah, she's better than last month. A *lot* better. A *lot* better than Marjorie, too."

He felt a twinge of guilt as he thought about his current wife. Then more guilt as he thought about his first wife and the kids he didn't see often.

"What's wrong with the two of them? Turn cold as soon as they hit the sheets. Don't want to do this and don't want to do that."

Maybe it was time to move on. Maybe he wouldn't get married this time. Maybe he'd just find someone to move in with, someone younger and firmer. He knew she was out there. There were lots of girls just like Miss September. After all, there was a new one in every issue. Girls who weren't busy with babies. Girls who didn't hassle you for grocery money. Girls who could be anything and do anything you wanted anytime you wanted. Yeah, maybe it was time to move on.

Sighing, he sank into the seat and fumbled for his zipper.

Just One of the Guys

Pete's not alone in this self-deception. Scenes like this one are reenacted every day by men who use pornography. Pornography appeals to masturbatory tendencies. Men become willing to trade the real human love they already have for a few self-absorbed moments with objects made of paper and ink. They know there's emptiness in what they're doing. They can see the lie in their eyes. They can feel it in the nagging doubts that haunt them.

Yet, at every turn, men like Pete rationalize their choice to commit adultery with figures printed on glossy stock. They are men "interacting with" and paying homage to engraved images. They may not remember their kids' birthdays or their wedding anniversaries or whether or not they've paid the mortgage this month, but they know exactly which day the latest issue of their favorite magazine comes out and they live for the moment when they can be consumed by the images in it. This is idolatry in its purest form.

And it's always someone else's fault. Someone else "gave" them permission to spill their strength on pretty paper dolls who'll never know them or care about the cost in enduring human relationships. Hey, if these magazines weren't at the corner quick stop, these guys would never think about going down to the slimy part of town to pick one up. If society says it's respectable, then it is. If society says boys will be boys, then boys will be boys. If the wife was just a bit warmer under the sheets, this wouldn't be necessary. Yes, it's always someone else's responsibility that ole Pete is out there doing his thing with Miss September.

Self-absorption, self-deception, rationalizations, and masturbation are common behaviors for men who use pornography. They are part of the primary nature of pornography. Much of pornography is specifically crafted to make sure this powerful conditioner kicks in. Researcher Harriet Koskoff wrote: "Pornography is primarily about masturbation, whether it is mental or actual."[2]

In a study done at the University of Manitoba and Winnipeg, researchers Neil Malamuth and Robert McIlwraith noted that *Penthouse*, in particular, searches for ways to increase its appeal as a stimulant for masturbatory fantasies.[3] According to Dr. Ron Miller, *Penthouse* and other pornographic magazines have been successful in this search. Dr. Miller said he never dealt with a man who was involved with pornography who wasn't also heavily involved in masturbation.[4]

Ah, Come On!

What's the big deal? Can't we grow up here? Why isn't it all right for guys to masturbate to a pretty picture if that's what they want to do? According to former U.S. Surgeon General Joycelyn Elders, masturbation could be the answer to the social problems brought on by unwed mothers and the deadly AIDS virus. After all, wouldn't it be better for guys to "relieve" themselves rather than go out and rape someone or impregnate someone or get a sexually transmitted disease? Is it only inhibited people who can't accept masturbation as a normal part of healthy sexuality? Not really.

Dr. Victor Cline, a prominent researcher on the psychological effects of pornography, said that masturbating to pornography can actually cause the very social problems it supposedly prevents: "In my view pornography is one contributor to sexual illness. It can provide anti-social sexual imagery which becomes *locked* into the man's mind and returns again and again to haunt and stimulate him. *When he masturbates to this image, **without realizing it,** he is engaging in a powerful form of learning called 'masturbatory conditioning' which can lead—in time—to acting out this imagery."*[5]

Thus, when a man masturbates to pornography he can open himself up to powerful forces that program his internal computer to respond in certain ways in the future. This programming happens without intention or awareness—it happens unconsciously. There are no internal buzzers that go off and say, "Alert! Alert! Value system has been infected. Do not proceed in this operation." A man can masturbate to pornography and not realize how he's being changed. There is almost a dualism that occurs, in that a man tries to make himself believe that the values he uses in relating to others in his everyday life are different from the values he masturbates to. But as a man thinks in his heart, so he is.

In the fantasy world of pornography, a man is lord and master of the woman, able to use her in any way he desires. She is completely subject to his will. This is especially true in some of the pornographic interactive software, like Dream Machine and Virtual Valerie.

In the fantasy world of pornography, a man is able to inflict pain to cause plea-sure. He becomes the final arbiter of what is good and evil. In his heart, the masturbator imagines himself participating in acts that defile and use other people. In the act of release, the masturbator rewards himself for having this kind of mind-set.

In the secret places of his heart, he begins to abandon his will to the fantasies that give him pleasure. This abandonment happens without awareness because he is going in the direction of least resistance. In the end, his imagination has redi-rected his will from inner control based on the principles of conscience to outer control based on the appetites of the flesh.

In his book *Spiritual Warfare,* Ed Murphy said, "During one of his crusades a few years ago, Dr. Billy Graham said, 'In any battle between the imagination and the will, the will loses out every time.'"[6] When your will surrenders its right to control you from within based on what your conscience says, you lose your power to protect yourself from evil. Now you react rather than act. Now you're outer-controlled rather than inner-controlled. Now you're governed the same way animals are, by the principle of stimulus-response, rather than the way God said you were to be governed, by self-control.

Once we surrender our wills to outer control, we experience the ultimate consequence of idolatry: a lack of proper personal boundaries. Without proper boundaries, we are vulnerable to a full-fledged attack by the enemy. Proverbs 25:28 says, "He that hath no rule over his own spirit is like a city that is broken down, and without walls" (KJV).

Sex Is About Being

It is impossible to separate our sexuality from our being. Sex isn't just something we do with our sex organs. Our sexuality is something we are. It is part of our essence; it flows through the whole of our being. Because of this, you cannot isolate sex and make it just something you do.

Yet, masturbation says that by keeping things strictly genital, you can have sex with yourself and not have it affect who you are. You can be both the star and the director of your own sexual production. But William Banowsky knows differently:

> Sex is not essentially something man does, but something he is: sex does not designate a simple function, it relates to the totality of existence. The biological side of sex cannot be isolated and viewed as autonomous because it is but one aspect of the whole, indivisible man. Sexual intercourse is not merely one physical act among many; *it is, instead, an act that engages and expresses the entire personality in such a way as to **provide insight into the nature of man**.*[7]

So, what kind of insight does masturbation give us into the nature of the man who engages in it? In *The Broken Image*, Leanne Payne shared a thank-you note from Randy, a young man who came to her for healing from obsessive masturbation. "Masturbation," Randy wrote, "physically is a self-bent thing. Its focus is inward. It doesn't share. It doesn't know the verb 'to give.' It is a fire that feeds itself."[8]

The Man Who Engages in Masturbation Hangs Out a "Do Not Disturb" Sign

Randy wrote that masturbation is self-bent and focused inward. This is in the opposite direction sex was designed to send us in. Sex was created to send us outward. The word *intercourse* means "communication, a connection between people." When we choose to make it on our own, we are saying we don't want to be bothered with the hard work of communication; we're not interested in connecting with anyone but ourselves. We are the center of our own universe.

Being both the star and the director of our own sexual production reduces sex to a mere physical hunger. Sex becomes a one-man show rather than an opportunity to relate intimately with another. In *Game Free: A Guide to the Meaning of Intimacy,* Professor Thomas C. Oden wrote: "Intimates are aware that their most significant exchanges are not merely body transactions, but as persons in encounter, of the meeting of spirit with spirit. What really happens in intimacy has to do with spirit-spirit communion or interpersonal communion, two persons experiencing their beings poignantly united."[9]

Yet, when the focus of sex is self-bent and inward, there can be no encounter with another. The masturbator is merely engaging in a bodily transaction with himself. When the focus of sex is self-bent and inward, there can be no spirit-to-spirit communion with the person we love. Instead, the masturbator is communing with an invisible spirit, one he totally controls. Instead of being a way to interpersonal communion with another, sex implodes a man, driving him further into himself.

When we are self-absorbed in our sexuality, we will be self-absorbed in every aspect of our daily lives. The wife of a man who is enslaved to masturbation will not only be shut out of his sexuality, she will also be shut out of daily decisions and daily occurrences. He jealously guards it all for himself. He cannot afford to let anyone in. To do so would destroy his illusion of control.

Thus, by its very nature, masturbation closes the doors to intimacy. When a wife approaches, she will find no handle on the door, only a quickly hung "Do Not Disturb" sign. The message is "Sex is a solo affair. I don't need you. Your presence gets in the way of what I'm trying to do here. I can make it on my own, thank you."

If sexual intercourse is the thing that makes a couple one flesh, how can a husband engage in a fantasy sexual relationship with himself and not have it affect the one flesh relationship he has with his wife? That which is supposed to be the seal of their covenant, the sexual relationship, becomes the very thing that says to the wife, "You are unwanted."

What's Mine Is Mine

Randy said that masturbation doesn't know how to share. Yet, sharing is the essence of relationship, especially in sex. Sex is about invitation, not exclusion. Sex is about taking down the barriers and welcoming our cherished one in to know us. But a man who is enslaved by masturbation doesn't know how to share his innermost being with anyone. He wants it all for himself. Thus, the very act that's supposed to be about giving and sharing with the object of our affections becomes a way to adore the self.

Adoring ourselves is different from loving and accepting ourselves. When we love and accept ourselves, we see ourselves as having value. We recognize that our opinions and feelings are as important as the opinions and feelings of others. We recognize that we have gifts and abilities that can make a positive difference in the world. We also recognize our limitations and we are gentle with ourselves about what we can't do.

In self-adoration, we become gods in our own eyes. We have no sense of our limitations. We are unbridled in our determination to affect our world. We think our values, opinions, and needs are far more important than anyone else's. In fact, we might not even see that anyone else has the right to values, opinions, and needs. We become objects of our own worship and live in a world according to us.

Adoration of the self is narcissism. Just as a small infant wants the world to revolve around him, so a narcissist wants those around him to bow to his every command. After all, he's in love with a wonderful guy—himself!

Leanne Payne wrote poignantly of the effect this has on a spouse:

> I remember only too well the young wife who realized her husband's narcissism in his very act of lovemaking. She said to me, "My husband is in love with his own body. I am most aware of this when he is making love to me. He doesn't really—can't really—make love to me, though I can hardly explain it to you. I have seen him nude, gesturing before a mirror. He gets the same pleasure out of that as in making love to me. I am not loved. I am merely a vessel through whom he loves himself."[10]

Masturbation Says "I Belong Only to Me"

Randy wrote: "[Masturbation] doesn't know the verb 'to give.'" The man who is enslaved to masturbation won't give his wife her sexual rights. He is saying, in effect, "My body, my sexuality, my innermost being, belong to me. No one else has prior claim. I can do whatever I want with myself because I belong to only me."

Yet, Scripture teaches that when we marry, we give up the right to own ourselves. When we say, "I do," we transfer the ownership of our bodies to our spouses. This is especially true in the area of sexuality. 1 Corinthians 7:4–5 says, "The wife hath not power of her own body, but the husband: and likewise also the husband hath not power of his own body, but the wife. Defraud ye not one the other, except it be with consent for a time that ye may give yourselves to fasting and prayer; and come together again, that Satan tempt you not for your incontinency" (KJV).

When a man masturbates, he repossesses the power of his own body, defrauding his wife of what is rightfully hers. And since masturbation is usually done on the sly, the masturbator defrauds his wife without her consent. A wife cannot consent to something she is unaware of. She is left completely out of the loop of her husband's sexuality.

For some men, masturbation becomes the preferred way to "have sex." Once he has satisfied himself several times in a day, a husband has nothing left to give to his wife. When she reaches for him at night, he jerks away. Why, he asks himself, should he put himself in a situation where he has to please another when he can so easily please himself? So, instead of warm responsiveness, she finds only cold hardness. If she responds to his rebuff by playfully teasing him, he is likely to hurl some put-down at her. He may even physically push her. Then he turns away and clings tightly to his side of the bed. Stunned, she wonders what in the world is wrong with her. Repeated sexual rejection kills the heart of a woman. It is a violent, painful death where the woman's heart is utterly consumed on the altar of a masturbatory fire that rages out of control.

A Fire Raging Out of Control

Finally, masturbation, as Randy wrote, is a fire that feeds on itself. It feeds on itself sexually. Because there is physical pleasure in release, the act of masturbation reinforces itself. We tend to repeat things that make us feel good. Masturbation also feeds on itself because it is intimately connected with fear.

This works in two ways. *The first way is when fear contributes to masturbation.* Payne wrote that the habit of masturbation may be

> rooted in infantile trauma and related to a severe dread and anxiety—those components accompanying the severest psychological injuries in infants. In these cases, a dread-ridden masturbation (rather than a merely lustful one) ensues. The infant, unable to receive the love of the mother or someone other than himself, will anxiously clutch at his own genitals. In this separation, the infant can fail to achieve a sense of well-being or even of being at all.
>
> There are differing degrees of damage here, but in cases where dread and anxiety are a factor, the counselor must help the sufferer not only to be released from the habit, but to exercise patience and understanding with himself while the underlying anxiety and identity crisis is being healed. And it will always be healed as the person

comes into his identity and relationship in Christ. Also, even though there is a pathological base to the habit, the sufferer who truly desires wholeness must consciously turn from it. The habit always contributes to self-revulsion and self-hatred, and will be found rankling at the bottom of a continuing bad self-image until the necessary freedom is gained. Such a sufferer needs to understand what such *a dread-ridden cycle of masturbation denotes: a love turned inward on oneself due to his primary disrelation to others.*[11]

Thus, masturbation may be caused by disrelation to others. Since masturbation contributes to self-hatred, it also reinforces disrelation to others. When we hate ourselves, we are completely unable to love others. As a consequence, we experience the terrifying sense of being disrelated. Since a sense of belonging is crucial to mental stability, isolation creates a mental health crisis. If we remain isolated long enough, we lose our sense of self. Now the pleasure of masturbation becomes a narcotic to dull the pain and fear of being disrelated.

Masturbation Contributes to Fear

The second way masturbation feeds on itself is when masturbation contributes to fear. Masturbation by its very nature is fearful. Because it's done in secret places on the sly, there's the fear of being caught, which becomes in some men a thrill in and of itself. There's also that nagging inner fear that maybe what they're doing isn't right—maybe there will be consequences.

Dr. James L. McGaugh of the University of California, in his research on memory, found that if a person is emotionally (including sexually) aroused at the time of experiencing or witnessing something, a chemical called epinephrine is released into the bloodstream. It goes to the brain and in a complicated way locks in a vivid memory of the experience or event.[12]

This vivid memory reappears over and over, like an LSD trip, and when it does, it brings with it the emotions associated with the experience, including the fear. The power of the trip is that it drives the masturbator to repeat the masturbation in order to seek solace from the fear. Thus sex causes fear and sex relieves fear.

Sex, in the masturbator's mind, now becomes intimately associated with fear. He will bring this fear into the marital bed and the intuitive wife will sense it during their sexual relationship. She won't know why she senses it; she'll just know there's a thick foreboding, bordering on panic, that settles in like a suffocating blanket whenever her husband approaches her sexually.

Masturbation Causes an Identity Crisis

In marriage, it is important for both the husband and wife to be secure in their sexual identities. In recent years, there has been much confusion about whether there is even such a thing as sexual identity. For instance, these days homosexuality is out and about. The homosexual denies that there can be a clear sexual identity and chooses, instead, to believe it is possible to be both male and female.

Feminists contend that there is no difference between men and women psychologically. A few even insist that there is no difference biologically. Some of the feminist hysteria has to do with the fact that in the past, the biological and psychological differences between men and women were used to restrict women to narrow roles and deny them the opportunity to develop their gifts.

Yet, understanding and celebrating our differences is a big part of what makes a marriage work. There are some things that men do better than women and some things that women do better than men. To use this truth to insist that men and women adhere to rigid roles flies in the face of the clear teaching of Scripture that both men and women are created in the image of God (Gen. 1:27) and that in Christ, we are one—neither male nor female (Gal. 3:28). However, to deny this truth, also flies in the face of the clear teaching of Scripture that men and women have separate but equally important tasks to accomplish (Gen. 1:26–28, 3:15–20). Embracing our sexual identities is crucial if we are to find contentment in our marriages and lives.

What does all this have to do with masturbation and pornography? Plenty. Both masturbation and pornography contribute to the general confusion about whether there is such a thing as sexual identity. Pornography, particularly interactive pornographic videos, does this by allowing a man to craft the sexual response of a woman so it is more like that of a man.

Whether manipulating a computer screen or manipulating his mind through fantasy, the porn viewer designs the woman's sexual response to suit himself. Because he allows no feedback, he believes the lie he has created. When a man believes a lie about a woman's sexual response, he will also be grossly out of touch with other parts of her nature.

You may recall an earlier quote from Dr. Victor Cline in which he said that pornography contains much scientifically inaccurate, false, and misleading information about human sexuality, especially female nature and response.[13] This false and misleading information about female sexual response blurs the distinction between men and women and feeds the confusion about sexual identity.

Masturbation to pornography contributes to sexual confusion because when he masturbates, a man imagines himself to be both self and other. He is both giver and receiver of pleasure, both male and female. His hand becomes a female hand caressing his male body. He is not a whole man responding to a whole woman, he is part man/part woman responding to himself. As a man, he communicates with his imaginary female, telling her what will give him pleasure. As a female, he thrills himself with her response to his communication.

The Dark Little Prison of Self

Masturbation can take a great deal of time out of life. Dr. Mark Laaser said, "There are sex addicts who masturbate as many as 20 times a day. The need to masturbate can take so much time, it causes addicts to lose valuable work, family, and social time."[14]

The more time he spends masturbating, the more the masturbator pulls into himself. C. S. Lewis wrote about this increasing isolation in a letter replying to a young man who asked Lewis what he thought about masturbation. Lewis wrote:

> For me the real evil of masturbation would be that it takes an appetite which, in lawful use, leads the individual out of himself to complete his own personality in that of another and turns it back; sends the man back into the prison of himself, there to keep a harem of imaginary brides.
>
> *And this harem, once admitted, works against his ever getting out and really uniting with a real woman. For the harem is: always accessible, always subservient, calls for no sacrifices or adjustments, and can be endowed with erotic and psychological attractions which no real woman can rival. Among those shadowy brides he is: always adored, always the perfect love, no demand is made on his unselfishness, no mortification ever imposed on his vanity. In the end, they become merely the medium through which he increasingly adores himself.*[15]

The Lonely Hearts Club

Once a man's ability to love has been consumed on the altar of a masturbatory fire raging out of control, both he and his wife will become charter members of the Lonely Hearts Club. In that dark and companionless place, with the band playing eternal encores of "Let Me Entertain Me," everyone dances alone. The dangers to the marriage are obvious.

CHAPTER 13

Liar, Liar, House Afire

Deceivers are the most dangerous members of society. They trifle with the best affections of our nature, and violate the most sacred obligations.

(George Crabbe¹)

When the Liar speaks, he makes it up out of his lying nature and fills the world with lies.

[John 8:44²]

M ost sex addicts are pathological liars. They lie about everything, not just their sexual behavior, and they do so with straight faces. They lie when telling the truth would save them time and money. They lie about little things as well as big ones. They lie to themselves about what they're doing. They lie to their wives and families about where they're going and what they're going to do when they get there, even if there's no sexually inappropriate behavior going on. Pornography itself is a lie, and they embrace it.

Roy Hession called lies a "forgotten factor" in adultery. "To the sin of the actual sexual behavior . . . has to be added the further sin of lies, deception, giving false impressions, play-acting, subterfuge, all to hide what has taken place or is still going on. In every situation of sexual misbehavior, . . . we can always assume that there has been woven a vast web of lies and deception before it came fully into the light."³

Many of us treat lying as a "lightweight" sin. Lying is so common today in

113

public discourse, including the discourse of leading politicians, that we've become desensitized to its power. Lying is a form of insanity. It denies reality and attempts to force others to deny the reality of a situation by manipulating their understanding of truth.

When we lie, we refuse to walk in truth. In lying, we deliberately take ourselves out of the light and plunge ourselves into the darkness. When we walk in the darkness, we are walking in Satan's jurisdiction.

For this reason, we are counseled to walk in the light as Christ is in the light. Scripture says there is a radical difference between light and darkness. Hession said that "in the New Testament, the words 'light' and 'darkness' are not merely vague synonyms for good and evil. The light simply means that which reveals, whereas the darkness means that which hides."[4]

Truth is that which reveals. Lying is that which conceals. And lying has dangerous consequences.

1. *Lying causes isolation.* 1 John 1:6–7 says, "If we say that we have fellowship with Him [God] and walk in darkness we lie and do not tell the truth. But if we walk in the light, as He is in the light, we have fellowship with one another, and the blood of Jesus Christ cleanses us from all sin." In other words, the basis for relationship is truth. Without truth, there can be no trust. Without trust, there is only the appearance of intimacy. The result is a terrifying isolation.

2. *Lying gives Satan legal ground to enter our lives.* In John 8:44 Jesus said, "Ye are of your father the devil and the lusts of your father ye will do; he was a murderer from the beginning, and abode not in the truth, because there is no truth in him. When he speaketh a lie he speaketh of his own, for he is a liar, and the father of it" (KJV). A person who lives a lie opens the door to spiritual oppression of himself and his family.

Things That Go Bump in the Night

Early one morning, four-year-old Tommy walked into his parents' bedroom. "Who's that man?" he asked, pulling on his mother to wake her up.

"What man?" Sue said, blinking herself awake.

"That man all dressed in black next to Daddy," he said.

She could see no one next to David. "Tommy, there's no one standing next to Daddy. You go back to bed."

"Yes there is, Mommy," and Tommy began to cry.

Over the next few weeks, Tommy saw the man several times. Sue dismissed each incident as the overactive imagination of a four-year-old. Then, one night, she was awakened by David reaching for her.

"Sue," he croaked, "pray for me."

She could see terror written across David's face. Quickly, she stammered out a prayer, asking God to come and be with them and take care of whatever was scaring her husband.

Later, David told her that he had awakened to see the form of a man hovering over him. "It was like a heaviness. I could hardly breathe, Sue," he said.

Although Sue was unaware of it at that time, David had been struggling with a secret sexual addiction that involved masturbation and exhibitionism.

Deliver Us from Evil

In *The Handbook for Spiritual Warfare*, Dr. Ed Murphy related the following story:

A fellow missionary with whom I often travel in ministry was experiencing increased sexual loneliness during his frequent absences from his wife. As he shared his loneliness with two missionary friends, both were amazed that he did not try masturbation as a means of temporary relief while away from home. They both said they did.

My friend began to follow their advice, at first infrequently. Then it became more and more often. . . . While it provided some relief, it actually made him feel very insecure. Mental images of what he was doing would cross his mind at the most inopportune times, often while he was praying and reading Scripture or preaching. He felt he must stop. He did for a while; then the desire would come upon him stronger than ever.

One night while in bed, the desire came upon him with the greatest intensity he had ever known. Suddenly, he became aware of an evil presence in the room with him. He was only beginning to learn the demonic dimension of spiritual warfare, but he sensed it was satan. He remembered James 4:7–8: "Submit therefore to God. Resist the devil and he will flee from you. Draw near to God, and He will draw near to you" [paraphrase].

He began to resubmit his sexuality and sexual organs to God, including his mind, his emotions, and his will. He then began to resist the devil and his sexual demons out loud. He took his position as reigning with Christ above all principalities and powers of evil. He claimed his victory through the One Who had defeated satan and his evil spirits on the Cross. Within a few minutes the evil presence left. The uncontrollable sexual passion was now under control. Though he still travels in a worldwide ministry usually without his wife, he has had no problems with masturbation or even strong temptations toward masturbation since that day.[5]

❧ Where Do We Go from Here?

What's going on in these two stories? I'm not a psychologist and I'm not a theologian; so I can't give definitive answers. At any rate, I'm not sure definitive answers are possible. But let me share some of my observations with you and tell you what some people who counsel sex addicts have discovered.

In both situations, there is a palpable sense of evil. Most of us have had experiences when we felt our backs tingle or our skin prickle when we met someone or walked into a room where we sensed something unusual had gone on. Usually, this awareness that "something evil there lurks" is brushed off because we tend to deal only with that which can be seen and known in the physical world.

Those things we feel in our gut but can't see with our eyes, we tend to intellectualize by making them into ideas. This is what we've done with good and evil because we can't hold them in our hands for scientific analysis. We know when we've been touched by them, but since we can't intellectually quantify them, we tend to deny that they are real in and of themselves. We prefer to look at good and evil as concepts. This allows us to neatly dispose of them by relegating them to lofty definitions. Then we congratulate ourselves for being such fine philosophers and hope the rest of society is able to come up to speed on these definitions so we can all live happily ever after.

But evil is not an abstract intellectual concept. It is a bone-chilling reality—more real than intellect. It is more powerful than the lofty words that try to reduce it to a mere curiosity as if it could be pickled in formaldehyde and displayed in a specimen jar for all to gawk at. And it is all the more terrifying because our finely tuned minds don't know what in the world is going on.

❧ The World Rulers of This Present Darkness

Scripture teaches us that there is a spirit world that lives alongside our physical world. The unseen beings in this spirit world are just as real as the seen beings in our physical world. These unseen beings have the ability to affect our lives in a profound way.

Paul reminded us of that in Ephesians 6:12: "For we are not wrestling with flesh and blood—contending only with physical opponents—but against the despotisms, against the powers, against the master spirits who are the world rulers of this present darkness, against the spirit forces of wickedness in the heavenly sphere."

It's been a struggle for me to believe it, but I finally had to accept that somehow, in some way, the spirit forces of wickedness have access to a family in which the father is involved in pornography. Until I was willing to accept this, I was fighting a losing battle because I was trying to respond to what was happening as if I were dealing with things I could see and touch.

Once I accepted that I was dealing with something beyond the realm of the physical, I had a whole new war chest of weapons to handle the situation. These new weapons helped me find peace in the midst of the storm.

✳ Sex Is a Physical Picture of a Spiritual Truth

It shouldn't surprise us that we encounter the spirit world when we're dealing with sex. Sex is a physical picture of a spiritual truth. In the past, the church has sometimes gone overboard on this concept by stressing the spiritual side of sex and downplaying (even denying) the physical side of it. "Religious" people can be uncomfortable with the idea that God wants us to have physical pleasure in the sexual act. But the good news is that He designed it that way, and He did it for a purpose. God creates something in the physical realm to teach us something about the spiritual realm.[6]

God designed sex so we could know something about Him. The word that is used for "know" in Genesis 4:1—"Adam *knew* Eve his wife"—is the same word that is used in Jeremiah 16:21—". . . and they shall *know* that my name is The Lord."

What can we *know* about God from the sexual relationship? We can know that God has a passionate desire to be in relationship with us. He compares this desire to the eagerness a bridegroom has to be with his bride: "For as a young man marrieth a virgin, so shall thy sons marry thee; and as the bridegroom rejoiceth over the bride, so shall thy God rejoice over thee" (Isa. 62:5, KJV).

Sex can also teach us something about the nature of the Godhead. Genesis 2:24 says, "Therefore shall a man leave his father and his mother, and shall cleave unto his wife: and they shall be *one* flesh" (KJV). The Hebrew word for "one" is *echad*, which denotes a oneness or unity that contains more than one entity. Interestingly, *echad* is also used in Deuteronomy 6:4: "Hear, O Israel, the Lord our God is *one* Lord" (KJV). In other words, God is one in the same way a man and woman become one through sexual intimacy.

What does it mean that God is one just like a husband and wife are one flesh? The meaning of the word for "flesh" ("they shall be one *flesh*") gives us a clue. In both the Old and New Testaments, this word means "nature." So, even though the Godhead contains three distinct persons (Father, Son, and Holy Spirit), the Trinity is one in nature. The hearts of all three Persons of the Godhead beat for the same things. In marriage, even though a husband and wife are two distinct persons, their hearts beat as one. When one weeps, the other tastes tears.

God feels so strongly about the picture He created in the sexual relationship that He repeatedly refers to it in Scripture. In the Old Testament, the nation of Israel is repeatedly called God's wife. Israel's turning away from Him to worship other gods is called "adultery" and "whoring" (Jer. 3:8, 13:27; Hosea 4:12, 9:1). God even calls His faithless wife a "whore" (Ezek. 16:28–42).

In the New Testament, the relationship between Christ and His church is compared to the relationship between a husband and wife (Eph. 5:22–33). There is even a "great whore" mentioned in Revelation. Better theologians than I have been arguing for centuries about the meaning of the symbolism in Revelation, so far be it from me to try and make any definitive statement about exactly what John was trying to convey when he wrote about this whore in Revelation 17:1–16 and 19:2. This much is clear, though: Whatever she represents, the great whore caused terrible devastation to God's people.

So, whether it's used in a positive sense, to convey a loving relationship between God and His people, or in a negative sense, to convey the people's rejection of Jehovah, sex, the seal of the marriage covenant, is a physical picture of a spiritual truth.

Painting the Picture Dark

Pornography distorts God's intentions for sex because it takes a picture that God wants to use to tell us about His desire to love us and paints that picture in the darkest colors. This contrast can be clearly seen when we compare God's model for relationships with the attitudes and actions perpetuated by pornography.

- God inflicted pain on Himself at the cross to buy our redemption (John 3:16); in pornography, the man inflicts pain on the woman to produce his own pleasure.
- God took upon Himself the form of a servant and made Himself of no reputation, becoming obedient unto death, even death on the cross, that He might use Himself up for us (Phil. 2:5–8); in pornography, the man dominates the woman in order to use her up for his own pleasure.

⊙God breathes life into us by redeeming our wasted years and constantly calling us to remember who we are in Him (Joel 2:25; 1 Cor. 3:16,17); in pornography, the man seeks to kill the woman by stealing her personhood and destroying her sense of self-worth.

⊙God is touched by our infirmities—He weeps with those who weep and comforts those who mourn (Heb. 4:15; Matt. 5:4) in pornography, the man never stops when the woman cries out in pain—the message is, if you keep hurting her long enough, she'll come to love it.

⊙Our relationship with Christ is joy unspeakable and full of glory (1 Pet. 1:8); in pornography, sex is often equated with pain.

These distortions of the sexual relationship are not accidental. God says the principles of eternity are written in our hearts. Our inner man instinctively knows that sex is a picture of our relationship with God. Satan knows if he can distort the picture by portraying God as a user and abuser, he can destroy the power of that picture to lead men and women to Christ.

The Act of Sex Causes a Lasting Impact

In sex, two people become one in *nature*. According to Dr. Gary Durham, senior pastor at Trinity Nazarene Church in Colorado Springs, Colorado, and director of research and instruction for Freedom Ministries Training Institute, a man is a living soul who has both a physical and spiritual nature. The "blending" and "mingling" of the spiritual with the physical and the physical with the spiritual goes deeper than we realize.

In Scripture, the functional soul of a man—where he is both spiritual and physical—is often called simply "the heart." The heart includes a man's self-conscious and unconscious mind. It also includes the functions of will, reason, and emotion, which determine his desires and attitudes.

In the sexual act, we open our hearts to our partners. This is one way the sexual act is a picture of our relationship with Christ, who calls us to open our hearts to Him (Matt. 22:37; Mark 12:30; Luke 10:27). This opening of the heart results in a spiritual as well as a physical "co-mingling" with each of our sexual partners.

This co-mingling of hearts occurs whether or not the people involved in the sexual act plan on it happening. It is as much a God-designed part of sexual intimacy as gravity is a God-designed part of the experience of jumping off a bridge. You literally give part of your heart to the other person and you literally take part of his or her heart into you. Scripture says this blending of hearts is so transforming that the two literally become *one* flesh.

Dr. Durham calls this co-mingling of hearts "spiritual transference." The implications of this concept are enormous. In the same way we become one with each of our sexual partners, we also enter a kind of "oneness" with everyone our partners have had sex with.[7]

✹ Getting More Than You Bargained For

An ad that circulated several years ago, warning people of the dangers of sexually transmitted diseases, illustrated the principles of transference on the physical level. The ad shows a couple in bed. Around the bed are the other men and women the couple have had sex with, as well as the men and women those men and women have had sex with. Even if the couple had only one other partner and each of those partners had one other partner and so on, you don't have to go too far back before the room is full of people.

The implication is that not only are you having sex with the person in bed with you, but you're also having sex with everyone who has ever had sex with that person. This is the degree of physical risk that is associated with having sex with someone. If any of the other partners have been exposed to a sexually transmitted disease, no matter how far back they are in the chain of sexual partners, you are now vulnerable.

Likewise, we open ourselves to a degree of spiritual risk when we have sex with someone. If we have sexual partners who have had a multitude of sexual partners, our hearts are exposed to the hearts of a multitude of people. Becoming "one" with a multitude of people has two effects.

➤ *The first effect is that we divide our hearts into many different pieces and we carry the pieces of many hearts within* James 1:8 says that when a person is double-minded (meaning "of two souls/hearts"), he will be unstable in everything he does because his inner being is fractured. In the same way a broken mirror gives a fractured reflection, so a broken heart can give only a fractured reflection of who someone is as a person. When a person is fractured in his inner man, he loses control of his behavior. He may do things he doesn't remember doing. This out-of-control behavior causes instability in the home. Because of the turmoil double-mindedness causes, Scripture urges us to seek an undivided heart (Ps. 119:2; Ps. 111:1).

➤ *The second effect of having multiple sexual partners is that we open ourselves up to whatever is in the spirit of the other person through the principle of spiritual transference.* In *Principles of Restoration*, Dr. Durham wrote:

> God created human nature so that sexual intimacy is concurrent
> with spiritual transference. In spiritual transference, God created our

spirits to open up not only to each other but also to Him. God intends this for good in marriage where it causes the husband and wife to complete each other and to impress more of His nature on each other.

But in immoral sexual union where God's blessing and protection have been disregarded, Satanic spiritual personalities take advantage of our sinful act as legal ground to oppress our unprotected spirits. If the person with which we have immoral sexual intimacy has deep spiritual bondage in a certain area, it will often transfer to us as oppression or even possession. While not every immoral transference will affect a certain person with the same power—some may have no visible symptom—they will still be a carrier and if they have immoral sexual union again it may show up in the second partner.[8]

Dr. Ron Miller applied the principle of spiritual transference to pornography. In *Personality Traits of the Carnal Mind*, he said, "Willfully seeking after pornographic material opens up one's spirit to demonic influence and even control by an unclean spirit."[9]

Because of the consequences of spiritual transference, Scripture warns us to flee immorality. To the church at Corinth, where temple prostitution was being practiced, Paul warned the Corinthians, "Flee fornication. Every sin that a man doeth is without the body; but he that committeth fornication sinneth against his own body" (1 Cor. 6:18). Back up a few verses and you'll see that the principle of spiritual transference is the reason why fornication is a sin against ourselves: "Do you not see and know that your bodies are members of Christ, the Messiah? Am I therefore to take the parts of Christ and make them parts of a prostitute? Never! Never! Or do you not know and realize that when a man joins himself to a prostitute he becomes one body with her? The two, it is written, shall become one flesh" (1 Cor. 6:15–16).

✗ This Thing Is Bigger Than You Think

Jesus' words in Matthew 12:30 describe a reality that we are often quick to deny: "This is war, and there's no neutral ground. If you're not on my side, you're the enemy; if you're not helping, you're making things worse."[10]

Jesus made no bones about it. He said that there is more to this life than meets the eye. He said that there are wide-reaching repercussions from the choices we make. He said the problem is always bigger than you think.

Are the things I've written about in this chapter the result of demonic activity? Or are they the result of a confused, sick mind? Perhaps no one can know for sure. But I do know this. In the war between good and evil, there's no neutral ground.

PART THREE

This Is War, and There's No Neutral Ground

How to Survive the Devastation

The Ground Rules of Engagement

Between stimulus and response, man has the freedom to choose.

(*Stephen Covey*)

Do what's right and don't be afraid.

[*1 Peter 3:6b*](*paraphrase*)

T here are a few ground rules that have to be followed in the war for the souls of your husband and children.

(1.) Figure Out Which Hills You're Willing to Die On

War takes a lot of energy. Military strategists will tell you that one of the greatest mistakes a general can make is to try to fight a war on too many fronts. When your manpower is running around putting out zillions of fires, your strength is squandered.

When your husband is addicted to pornography, you've got major dysfunction in your life. There will be many fronts where it appears the enemy is about to overwhelm you and yours. If you try to deal with all of them, you'll be spending your energy reacting instead of using it to act. Besides, you don't have the strength to fight every fire. So, you have to figure out where your energy is best spent.

I sat down one day and made a list of all the things that were causing me anxiety. I listed everything, all the way from bills that needed to be paid to whether my children would make a good choice of marriage partners to the daily cares of running a home. After everything was down (it was a long list), I went back and separated the goals from the desires.

I like the way I heard goals and desires defined at a conference I attended several years ago.

➤ A GOAL is something you can achieve by yourself with little or no help from others.

➤ A DESIRE is something that you need the cooperation of others to accomplish.[2]

For example, having a happy family is a desire. You need the cooperation of others to achieve that. But being a good mother by cooking favorite things or tucking notes into lunch boxes to create a sense of belonging in your children is something you can do by yourself. Having a good marriage is a desire. You need the cooperation of your husband to achieve that. But being a wife who is a blessing to her husband is a goal. It is something you can do by yourself.

You work for goals. I made my goals part of my daily "To Do" list. I did what I could by myself and I did them with all my heart (some days I didn't have much heart to put into anything).

You pray for desires. I took my desires and made them into a prayer list. Daily I brought them before the Lord and left them there. Leaving my hopes and dreams with the Lord was rarely easy. I suffered a lot of separation anxiety. My desires for a happy home and good marriage meant so much to me, I often felt as if I were ripping my heart out. But it was freeing to admit that I couldn't make choices for others.

Separating goals from desires gets you off the manipulation and control seesaw. Separating goals from desires will save you a lot of energy. You fight only your own battles. You clean up only your own messes.

2. Fully Occupy Your Place of Functional Authority, But Refuse to Seize the Place of Positional Authority

In Matthew 20:25–27, Jesus explained the two ways we get authority. Jesus said that in the world, people obtain authority because of position. These positions are offices that God has ordained as seats of governing authority. Jesus lamented that the men in these offices often use their authority to exploit, rather than serve, those under them. These "leaders" often have to use force to maintain their authority.

But, Jesus said, there is a greater authority than positional authority. This authority comes through the acts of caring and kindness we do for others. Jesus said those who serve others have the truest authority, whether or not they occupy a seat of governing authority. ". . . Whosoever will be great among you, let him be your minister; and whosoever will be chief among you, let him be your servant" (Matt. 20:26–27, KJV). People naturally look to those they know have their best interests at heart. This is functional authority. No title, no perks, but great power.

Authority in the Home

So, how does this work in the home? The husband has positional authority. He occupies the office of head of the home. If, in that office, he is serving his family by truly loving and caring for them, he will also have functional authority. His family will naturally look to him to lead.

In the preceding chapters, we have talked about how lust makes a man a user of his family. Users are unable to serve; they only seek to get. When a man has defiled his marriage bed and used his family, he has forfeited his right to be heard by his wife and children. (Where there is no purity, there is no power to lead.) Therefore, when a husband is involved with pornography, although he will still occupy the position of head of the home, he will have no functional authority to exercise his headship.

It Ain't Easy Being Point Man

As the wife puts her energy toward accomplishing her goals of being the kind of wife and mother she wants to be, she will obtain much functional authority. The children will naturally look to her because they can trust her to have their best interests at heart. She should not discourage this because the children are only doing what's natural, but she needs to be very careful that she doesn't exploit it.

Whether she exploits her growing authority or not, the husband will see that the children look more to their mother than they do to him and it will often make him jealous. He will resent the wife for receiving honor he feels is due him. A man who has been the hero of numerous fantasies is a legend in his own mind, and he craves all the glory that goes with being a legend. Anyone who gets what he feels belongs to him is a threat.

Resentful, jealous people play games. Do not allow him to make you feel guilty for having the children's trust, but don't flaunt it either. Even though he might demand it, even though you might try to give it, until he changes his behavior and proves he's worthy of respect, it is impossible to restore the authority your husband has stolen from himself by his own actions. But don't grind his face into his powerlessness. Positionally, he is the head of your home. So, train your children to honor him. (Respect has to be earned, but honor is a choice.)

Honoring their father doesn't mean children put up with abuse or keep quiet about how much they're hurting. Honoring their father means they treat him like a man instead of a child. A man can take what other people think about him, a child cannot. But when the children tell him what they think of his behavior, they must do it with honor for his position as their father and as a human being. He may be acting like a jerk, but he's a jerk created in the image of God.

I remember one powerful night when our son, Ian, confronted Jack about the way he had violated a promise he had made to the children about how he was going to handle a meeting with Sandy and her future husband about standards for their dating. Sandy and her fiancé wanted Ian at the meeting because they were very close and felt comfortable talking about these matters together.

But all of them felt Jack had forfeited his right to have any say about sexual standards in a dating relationship. They were quite resistant to the idea of him being present during the discussion. Jack was feeling left out, so we made a compromise that allowed him to come if he remained a silent observer as the four of us worked out an agreement.

As the older brother, Ian headed up the meeting and all was going well until Jack couldn't stand feeling left out. He interrupted what we were doing by saying some bizarre things. The meeting ended with everyone feeling upset about how things had gone.

Afterward, Ian came to me incensed. He was angry with Jack. My first thought was to remind him that he needed to honor his father, but I bit the words back as the Lord said to me, "That's not honoring Jack." Suddenly, I saw that protecting Jack from Ian's wrath was treating him like a child instead of a man. So, I encouraged Ian to tell his dad how he felt. "But as you're telling him how you feel, remember that he's created in the image of God," I said.

Later that night, I heard Ian talking with Jack and I was so proud of him. He spoke to his father like a Dutch uncle. He called a spade a spade, but he reminded Jack that he could be something greater than he was. It was a mighty testimony to the power of speaking the truth in love. Jack cried for hours after that meeting. Ian's words pierced his heart and showed him that no matter how much he wanted to believe otherwise, his children knew that the emperor had no clothes. It was a pivotal point in Jack's healing.

Dangerous Places on the Road to Healing

Learning how to honor someone who is living in a dishonorable way is a place of danger for the wife, for the marriage, and for the children. If a wife reacts to her husband's failures by treating her husband with disdain, she will eventually destroy her own position of authority. Only those under authority have authority. When children see a wrestling match for control going on between their parents, they not only feel insecure, they use the resulting confusion as an excuse to justify their own rebellion. It has been well and wisely said that children will obey their mother to the degree that she honors their father.

The wife will also destroy her position of authority if she denies there is a problem or if she refuses to allow the children to express their hurt and dismay over their father's behavior. Authority flows from trust, and trust flows from truth. The truth is, your husband's behavior is hurtful. It is out of control. It is outrageous. Denying that is not love or honor. It's insanity. So, a wife in this situation must be wise as a serpent and harmless as a dove. She must fully embrace her functional authority and do justly, while at the same time she loves mercy and walks humbly with her God (see Micah 6:8).

3. Learn How to Use Your Strengths to Build Your House

Proverbs 14:1 says, "Every wise woman builds her house: but the foolish one tears it down with her own hands." That word for "hands" means "strength." In other words, don't use your strengths to tear down your house, use them to build your house.

Interestingly, the same point is made in Genesis 2:24: "Therefore shall a man leave his father and his mother, and shall cleave unto his wife and they shall be one *flesh*" (KJV). That word for "flesh" is *basar*. It means "the musculature" or "strength," and in general, refers to the external form of a person.

So, what we're talking about is a yoking together, a combining of strengths, to gain forward momentum. If marriage is a yoking together of strengths, you can see why 2 Corinthians 6:14 gives this strong warning: "Be ye not unequally yoked together" (KJV). If you are the stronger party, you will have to pull an inordinate share of the load. It will be difficult to keep going straight ahead, and the yoke will bite into your shoulders.

Coming alongside someone to share your strength is entirely different from using your strength to maintain your own position. Coming alongside means you have an attitude of wanting to use your strengths to restore the relationship and seek your husband's good.

In *Covenant Relationships,* Keith Intrater said, "A person who sees covenantal dialogue as protecting what belongs to him or gaining what he deserves, misses the purpose of being reconciled to the other person. Covenantal dialogue has nothing to do with getting something for yourself. Its motivation is to restore relationship and to seek the other person's good."[3] I'm not talking about being a "good girl," I'm talking about being a strong woman who has the courage to do what's right and brave the consequences. As you do what's right, you begin to rebuild your house. As you do what's right, you model strength and goodness to your children. As you do what's right, you show your husband that there's a happier, healthier way to live.

(4.) Learn That This Is a Spiritual Battle

God designed us to be controlled from the inside out. (We are to be spirit-led.) Pornography controls from the outside in. It seeks to lead us by our flesh.

Pornography starts by using the desires of our flesh to lure us into its clutches. It seeks to bring about the destruction of the body through abuse, venereal disease, abortion, and suicide (all traumas that occur to the body as a result of involvement with pornography).

Through the imagination, it gains access into our souls where it affects our belief systems, seeks to bend our wills to evil, and causes devastation in our emotions. Then it closes in for the kill in our spirits. It violates our consciences, quenches our ability to know right from wrong, and shuts down our ability to talk with God. (Once the spirit is dead, there is no real life in the body.) We may be going through the motions of living, but no one is really home inside.

Even if you've never looked at pornography yourself, if you are one flesh with someone who has, your spirit, soul, and body are probably also on the critical list. Some women talk about feeling "numb" inside. It hurts too much to feel anymore, so they just shut down. Used up and wasted, they wander about in an emotional daze. Life has been sucked right out of them.

I was like that. I had to be called forth from the dead. I had to be made whole again. In order to recover wholeness, I had to start rebuilding from the inside out. I had to learn how to stand on what I knew was true, *no matter what anyone else said*. I had to learn how to listen to my conscience, even when that meant I had to pay a painful consequence. I had to learn how to meet my needs in healthy ways so I wouldn't end up doing something self-destructive. I had to learn how to deal with gossip and the hurtful things people said to me. I had to learn how to listen to God and find my comfort in Him. I had to learn how to forgive the unforgivable.

None of these was an easy lesson. God had a lot of work to do. Patiently and gently, He continued the good work He began in me that night when He showed me His promise in 1 Peter 1:3. If you or someone you love is being affected by pornography, I suspect you will have to learn these lessons, too. In the rest of the book, I want to show you how I learned to choose to do what was right when I was being so terribly pressured to choose to do what was wrong.

Learning How to Get Direction from God

All of God's actions on the earth are done through the mechanism of covenant. There must be a human being prophetically coming into agreement with God. Through this joint authority, the intervention of God takes place. Without such joint authority, there will be no divine interference.

(Keith Intrater)

Pray also for one another, that you may be healed and restored to a spiritual tone of mind and heart. The earnest, heartfelt, and continued prayer of a righteous man makes tremendous power available— dynamic in its working. Elijah was a human being with a nature such as we have—with feelings, affections, and constitution as ourselves; and he prayed earnestly for it not to rain, and no rain fell on the earth for three years and six months. And then he prayed again and the heavens supplied rain and the land produced its crops as usual.

[James 5:16b–18]

If we're going to be healed, we have to be able to recognize the feel, smell, sound, and look of real life. Once we begin to see what real life is, our eyes will be opened to the ways in which we have behaved like dead people. Rather than studying the darkness, we turn on the light. Then we can see what the darkness has hidden. We see the obstacles we have been stumbling over, and we see where we have sustained bruises from that stumbling.

Getting from Point A to Point B

So, where do we go to learn about real life? *Prayer* and the *Word of God* are the tools that will train us how to recognize the deadness in our lives by showing what real life is all about. I can't begin to explain how important these have been to me. Without them, I would have stayed stuck in darkness, and I would have sustained many more bruises than I did. Without them, I would have had no hope.

I remember the extreme stress I felt when I didn't know how to get from point A to point B. Point A, of course, is where I thought I was, and point B is where I thought I needed to be. Point B seemed to be on the other side of a huge abyss. I stood on the edge of the cliff and looked longingly across the chasm at what I thought was the solution to all my problems. But I had no idea where I really was, and I certainly had no idea where I needed to go. What prayer and Bible reading did for me was to show me where point A and point B really were. They also showed me how to build a bridge to span the chasm between them.

Each of Us Has to Build His or Her Own Bridge

Throughout this book, I have been showing you my bridges. My prayer is that you will find my observations helpful. But there are no one-size-fits-all answers. Each person has a unique situation. True, there are some common behaviors associated with pornography. But each man has his own set of issues, and those issues will affect the way he acts out those behaviors. Each wife has her own set of issues, and those issues will affect the way she responds to her situation.

I don't want this book to provide answers as much as I want it to provide a way you can find answers for yourself. It's easy for us to think that someone else might be able to hear God better than we can, so we tend to build our bridges by following another person's blueprint. In our fallenness, we tend to run around looking for other people to solve our problems, instead of asking God what He wants us to do. We tend to be controlled by others' opinions rather than be guided by the dictates of our consciences. We tend to shape our behavior to gain other people's approval rather than risk their wrath by doing what we know is right.

God knows we *do* need each other. Outside counsel can be helpful, but it has a limitation: No one knows our whole situation. And because our advisers' knowledge is limited to their own experiences, the advice they give us may sometimes be helpful and other times disastrous.

We apply the advice and sometimes things change for the better, but other times,we experience greater turmoil than ever. And even though we may get good counsel or be able to avoid bad counsel, if we've only learned how to decorate the outside with healthier behavior but haven't been changed on the inside by having the light of liberating truth shine on our darkened understanding, we have only received a quick fix. We are not healed.

God isn't interested in quick fixes. He's not interested in formulas or clichés that promise more than they can deliver. The end result of quick fixes, formulas, and clichés is often just more despair. God is interested in healing the wounds in our spirits and redeeming the brokenness that's destroying us.

This means we must go beyond merely managing our behavior by controlling it from the outside. We must become whole people who are controlled from the inside. The difference between managing and being whole is learning *self-control*—a fruit of the Holy Spirit. In the end, each of us has to build his or her own bridge.

This is one of the most important chapters in this book because it is about how to build your *own* bridge by learning how to listen to God. You don't have to be a spiritual giant to receive God's guidance for how to live your life. All you have to do is ask for it (pray), then go to the place where it is found (the Bible). You also need to leave your agendas and expectations at the starting gate. Otherwise, you won't be able to recognize the answers when they come.

Getting Our Brains Washed

We talked earlier about how our minds and consciences can be filled with misbeliefs. These misbeliefs write the script of our lives. They dictate the way we respond to our circumstances, and they form the basis of our self-talk. They misinform us about where point A and point B are. They give us some pretty crummy bridge-building instructions. Since we can't live beyond what we believe, these misbeliefs have to be identified and replaced with truth, or we'll be building a bridge that stops in the middle of the chasm.

We identify these misbeliefs by knowing what the true beliefs are. The truth is what sets us free. As we fill our minds with truth, they will be renewed. The result is a spiritual transformation. Romans 12:2 says we will be transformed by the renewing of our minds by the washing of the water of the Word.

So, the Word of God is our bridge-building guide in this journey. But the Bible is more than that; it is a living thing that has the ability to get inside our souls and spirits. Paul says it's like a two-edged sword that gets inside and cuts to the quick of who we are and how we operate (see Heb. 4:12).

⸱ How to Get Started Reading the Bible

(1.) Find a Bible That's Easy to Read

Everyone has their favorite translation of the Bible. I love the Amplified because it makes passages so clear to me. I feel the earth move under my feet in Genesis, and I feel the passion of God in the prophets. I bought the large-print version, because it's easier to read early in the morning and late at night.

I also have a Spiro Zodhiates *Hebrew-Greek Key Study Bible*. This King James Version Bible has an easy-to-use lexicon at the back where some of the Hebrew and Greek words are defined more clearly. I find this resource absolutely invaluable in understanding what the Bible is really saying.

Finally, I have a copy of Eugene Peterson's *The Message*. This is a raw and powerful translation of the New Testament, Psalms, and Proverbs. When you read it, you laugh, you cheer, you weep; you feel like you have a ringside seat where you can watch the whole story unfold.

(2.) Set Aside a Certain Time of Day to Read Your Bible

I find if I don't have a set time to read my Bible, I don't get around to it. It works best for me to get up early and spend some time in the Word. The house is quiet and the distractions of the day haven't settled in yet. I also like to read a chapter every night when I go to bed—but I find my best time to study the Bible is in the morning.

(3) Make a Commitment to Read the Whole Bible

Begin by reading the Bible through from cover to cover. I've seen these read-through-the-Bible-in-a-year plans where they have you skipping around reading three chapters here and three chapters there. I think it's easy to misinterpret what's being said if you read the Bible like that. You're trying to get the big picture, so read it sequentially and if you get hung up on the "begats," skim through them, but don't skip over anything because there are some really great stories you might miss.

You can't really understand the New Testament if you don't know the Old Testament, because Jesus and the apostles constantly referred to the Old Testament in their teachings. Once you begin to read it with an open mind, you'll find the Old Testament quite exciting. It's filled with powerful stories that give you the ability to see God work in entire lifetimes. You'll learn so much about human nature in its pages. You'll see how people did what was right and what

the rewards were. You'll see how they fell on their faces and what the consequences of their choices were.

You're not in a race here, so you don't have to promise yourself you'll read so
many chapters a day. That's a great way to discourage yourself before you even
begin. Besides, reading so many chapters a day develops a mind-set that you're
trying to get through something. You don't want to get through the Bible, you
want the Bible to get through you. My rule is to read until something grabs me
and then stop and meditate on it for the day.

4. Go Back and Marinate in the "Good Stuff"

As you're reading, note the books that piqued your curiosity. Then, when
you've read the whole Bible cover to cover, go back and reread those books
several times until the truths inside them begin to "get you." Genesis, Exodus,
Deuteronomy, the Kings and Chronicles, Isaiah, Jeremiah, Ezekiel, the Gospels,
Romans, and Hebrews were the books that grabbed me. I also spent a lot of time
in 1 Peter, which is a book about suffering in relationships. It's only five chapters
long, so I read it through every day for months, until I was changed.

It is good if you have a friend who is also searching to know God. I was privileged
to have several, and we'd call each other every couple of days and say, "You
wouldn't believe what I learned in my devotions today." Often, the other person was
learning the same truth in a different place in Scripture. I found this reassuring since
some of the "new" truths I was learning challenged old things I had been taught.

5. Make a Note of New Truths

As you read, certain verses will stand out as very important. You may not
know why they're important, but you have a sense that they are part of new
truth God is trying to help you understand. I don't mean that you are suddenly
discovering a truth that no one else in all Christendom has ever known before.
I'm talking about an essential biblical truth that YOU have never known before,
either because of lack of teaching or wrong teaching, or because your own
mental baggage caused you not to be able to properly understand and lay hold
of this truth, even when it was plainly taught to you.

For example, a pastor who grew up in a home where there was an abusive
father will have a difficult time preaching about the love and mercy of God. His
messages will tend to emphasize passages that talk about God's judgment of
sinners. Unless they spend substantial time in the Word on their own, this man's
congregation will probably remain untaught in God's love and mercy. Likewise,

a layperson who grew up in an abusive home, will have difficulty properly interpreting messages on repentance. Even if the preacher is careful to stress the unconditional love of the Father, the man in the pews may only hear the part of the message that tells him he is an especially wicked sinner, because of the sense of shame and worthlessness that are often part of the mind-set of a person from an abusive background. Whether our wrong understandings about God have been caused by incorrect teaching, no teaching, or a warped mind-set, the exciting promise is that life will begin to spring up in us once our minds have a correct biblical understanding of who God is.

6. Pay Attention to Special Verses

As you're reading, some verses will stand out as special promises. Underline them and put a date next to them. Use them as rainbows to light up your night. For example, I spent a lot of time in the psalms because they seemed to express my emotions so well, especially David's frequent cries of "Where are You, Lord?" One day, when I was feeling especially abandoned by God, I came across Psalm 31:22, "As for me, I said in my haste and alarm, I am cut off from before Your eyes. But You heard the voice of my supplications when I cried to You for aid." On August 22, 1987, God spoke to me through that verse and assured me that He did hear my prayers and that He would answer when the time was right. Whenever I felt abandoned, I came back to that verse and reminded myself of His promise.

Another passage that was a special promise was 2 Peter 1:2–11. This came to me after I'd spent much time in prayer, telling the Lord how I was afraid I'd fall into sin because of the stresses I felt in my marriage. Whether it was adultery, bitterness, jealousy, envy, hopelessness, gluttony, or rage, they certainly all were waiting to get a hold of me. "How do I keep on the right path, Lord?" I kept crying. Then, on September 8, 1996, He brought me to this passage. It lists seven character qualities that God says He wants to develop in us so we won't stumble. After that, every time when I faced a temptation, I would go back to that passage and ask God to show me which character quality He needed to build into me so I wouldn't fall. Each quality has a date listed next to it and as I struggled to let Him work that quality in me, He gave me the grace to overcome the particular temptation I was facing.

7. Use a Concordance to Help You Link New Truths

A little knowledge can be a dangerous thing. Remember that Satan used Scripture to tempt Jesus. In Matthew 4:6, he tried to get Jesus to jump off a pinnacle of the temple by emphasizing one part of a scriptural principle: "He will give His angels charge over you." But Jesus knew the *whole* truth, so He answered Satan's lies with the balancing truth: "It is written also, You shall not tempt, test thoroughly or try exceeding the Lord your God"(Matt. 4:7; Deut. 6:16).

It is wisdom to know that Scripture explains Scripture. Truth is like a many-faceted diamond. We need to understand the different angles of it or we won't get healed—we'll just get weird.

Here's where having read the whole Bible will come in handy. You'll suddenly remember a fragment of a verse that expresses an idea similar to the passage you're reading now. Use your concordance to find that verse. I began my own chain-reference Bible by using the margin to jot down the address of verses that expressed similar thoughts. It's when you pull the same concept from many different parts of Scripture that you begin to grab hold of how its truth can transform your life.

8. Ask the Holy Spirit to Lead You into All Truth

What you are looking for as you read each book is a better understanding of the character of God. You're also looking for an understanding of how human nature operates—the kinds of things we tell ourselves and the consequences of the choices we make. Because you're created in the image of God, as you get a clearer understanding of how He operates, you will get a clearer understanding of how you should operate. You will begin to see how a lot of your inner turmoil comes from failing to operate based on the Manufacturer's User's Guide—the Bible.

I must be a hard case. I found that God had to till a lot of soil before He could plant new truth in my life. Sometimes He'd take months preparing the soil. First, He'd teach me something that would thrill me. Next, He'd teach me another thing that would thrill me. Then, He'd teach me something else that I thought was just great. I would never see how these things could possibly be related. So, they successfully slipped past my mental blocks.

Then, as I became all excited about the new things I'd learned, God would slip in the zinger. Suddenly, I'd see how all these new ideas were connected. And their combined force would assault a long-cherished misbelief and behavior pattern. It was a heavenly "*Gotcha!*" Sometimes I was sure I heard a chuckle.

ӑ Talking It Out in Prayer

Getting a good understanding of what God's Word has to say about life is important, but it's only the starting point. You have to wrestle through how that applies to your situation. You do that through prayer.

Prayer is talking it out with God. I don't understand prayer. I'm not sure how it works or why; I just know that it does. I've been shaken by its power, and to tell you the truth, I'm afraid of it. You see, I've had my prayers answered, and the answers were always what I needed but never what I expected.

No matter how much of the issue was Jack's responsibility, prayer always changed me first. Prayer gave me new eyes to see my situation from God's perspective. That new perspective empowered me to change my responses to what was going on. As I changed, my situation began to change.

Diagnosing the Problem

Suppose you went to your doctor because you had a serious pain in your hip. After hearing your complaint, he writes out a prescription for a pain reliever. After a few days of being on the medication, the pain goes away. Would you say you're better off than you were before you went on the medication?

"Well, the pain went away," you say, "so I suppose I'm better."

Maybe. But pain rarely exists by itself. It is usually an alarm alerting us to an underlying problem. Medication only shuts off the alarm, it doesn't fix the thing that caused the pain. What if I told you that the pain came from a cancer growing in your hip? Armed with that knowledge, your perspective on the situation would probably change. Now you would probably want to begin an aggressive program to eradicate the cancer. Once the cancer was eliminated, the pain would go away by itself.

I discovered that prayer often works the same way. When we first start praying about our situation, we usually begin by praying about symptoms. We may start by asking God to fix some of the things that are causing us pain, such as, "Dear God, please work in Jack's heart so he wants to stay home more," or "Dear God, please let him stop doing the pornography."

In the beginning, a wife may think that her husband's absence from home or his preoccupation with pornography is the problem. But these things are not the problem; they are symptoms of the problem. Sometimes God "fixes" symptoms, but more often, He is interested in dealing with the issue behind the symptoms.

Our prayers change direction and gain power when we start asking God to reveal the issues that create the pain our behavior is trying to anesthetize. We ask Him to search us and know our hearts, and then to guide us on the road to eternal life (Ps. 139:23,24). We ask Him to transform us by renewing our minds (Rom. 12:2). Prayer now serves as a diagnostic tool to uncover the problem. Of course, the Great Physician already knows what the problem is; He just wants to clue us in, but He waits for us to ask Him first.

For with the Mouth, Confession Is Made unto Salvation

I found the diagnostic process began happening as I prayed Scripture *out loud*. Again, I don't understand exactly how it works, but I know what Hebrews 4:12 says: "For the Word that God speaks is alive and full of power—making it active, operative, energizing and effective; it is sharper than any two-edged sword, penetrating to the dividing line of the breath of life (soul) and spirit, and of joints and marrow [that is, of the deepest parts of one's nature], exposing and sifting and analyzing and judging the very thoughts and purposes of the heart."

I also know what Psalm 119:130 says: "The entrance and unfolding of Your words gives light; it gives understanding—discernment and comprehension—to the simple." As I prayed passages of Scripture, out loud, day after day, the words cut deep into the center of my innermost being, exposing my true thoughts and feelings. They showed me where my mind was messed up. They opened my blinded eyes, strengthened my feeble knees, and gave me the freedom to move ahead instead of staying stuck.

Prayer is so important in this whole process that I would strongly caution you not to apply a single thing you have read in this book until you've spent some serious time praying about it. We often say, "I'll pray about it," when what we really mean is, "I'll mull it over for a while and if it makes sense, then I'll do it." That's *not* praying about it. You won't get the same results—I guarantee it.

Prayer Is About Coming into Covenant Agreement with God

When we begin praying Scripture, we come into covenant agreement with God. The Bible is the written record of God's covenant with us. It tells us what He plans to do in our lives. By praying Scripture, we are simply coming into agreement with God's plan for our lives. "Amen" means "So be it," so when we say "Amen" at the end of our prayers, we are reaffirming our agreement with what God has said.

Keith Intrater said, "All of God's actions on the earth are done through the mechanism of covenant. There must be a human being prophetically coming into agreement with God. Through this joint authority, the intervention of God takes place. Without such joint authority, there will be no divine interference."[2]

James 5:16b–18 urges us to "pray also for one another, that you may be healed and restored to a spiritual tone of mind and heart. The earnest, heartfelt and continued prayer of a righteous man makes tremendous power available—dynamic in its working. Elijah was a human being with a nature such as we have—with feelings, affections and constitution as ourselves; and he prayed earnestly for it not to rain, and no rain fell on the earth for three years and six months. And then he prayed again and the heavens supplied rain and the land produced its crops as usual."

Now, here's the interesting thing. Elijah didn't just get it into his head that a three-year drought might be a good way to teach Israel a lesson. He went back to Deuteronomy, the book of the covenant, where God told His people that if they obeyed Him, He would send rain in due season, but if they disobeyed Him, He would withhold the rain. All Elijah was doing was coming into covenant agreement with God about what God had *already* said He wanted to do.

When you are praying Scripture for your situation, you have the same authority to get your prayers answered that Elijah had. Remember, Elijah's authority wasn't in himself; it was in the One who had made the covenant with Israel. God is a covenant keeper. This is good news since your marriage is a covenant whose vows were made before God. Therefore, you can remind Him of those vows in prayer. You can ask Him to do whatever is necessary to see that those vows are kept. He witnessed those vows and He cares passionately that they be honored.

But Why Does It Take So Long?

My friend Teresa and I were talking one day about why God often waits so long to answer our prayers.

"I think it's because He wants us to get real with Him," Teresa said.

I agree. One thing prevailing prayer does is take off the layers of our denial. When you pray about something for 20 years, you either get past the "Now I lay me down to sleep" stage, or you didn't have much invested in the situation to begin with.

We may start our prayers by trying to be super spiritual, praying what we think God wants us to say—something like "Help me to be a good testimony through all this." As the answer tarries, He urges us to look a little deeper. Do we care about the outcome? Do we care passionately about the outcome? Then, where is the urgency and agony in our prayers?

As the answer continues to tarry, He pulls off a few more layers of denial. How do we really feel about the situation? What are our risks, losses, possible gains? Now that we've finally been honest with Him about what's precious to us, will we trust Him with those things? And what does it mean to trust Him?

Finally, as year after year rolls by, He asks us to carefully consider the way we view Him. Is He only a heavenly Santa? A "bless me" God? Do we love Him and trust Him even when we can't see with our own eyes that He is good and in control of our situation? Are we willing to abandon our hopes for relief to the bigger plan that God is working out through our suffering?

God consistently answered my prayers, but His answers were always much bigger than I thought they would be. He had to enlarge me to make room for them and the stretching was painful. Just as a long-distance runner has to slowly stretch before running so that he won't damage his muscles, so God slowly stretches us so that our hearts and minds are able to go the distance in the race He has called us to run.

Prayer Is About Recovering the Ability to Be Intimate

Being intimate means we reveal our true selves. When we have garbage in our lives, we avoid intimacy. We want to hide the stink of our garbage behind locked doors. We guard these doors with eternal vigilance, lest someone should discover our shameful secret. Prayer works together with the Word of God to diagnose and painstakingly remove the garbage in our lives by smashing the shame that keeps the doors locked.

In prayer, we stop hiding from God and we stop hiding from ourselves. We recover true intimacy. Whenever I get stuck in prayer, it's because I'm afraid to be intimate with God. I'm afraid to reveal the full intentions of my heart. Fortunately, as I've learned to trust His love for me, those times are getting to be fewer and fewer.

Recently, I read *The Message* translation of Psalm 109 to a friend of mine who was struggling with the pain of wounds inflicted by "friends." She had tried to deal with it by being "nice" in her prayers. But Psalm 109 shows a slightly different approach.

This psalm deals with David's feelings about being betrayed by people he had been good to. It has phrases like "Get me out of here" and "Send the Evil One to accuse my accusing judge; dispatch Satan to prosecute him. When he's judged, let the verdict be guilty, and when he prays, let his prayer be turned to sin."

My friend gasped. "Do you think God can answer a prayer like that?"

"I think God loves those kinds of prayers because they're honest," I replied.

God sees our hearts. He knows what's in there, and He wants us to know, too. But here's the beautiful thing: Hebrews 4:12–16 says we don't have to be afraid of our nakedness before God. He is a High Priest who is able to understand and have fellow-feeling with our weaknesses. Therefore, we can come boldly before His throne and receive the grace we need to get through the mess our lives have become.

In the Garden, the Lion Roared

Jesus, the Lion of the Tribe of Judah, is our example when it comes to revealing our weaknesses to God. When He was facing His crucifixion, He knew exactly what was going to happen. He knew all about the resurrection, too.

Yet, in the Garden of Gethsemane, Jesus didn't say, "If I can just get through the next three days, I've got it made." He didn't say, "Hey, all they're going to do is beat Me for a while and then nail Me to a tree. After a few excruciating hours, I'll die. Then it's over. Yeah, I can deal with this." He didn't say, "In a few days, You'll be back to Your old self, so lighten up. Remember, God is working good through all this."

In the Garden, the Lion roared! When you are praying, it's okay to roar, too.

Prayer Is a Catalyst

Prayer unleashes a chain of events that brings about God's desired outcome for the situation. It's as if I asked God for bread, and in order to grant my request, He chops down trees, pulls out stumps, plows the field, plants and tends the wheat, all before finally threshing it, grinding it, and baking it. I get my bread, but there's a whole lot of other stuff going on. It's the other stuff that makes prayer so scary. It's the sudden awareness of "God, I didn't know you were going to have to chop down *that* tree to get me my bread." It's the uh-oh feeling of "God, I didn't know you needed my sacred cow for the butter."

When we start praying, we're thinking He's just going to hand us a slab of bread. But He wants to feed us with Living Bread, so He goes to the heart of the matter and takes care of the reason we were hungry in the first place. He does abundantly *above* all that we ask or think.

James 1:5 says, "If any of you is deficient in wisdom, let him ask of the giving God, Who gives to everyone liberally and ungrudgingly, without reproaching or faultfinding, and it will be given him." I found there were many times when I lacked the wisdom to know what to do. But I also found that God never failed to give me direction when I went to His Word or sought Him in prayer. Sometimes it took awhile for me to understand what He was trying to say, but He never left me comfortless. If you spend time seeking Him, you will find Him, and He will lead you in the way you should choose.

Possible Passages for Prayer

I've pulled together a few passages that you might find helpful as you learn to draw closer to God through prayer. In some instances, you might want to personalize them to make them more relevant for you—for example, if it says, "man," you can say "woman." I like to use the Amplified Bible.

- Psalms 17, 25, 103, 109, 136—Any of the psalms are great, but these are especially good.
- Isaiah 54:4–17—This passage is a comforting prayer for rejected wives.
- Malachi 4:5–6—I prayed this for Jack.
- 2 Corinthians 10:3–7—I prayed this for our whole family.
- Ephesians 1:15–23
- Ephesians 3:14–21—This is the passage I prayed for my children.
- Philippians 1:5–11—I prayed this for our marriage.
- Colossians 1:9–14—I prayed this for Jack.
- Colossians 2:2–3,6–10
- Hebrews 1:1–14 and 2:1,6–8,10–11,17 18
- James 1:5—I prayed this when I needed wisdom.
- 1 Peter 3:1–10—I prayed this for our whole family.
- 2 Peter 1:3–11—I prayed this to make sure I stayed on track.
- 1 John 1:9

Telling Yourself the Truth, the Whole Truth, and Nothing But the Truth

Stand therefore—hold your ground—having tightened the belt of truth around your loins. . . . For God's holy wrath and indignation are revealed from heaven against all ungodliness and unrighteous-ness of men, who in their wickedness repress and hinder the truth and make it inoperative. For that which is known about God is evident to them and made plain in their inner consciousness, because God Himself has shown it to them.

(Ephesians 6:14, Romans 1:18,19)

Truth: Conformity to fact or reality.

(Noah Webster)

In Ephesians 6, Paul said that when we find ourselves between a rock and a hard place, we need to realize that we're engaged in a battle. At times like this, he said, the first weapon of our warfare is the loinbelt of truth. Historically, the loins have been viewed as the location of our physical strength and genera-tive powers. So, what are the loins anyway? Externally, they are our hips. Internally, they represent our procreative powers.

The loinbelt of truth is a crucial weapon for a woman whose husband is involved in pornography, because pornography is specifically designed to affect our procreative powers. In fact, pornography uses our procreative powers to lure us into its clutches. By a swivel of the hips, pornography entices men and women to abandon themselves to the mesmerizing power of sexuality.

Once pornography has us in its grip, it attacks our procreativity. It does this in several ways. First, because it encourages casual sexual encounters, pornography puts us at risk for producing children by someone with whom we have no ongoing commitment. This leaves the children holding the bag with no dad to provide for them and a mom who has to scramble to make ends meet and whose stress level and unmet personal needs make it tough for her to give her children the unconditional love they need to grow into healthy people.

Second, pornography attacks our procreative powers by encouraging behavior that will expose us to a wide range of sexually transmitted diseases. STDs have a devastating effect on our fertility. Many of these diseases affect our ability to conceive, and some even render us sterile.[2] If we are able to conceive, STDs expose the developing baby to serious risks, such as miscarriage, stillbirth, blindness, and a host of other physical maladies.

Third, pornography attacks our procreative powers by promoting abortion, the ultimate assault on our procreativity. When you study the history of ancient Israel, you see that whenever they became wanton in their sexuality, child sacrifice followed. Abortion is modern-day child sacrifice. Hugh Hefner, king of the *Playboy* philosophy, has said one of his most important accomplishments is making abortion the law of the land.[3]

Finally, pornography attacks our procreative powers by promoting incest. You don't have to go hardcore to find incest as a theme, even the so-called soft-porn magazines promote it. Incest is the ultimate perversion of the love of a parent for a child. Children who have been incested are tremendously damaged in their inner person. It can take them a lifetime to work through the pain.

Susan Smith, the Union, South Carolina, mother who in October 1994 murdered her two young sons, is a perfect example of how perverted sexuality affects our procreative powers. First, Susan was incested by her stepfather. Then, she married a man who had a series of affairs on her. Finally, after she separated from her husband, she met a man who was interested in her but didn't want her children. The resulting confusion and despair so perverted her heart that she ended up sacrificing her children.

Please don't misunderstand. Nothing that happened to Susan justified what she did to her children. We make our own choices, and the choice Susan made was evil. What I am saying is that she was provoked to evil by evil. Susan followed the ancient pattern: wanton sexuality leads to child sacrifice.

I don't know if Susan's stepfather, husband, and lover were somehow involved in pornography, but they certainly acted in the spirit of the behaviors pornography promotes. Porn glorifies incest, adultery, no ongoing responsibility for sexual acts, and the attitude that the parents' needs for sexual conquest come before their children's needs for a secure home. All these things are devastating attacks on our procreative powers.

There's a Difference Between Being in Denial and Being in the Dark

In Ephesians 6:14, Paul said the first way we protect ourselves from danger is by operating based on truth. We have to make a radical departure from the old way of doing things by telling ourselves the truth, the whole truth, and nothing but the truth. But sometimes it's difficult to know what the truth is.

You've probably heard people say, "She's been in denial." People often say this after they've been informed of a husband's longtime struggle with an affair or alcoholism or drugs. What they mean is that the woman hasn't been telling herself the truth about what's been going on in her life. The implication is that somehow this woman blinded herself to what was obvious. Often those making such statements think that if the same thing were going on in *their* lives, they would be quick to catch on. But it's not always as simple as those looking in from the outside want to believe.

Sure, if your husband is coming home from work staggering drunk, the evidence that something is wrong is all around you. While it may be painful to admit it, at least the "sin" is out in the open. If your husband has fallen down drunk and you told the children he was just sleeping on the floor, then you *have been* in denial.

But when your husband is living a cleverly concealed private life, it's a little more difficult to catch on to the truth. You don't want to operate from a position of suspicion. You want to act from a place of trust. If your husband is taking advantage of that by lying to you about the choices he is making, it doesn't necessarily mean you are in denial. It does mean that you need to find out what the truth is.

Get Ready

The second reason it's important to tell ourselves the truth is that any action we take must be based on truth. Truth is the preparation for action. It is the foundation on which all our decisions must rest. If it's not, if our actions are based merely on what we think is true or if they're based on a total denial of the situation, we'll go off in the wrong direction and the results won't be at all what we want. Proverbs 14:12 says, "There is a way which seems right to a man and appears straight before him, but at the end of it are the ways of death." That's because whenever we act on anything other than truth, we reap the consequence, no matter how sincere our misbelief. Jesus constantly warned His followers to make sure they were living their lives based on truth.

As we've discussed previously, a man who is involved in pornography hasn't just exposed the procreative part of his loins to assault, he's screwed up his own ability to see and act on truth. When your husband is living a lie, you cannot depend on him to verify truth for you because, as 1 John 2:21 says, "No lie is of the Truth" (KJV). He is not capable of telling truth, and he does not desire that you know the truth.

A woman in this situation desperately needs a reliable plumb line so she can measure where she is in relationship to what is true. Fortunately, God's plan is to "grant you a spirit of wisdom and revelation . . . in the knowledge of Him, by having the eyes of your heart flooded with light, so that you can know and understand the hope to which He has called you and how rich is His glorious inheritance in the saints" (Eph. 1:17–18).

Uh, How Do I Get This Thing On Anyway?

How do you learn the truth about your situation? Ask God to reveal it to you. James 1:5 says, "If any of you is deficient in wisdom, let him ask of the giving God Who gives to everyone liberally and ungrudgingly, without reproaching or fault-finding, and it will be given him." In other words, if you can't figure out what's going on, ask God. He'll let you in on things without making you feel like an idiot.

I started out praying Psalm 25 every day. It repeatedly says things like, "Show me your ways," "Guide me in Your truth," and "Lead me in what is right." The whole psalm is a prayer for guidance. The funny thing about prayer is that we never really know what we're asking for. When I started praying Psalm 25, I thought I might need a minor tune-up in a few areas. What I needed was a major overhaul. Even though I didn't know what I was asking for, God did, and He wasn't at all hindered by my ignorance.

He answered my prayers by taking me through some horrendous experiences ("adventures," I came to call them) specifically designed to shine the light of truth on some things that I believed weren't true. "Oh no, not another one!" I kept having to say as another sacred belief was shattered. But He *never* made me feel like an idiot or a jerk. There was never any condemnation from Him, only a quiet delight that I was finally catching on.

Proverbs 2:2–6 says, "Making your ear attentive to skillful and godly wisdom, and inclining and directing your heart and mind to understanding—applying all your powers to the quest for it; yes, if you cry out for insight and raise your voice for understanding, if you seek wisdom as silver, and search for skillful and godly Wisdom as for hid treasures; then you will understand the reverent and worshipful fear of the Lord and find the knowledge of God. For the Lord gives skillful and godly Wisdom; from His mouth come knowledge and understanding." In the beginning of the book, I related how, after three days of fasting and prayer, the Lord showed me that Jack had taken $350 that didn't belong to him, had committed adultery, and had a lot of pride. This knowledge came through my communion with God, apart from any intellectual awareness I had.

If God is going to let us in on things, we have to spend time with Him, both in prayer and Bible reading. That's how we commune with Him. Don't expect to get answers if you don't spend time with Him—there's just no shortcut to becoming wise.

Forget the Magnum, P.I., Stuff

The only thing harder than being in the dark is waiting for the light to shine. Once you make up your mind that you want to know the truth, waiting to find out what the truth is can be excruciating. To make up for lost time, it's easy to go overboard by searching for answers. But finding truth is not about becoming your own personal private eye. We're not talking about snooping in wallets, asking leading questions, listening in on phone conversations, or opening mail. That's controlling. Remember, this is about asking God to reveal things to you and then waiting quietly until He does.

After I shared this principle with Alice, she began to pray and ask God to show her the truth. Like me, she couldn't figure out what was going on in her marriage. Her husband was distant emotionally and he had lost all sexual interest in her.

One day when Alice was cleaning her husband's hobby room, the Lord impressed on her that she needed to go look in the middle of a pile of old magazines. "What a ridiculous thought," she told herself. But it wouldn't go away. Finally, she walked over to the pile and pulled out the middle magazine. It was a copy of the latest edition of *Playboy*. Now the wadded-up, crispy towel she had found in Bob's underwear drawer when she was putting away his clean socks made sense. He'd been masturbating to the pornography.

"I never would have believed he was into that stuff," she told me.

The Lord also opened Helen's eyes. Her husband, a deacon in their church, was extemely jealous and given to mood swings. One night, after Helen had been asking the Lord to reveal what was going on, the Lord woke her up and urged her to go to the family room.

"You've got to be kidding, Lord," she said, looking at the alarm clock. "It's 3:00 in the morning!" Then she became aware that Paul wasn't in bed. Walking into the family room, she was stunned to find her husband watching the Playboy channel.

Alice and Helen are just at the beginning of their adventure in learning how to discover the truth in the midst of deception. But already they're finding greater freedom from fear. They've discovered that their fears came not from the truth but from not knowing the truth. They've also discovered that their God wants to give them a lamp to light up their darkness—if they'll only stop quenching it.

No Trespassing

If God wants to give us a lamp to light up our darkness, why do we keep quenching it? Because we're afraid that the darkness will destroy us. That fear causes us to shove the darkness into a room, bolt the door, and hang up a No Trespassing sign. Then, just in case the lock doesn't work, with our hearts beating furiously and our breath coming in rapid, shallow gulps, we press our backs into the door with all our might. We dedicate ourselves to this post with eternal vigilance.

Let me tell you something. The power isn't in what's behind the door. The power is in the fear that keeps the door locked. Yes, there's a lot of pain behind the door, and yes, you will have to grieve your losses, but it will not destroy you. The pain will not kill you. Not taking the pain out is what will kill you. Not shining the light into the darkness is what will destroy you.

Here's the promise that can give you the courage to let God shine His light of truth into that locked darkness of denial: "The Light shines on in the darkness, for the darkness has never overpowered it—put it out, or . . . absorbed it" (John 1:5).

Where Do We Go from Here?

As God begins to reveal truth to you, you will find that truth requires a response. You can flee from it ("I'm outta here!"), you can rationalize it ("It's really like this"), you can suppress it ("It's not hot, and I'm not here")—or, you can deal with it.

Get Real

Our principles are the springs of our actions; our actions, the springs of our happiness or misery. Too much care, therefore, cannot be taken in forming our principles.

('Skelton')

Guard your heart with all diligence, for out of it are the issues of life.

Proverbs 4:23 (KJV)

Those who have fasted have found that the first few days, they miss food like crazy. Then, about the fourth day, their sense of hunger starts to shut down. A person can coast along for about 36 more days without feeling ravenous hunger; but along about day 40, tremendous hunger pangs strike. This is because the body has used up its reserves. If it doesn't get food soon, it will begin to digest the organs to get the energy it needs.

Matthew 4:1–11 tells the story of Jesus being tempted in the wilderness. The devil came to Jesus after He had fasted for 40 days—when He was *very* hungry, even starving to death. Food wasn't just a good idea, it was essential. That's when the tempter struck. He did it cleverly, too. First he suggested that Jesus could prove who He was by meeting His legitimate physical needs.

"If you're God's Son, prove it by turning these stones into bread so you can feed yourself," Satan coaxed. "You *are* hungry, aren't you?" was the hook.

Jesus refused to be taken in.

Then Satan asked Jesus to prove who He was by meeting His legitimate emotional needs.

"If you're God's Son, prove it by making Him show up to save you from yourself," he wheedled. "It would be nice to know He really loves you," was the hook this time.

Failing at that, Satan tried playing on Jesus' legitimate spiritual need to have others look up to Him.

"If you'll just bow down and worship me, I'll give you the kingdoms of this world," the devil cooed. "Millions will be falling at *your* feet," was the hook.

Notice the word *if*. "*If* you're God's Son . . ." That's the ammunition Satan loaded his gun with. The approach was simple: Attack Jesus' sense of self. Was He the Son of God or not? Prove it, Jesus, was the taunt. Dare ya. Double dare ya.

Notice also that Jesus never responded to the temptations by saying that He didn't have the need He was tempted with.

He never said, "Food? How ridiculous. I'm not hungry at all."

He never said, "I don't need anybody or anything."

He never said, "Hey, I don't care what other people think."

Jesus never denied His legitimate emotional, physical, and spiritual needs. He just refused to be derailed by meeting His needs in a way that would deny who He was and whose He was.

If You Were Woman Enough . . .

What does this have to do with the wife of a man involved in pornography? Plenty. First, there's a temptation to prove herself. A woman whose husband wants to be with an imaginery woman or a hooker more than he wants to be with her feels like a failure as a woman, a lover, and a companion.

Second, she has legitimate physical, emotional, and spiritual needs that aren't being met. Lust is totally self-absorbed. Everything revolves around the needs and desires of the one lusting. A man who is involved in pornography is incapable of looking past his own needs to see and meet the needs of his wife. In his selfishness, he sucks out her meager reserves, leaving her nothing to meet her own needs.

Yet, those unmet needs aren't going to go away. Just as Jesus' body was dying for food after His 40-day fast, her body is dying for fulfilling sex, not the degrading quickie stuff her husband learned from porn. Just as Jesus longed for the loving companionship of His Father, her soul longs to have her husband be a loving companion, not someone who's going to think of her as a plaything. Just as Jesus deserved to have others recognize His value, she may be dying to be affirmed rather than viewed as a tool to be compared, criticized, and manipulated.

Long about now, when she's good and hungry, the temptations come. What's the bait? Unmet physical needs, unmet emotional needs, unmet spiritual needs. The hook is to prove yourself—prove you're attractive, prove someone can love you, prove you're worth it—because if you don't take care of number one, who will? You know what everyone's saying, don't you? If you were woman enough, he wouldn't need anyone else, so why not prove it?

Human nature is always tempted in the same ways. And while the hook and bait didn't work with Jesus (because He knew who He was and whose He was), they often work with a woman who's desperate to shore up her shaky self-esteem by proving to herself and others that she's "woman enough" (because she doesn't have a clue who she is and she's desperate to feel she belongs to somebody—anybody).

Feelings, Nothing More Than Feelings

Proverbs 4:23 says to guard your heart with all diligence for out of it flow the issues of life. That word "heart" means the innermost part of our being, the place where our motivations and feelings arise. Feelings are important to God. If you've ever read through the whole Bible, you've probably noticed how many times there are references to the "feelings" God has about our refusal to be in loving relationship with Him. There's yearning (Isa. 1:18), anger (Deut. 9:7–8), jealousy (Exod. 34:14), loneliness (Matt. 26:38, 40), and frustration (Luke 13:34).

Feelings are part of being made in the image of God, especially the feelings a husband has for his wife and a wife has for her husband, because God says He created the marriage relationship to be a picture of our relationship with Him. When one spouse is committing multiple adulteries through the use of pornography and its twisted sisters—strip shows and prostitutes—the other spouse is going to experience the same feelings God did about His adulterous wife—yearning, anger, jealousy, loneliness, and frustration.

What should you do? The same thing God did. Express your feelings, but base your actions on what's right. That's righteousness. Righteousness makes choices based on what's right, not what's convenient and not what's urgent. The Greek word for "righteousness"—*dikaiōsunē*—means there's a claim on our lives by a higher authority. Now, there's an unpopular concept.

There's a higher authority than our feelings. Our feelings are value-neutral, neither right nor wrong; however, the choices we make about how we will express our feelings are either right or wrong. The idea that there's a right and wrong is considered old-fashioned today. We're told that there are no absolutes.

If there are no absolutes, there can be no right or wrong, so "what's right for you might not be right for me." We're told "The times they are achangin'" and "What I said yesterday isn't what I mean today." It's the same line of reasoning a husband uses to justify his use of pornography. "Sure I said I'd forsake all others and keep myself only unto you, but that was yesterday. Today, I want to get my jollies looking at and being with other women, and you can't tell me it's wrong because it's only wrong if I think it's wrong."

It's not my purpose to argue the folly of that kind of thinking. Let's just say that the grief of the wife and children in this situation testifies eloquently to the destructiveness of situation ethics.

Now, here's the tricky part. Although she will be sorely tempted to react to her husband's abandonment of his vows by proving herself in some way, a wise wife will refuse Satan's bait and act based on what she knows is right. She will own her feelings, but she will make her choices based on God's principles.

Some Things Never Change

Principles are things that are always right, true, and just. Principles don't change with the situation; they are eternal. Principles are guardrails on the highway of life that keep us from going off the edge and crashing onto the rocky shoals below.

God gave us 10 eternal principles to govern our lives and keep us safely on life's highway. Theologians call them the Ten Commandments. Four of them discuss our relationship with God and six discuss our relationship with each other. In the New Testament, Jesus boiled these 10 principles down to two: "Love the Lord your God with all your heart, soul, mind, and strength and your neighbor as yourself. On these two commandments, hang all the law and the prophets" (Matt. 22:37-40).

That phrase "hang all the law and the prophets" is important because it means you can use these two principles to figure out how to respond righteously to any situation. That's called discernment. Discernment is a gift that accompanies righteousness. If you don't have discernment, your only option is to have zillions of rules to cover every conceivable situation. That's what the Pharisees did. Jesus preferred to keep it simple: "Use these two principles as guidelines to guard your heart when you decide which course of action to take."

Living by principles, rather than feelings, is the only way a woman can guard her heart and keep herself from plummeting into the abyss of her needs while the Lord works to show her what the truth of her marriage situation is. Living by principles, rather than feelings, is the only way a woman can keep herself from being controlled by external circumstances and honestly answer the question "What do I need to do so I don't destroy myself on the shoals of a rocky marriage?"

Your Worth Is Not Determined by What Others Think of You

If we try to prove to ourselves and others that we are attractive enough to hold a man by going out and finding someone else, we'll end up denying who we really are. If we try to prove to the world that we really aren't the failures everyone thinks we are by living up to other people's expectations, we'll end up denying who we really are. If we try to get rid of that feeling of failure and shame by winning other people's approval, we'll also end up denying who we really are.

No one can validate who you are, not even you. To grant someone the power to validate your worth is to put them in the position of God. If they say we're worth something, then we are. If they reject us, then we're less than worthless. These are all lies.

Your worth depends on what God says about you, not what others say about you, or even what you say about yourself. And here's what God says: "Fear not, for you shall not be ashamed; neither be confounded and depressed, for you shall not be put to shame; for you shall forget the shame of your youth and you shall not remember the reproach of your widowhood any more [the word for *widowhood* means "forsaken" or "discarded," just as the wife of a porn addict has been forsaken and discarded for others]. For your maker is your husband, the Lord of hosts is His name; and the Holy One of Israel is your Redeemer, the God of the whole earth, He is called. For the Lord has called you like a woman forsaken, grieved in spirit and heartsore, even a wife wooed and won in youth, when she is later refused and scorned, says your God. For though the mountains should depart and the hills be shaken or removed, yet My love and kindness shall not depart from you, nor shall My covenant of peace be removed, says the Lord, Who has compassion on you" (Isa. 54:4–6,10).

We've all at one time or another swallowed that bait to prove ourselves and ended up gutted and filleted. But here's the gift of grace: Jesus doesn't condemn a heartbroken woman for denying who she really is when she tries to prove herself. But He does want her to go her way and sin no more by remembering that who she is isn't a function of what others think about her. Rather, she needs to get her identity from what God says about her, and He says she is chosen of God, holy and dearly beloved, to be His precious daughter and a joint heir with Jesus Christ (Col. 3:12; 1 Thess. 1:4; Rom. 8:17; Gal. 3:26,28–29).

As a woman learns to rest in who God says she is, she finds peace and true security. She can now make the choice to act based on her principles, rather than react based on her needs. But first she has to tell herself the truth about what those needs are.

♦ Watch Out for the Smell of Burning Martyr

Mary's husband, Jim, was a Vietnam vet. Lonely and scared during the war, he took comfort in the prostitutes that were readily available to the troops. When he came home, he was treated for a venereal disease. Mary forgave him, but he couldn't forgive himself. Even though his body had been pronounced whole, his conscience was still on the critical list. His guilt kept him from being able to approach Mary. They had sex only a few times a year and Mary always had to initiate it.

Mary was terribly vulnerable. Her normal sexual needs were not being met and she felt rejected by her husband. Not wanting to fall into an adulterous relationship, she did what many women do—she gained weight.

"If I'm heavy enough, maybe no one will notice me and then I won't be tempted," she reasoned.

Mary dealt with her vulnerability to an affair in a self-destructive way—similar to the old "pick-your-nose-and-act-weird-so-you'll-turn-'em-off" mentality that I learned when I was a secretary in Washington, D.C. My bus stop was several blocks from my workplace, so I had to walk some distance in a city known for muggings and rapes. When I asked a coworker what she did to keep safe, she told me she kept her purse tucked under her arm and when a strange man approached her, she started picking her nose and acting weird. "It's always worked for me," she said.

Just like Mary and my coworker, when I realized I was no longer attractive to Jack, I used this approach to protect myself from getting involved with anyone else. It wasn't anything I did consciously. I wasn't honest enough to admit to myself how vulnerable I was, but in the hidden places of my heart, I knew. So, I sabotaged myself. I stopped taking care of myself and I gained weight. If men showed any interest in me at all, I'd cover up my tender places by acting weird.

One day, a coworker let me know that he was interested in more than a working relationship. Suddenly, I felt that old weirdness coming back.

"Okay, that's it. I don't wear makeup anymore, and I don't set my hair. Maybe I won't even work here anymore," I told myself.

Running away? the Lord asked.

Startled, I realized for the first time that that was exactly what I was doing. It had been my modus operandi for years: don't deal, just peel (out).

"I guess I am."

From what? The voice was gentle but insistent.

"You know—screwing up." This was hard. I was having to admit that I was scared to death of myself. I was terrified that the great whirlpool of unmet needs was going to suck me into its vortex. Suddenly, I could see that fear was causing me to destroy myself.

That's a pretty shabby shield you're wielding, the Lord continued.

He was right. The thing was junk—the 90-pound weakling of mind games, the fast-buck artist of the "It's not hot, and I'm not here" gang. Self-destruction is never good protection. At best, it's mental Swiss cheese: just enough substance to make you think you've got something, but so full of holes that the mayo squeezes through anyway.

Why don't you just be yourself behind My protection?

It was an offer I couldn't refuse because I really wanted that job and I was beginning to realize how weary I was of hiding my light under a bushel basket.

So, instead of running away from myself, I learned how to stand my ground and confront my coworker with the truth of my principles. I also learned that "getting down and ugly" is no protection from failure. Look around and see who's having affairs. They come in all sizes and shapes. Uglification can't keep you from sin; only holding fast to who you are and whose you are can.

This approach worked well for several years and then I ran into a big problem.

Uh-Oh Time

My tremendous vulnerability was brought sharply home to me when I observed several relationships in which love was both given and received. It stung me as I realized afresh that my desperate, long-buried yearnings weren't unrealistic. It was possible to love someone and have him love and cherish you back. People were doing it. People I knew were feeling the joy of it.

Have you ever walked by a restaurant around mealtime and had the aroma knock you off your feet? Did your stomach suddenly growl and say, "Hey, I've gotta have some of that?"

Well, that's what happened to me—only in a different dimension. I wasn't just hungry, I was starving. Folks who are starving have gone so long without food that they've lost their sense of hunger. That had happened to me. I'd gone so long without love that I'd lost my sense of needing it. I thought I could go on forever giving and never receiving. But then I walked by the homes of these loving relationships, and the fragrance wafting out knocked me off my feet. Peering into the window, I saw a sumptuous banquet spread, and I didn't just feel hunger pangs, I felt gut-wrenching cramps.

"I've got to have some of that or I'm going to die," I told myself.

And then something happened that had never happened before. I started thinking about someone. I thought about him a lot—about how kind and funny he was and how much integrity he had. Yes, he was good-looking, but what really attracted me was his character. I'd known him for a long time. I knew his strengths and his weaknesses. I knew he was real and trustworthy. He thought about life, he cared about people, he worked hard, and he lived by his principles. His virtue made him enormously attractive to me.

What I wouldn't give to be loved by someone like that, I thought. Because I knew the thought is mother to the act, I was afraid I would do something I would regret. So I made up a lot of rules for myself about how I wouldn't talk to this man or even get near him. I even tried the old acting weird syndrome when he happened to get near me. But inside, the need that drove the thoughts of him wouldn't go away. I couldn't seem to make the thoughts stop by an act of my will. And I tried—I really tried. Something way down in my soul was screaming, "Pay attention! We're dying down here."

I never realized before how vulnerable a woman in this situation is. Lost, lonely, and rejected, women whose husbands have been committing adultery desperately need to feel loved and attractive. For the first time, I was terrified that I wouldn't have the inner strength to make the right choices.

I tried the old denial thing: *If I don't think about the fact that I'm thinking about this, then I'm not really thinking about it.* But by then, I had enough integrity to realize the shabbiness of that approach.

Then I tried the old guilt and shame approach: *You're scum! How can you do this? And you call yourself a Christian!* But by then, I'd learned that guilt and shame beat you so far into the ground that you couldn't move if your life depended on it.

Then 1 John 1:9 popped into my mind: "If we admit we have sinned and confess our sins, He is faithful and just and will forgive us our sins and continually cleanse us from all unrighteousness."

Just confess what I'm thinking to God and ask Him to set me free. Ah, what a novel approach! But was it safe? By now, I'd learned enough about God to know that He wasn't going to condemn me for being honest with Him. I knew He felt tenderly toward me and that He wanted me to trust Him. I'd learned that I could be naked before Him and not be ashamed.

With the condemnation factor settled, I still had the tricky part to deal with:

Did I really want to give this fantasy up? After a lot of internal struggle, I realized I could no longer deny my needs, but if I had my needs met and lost myself in the process, I'd create a whole new set of problems and needs for myself.

So, I prayed: "It's me, God. And I can't believe it, but I'm thinking about adultery. I'm so ashamed and I feel so ugly inside."

As soon as the words were out of my mouth, the raging thoughts lost some of their power over me.

"That feels better, but here's the thing. I've got this great big hole inside, and it's creating a terrific vacuum. If you don't plug it, I'm going to suck something in I don't want to be there. Besides, I'm sick of pretending I'm above needing. I want to be able to lay my head down at night on the chest of someone I can trust. I want to feel all the way down to my toes that I'm loved. I want someone to cherish me, not abuse me. I want a partner, not a persecutor. I'm just going to die if I don't get some of this."

The reply was stunning. *I'm glad you finally realize that you're just flesh and blood, not some paragon of virtue who's so spiritual she's above human need.*

Wake-up call. Suddenly, I realized I was holding myself to a higher standard than God did. There is nothing wrong with needing. There is nothing wrong with wanting to be loved by someone who is trustworthy. There is nothing wrong with wanting to be cherished and protected. There is no sin in wanting a true companion for life's journey.

These things are the mark of being created in the image of God. God aggressively pursued these things in His relationship with his wife, Israel. Her refusal to be a loving wife grieved Him. Her unfaithfulness broke His heart. Didn't He repeatedly confront her about the mind games she played with Him—pretending to worship and serve Him by offering token sacrifices while her heart was far from Him? Denying the need to be in a relationship in which love is both given and received is not a mark of spirituality, it is a symptom of the sickness of self-righteousness. Embracing that need was a sign of *health* in me.

"Thank you, Lord," I breathed. "I see now that there's nothing wrong with me. I'm getting healthier. I'm stopping the sickness of pretending I'm self-sufficient. It's not good for me to be alone. It's lunacy to pretend my marriage is all you want it to be."

Right. Now, don't be afraid of the hunger, but don't get lost on your way to the table.

Bringing in Reinforcements

Handling a situation like this by yourself doesn't work well. It's tough to be totally honest with yourself when you feel overwhelmed by personal needs. That's what the body of Christ is for. James 5:16 says, "Confess to one another therefore your faults, . . . and pray for one another, that you may be healed and restored to a spiritual tone of mind and heart. The earnest prayer of a righteous man makes tremendous power available."

But a word of warning: Choose your confidant carefully. After Jack and I separated, during a meeting with the deacons of our church, I asked them to appoint an older woman in the church for me to be accountable to. Why? Because a separation is just that—a separation. It is not a divorce. A separated couple is not free to form new relationships. A separated couple is still married in the eyes of God and in the eyes of the state. The purpose of the separation should be to decide what to do about the marriage. You can't do that if you're involved with someone else.

"I know there's a tendency for women who are separated from their husbands to get involved with someone else. I don't want to do that, but I'm afraid if I'm not accountable to someone, I might," I told them.

I shocked them. It was uncomfortable for them to hear someone be honest about her vulnerabilities. Embarrassed, they shut me off without a word. Over the next three months, I received one call (which was precious to me) checking to see how I was. But no one dared to ask me if I was dating anyone.

It was when I realized there was no real help for me in my church that I reached out to a special friend who lived several hours away. Normally, friends aren't the best people to keep you accountable. If they love you, they want to see you happy. If a new man is making you happy, well, they're reluctant to tell you, you can't have a bit of joy, even though they know in a few months you're going to be kicking yourself.

"Pray for me," I asked her after pouring out my heart about this man. She not only prayed for me, she shared with me that she had struggled the same way. Suddenly, I was not alone. Suddenly, the shame lost its grip and the attraction lost its power. The love of a friend is like that: It sets you free. If I had it to do over again, when looking for someone to be accountable to, I'd start with a friend— but a friend who would truly hold me accountable.

Cutting Off Our Noses to Spite Our Faces

If we're going to guard our hearts, we have to stop trying to manufacture our own self-righteousness by pretending we don't have needs. In reacting to the world's philosophy of "Looking out for number one" and "If it feels good, do it," Christians often try to pretend that there's no real basis of need in our lives. We don't want to abandon our principles by meeting our needs in sinful ways, so we grit our teeth and hold on tightly to the end of our ropes as if by sheer willpower, we could demand that our humanness cower in submission. And the fact is, this approach works much of the time. It works so well that entire religions have been created out of it. All you have to do is create enough rules. Push down the flesh enough and you'll look spiritual. The Pharisees were masters at it.

Bind the needs up in rules, they taught. The greater the need, the more rules they devised to subjugate it. In so doing, they created a religion where they could outwardly appear to have it all together, while inwardly they were filled with desperation. This is why Jesus called them whited sepulchres—spiffed up on the outside while they ignored the rotting needs inside. That's about all self-righteousness can do for us—keep us looking pretty while we rot to death.

Jesus said there's no way we can enter heaven if our righteousness doesn't exceed the forced righteousness of the Pharisees. He knew that a long list of rules doesn't make the needs go away. A woman who determines to avoid moral failure by gaining weight or looking dowdy or acting weird has made becoming unattractive her rule for how she's going to keep from succumbing to her needs. But inside, she's as needy as ever. Likewise, a woman who determines to prove herself attractive by dressing seductively and flirting has made a rule for how she's going to prove she's got what it takes to be interesting to a man. But inside, she's still as confused as ever about whether she has anything to offer anyone. Finally, a woman who determines to gain the approval of others by being a good girl, and always doing what they tell her a good girl should do, has made a rule for how she's going to avoid condemnation. But inside, she still feels as rejected and unsure of herself as ever.

It's not admitting the need that makes us vulnerable. It's the self-righteous denial that the need is there in the first place. Denied needs don't go away; they just tunnel a little deeper and come out sideways. Denying needs just makes us numb to them, and being numb can have serious consequences.

When a body part is numb, you have no way of knowing when it's being exposed to danger. If your emotions are numb, you have no way of knowing when you're exposing yourself to a situation that has the potential to destroy you. Jesus knew it was better to acknowledge the need, but to refuse to meet the need in a way that would derail us from our chosen paths. Jesus knew that the secret of guarding our hearts is to get real and remember who we are and whose we are.

So, let me ask the question again. Can a woman in this situation avoid moral failure? Yes, but she can't do it by white-knuckling or denying that she has needs. To avoid moral failure, a woman has to guard her heart with the truth of who

God has created her to be. Then she has to find healthy ways to cherish herself (we'll talk more about that in chapter 25). That's the only way she can find the strength to refuse to sacrifice even one ounce of her potential to the pressing needs of her flesh.

CHAPTER 18

Let Your Conscience Be Your Guide

By this shall we come to know . . . that we are of the Truth, and can reassure and quiet our hearts in His presence. In whatever our hearts in tormenting self-accusation make us feel guilty and condemn us. For we are in God's hands, He is above and greater than our consciences, and He knows and understands everything—nothing is hidden from Him. And, beloved, if our consciences do not accuse us—if they do not make us feel guilty and condemn us—we have confidence and complete assurance and boldness before God; and we receive from Him whatever we ask for, because we watchfully obey His orders—observe His suggestions and injunctions, follow His plan for us—and habitually practice what is pleasing to Him.

1 John 3:19–22

Conscience never argues or reasons. Explanation may satisfy the mind, but never the conscience.

Watchman Nee[1]

Once we've begun to tell ourselves the truth about our situation, and made a decision to do what's right, no matter what the cost, we will begin to see that in many ways we have not been listening to our consciences. There's a disturbing story in 1 Kings 12–13. I'm going to tell it to you because it has a lot to do with listening to our consciences, which is something women who are married to men who use pornography have to learn how to do.

163

The story goes like this. Once upon a time, King Jeroboam made two golden calves and encouraged his people to worship them because he was afraid if they went to worship the Lord in Jerusalem, they'd decide to make his rival, Rehoboam, their king.

As King Jeroboam was burning incense on the altar, a man of God came and said to him, "You're in big trouble."

Jeroboam didn't appreciate the message, so he stretched out his hand to grab the man of God, whereupon Jeroboam's hand withered.

Shocked, Jeroboam pleaded with the man of God to pray and ask God to restore his hand. The man did, and God answered the prayer and healed Jeroboam's hand. The king invited the man of God to come home with him to receive a reward and take a break before he returned to his own country.

But the man of God said, "No, thank you," because God had told him he wasn't to eat or drink or return by the same way.

Meanwhile, another prophet got wind of the whole thing and set out on his donkey to intercept the man of God. He found him sitting under an oak, and he said to him, "Are you the man of God who came from Judah?"

And he said, "I am."

Then he said to him, "Come home with me and have something to eat."

But the man of God said, "God told me not to have anything to eat or drink in this country. I'm even supposed to go home a different way than I came."

Then the other prophet said, "I'm a prophet just like you, and God sent an angel to tell me to tell you that you're supposed to come back to my house and have something to eat." But he had lied to him.

So the man of God went to the other prophet's house and after he ate, the word of the Lord came to the prophet's house and he said to the man of God, "Because you disobeyed the Lord, you will die."

So, after the man of God finished eating, he got on a donkey and went his way—right in the path of a lion, which killed him.

A Blow-by-Blow Analysis of the Losing Play

This story starts with a man of God going out and doing a powerful work for God. He has been given explicit instructions about what he's *not* supposed to do—and the plot thickens when other people try to persuade him to rethink what God has told him.

He doesn't have any problem brushing off Jeroboam's suggestion that he compromise his understanding of what God said to him. Of course, turning

Jeroboam down was somewhat risky, because Jeroboam was the king, and kings are to be obeyed. But the man of God felt confident enough in what God had told him that he was able to turn down Jeroboam's offer of dinner and a reward.

However, when another prophet approached him and told him he had a message for him from God, suddenly the man of God is unsure of which end is up. Now, it doesn't say this in Scripture, but I think this guy's interior monologue went something like this:

You know, maybe I didn't get it right. I mean, this is the second time I've been invited to dinner. Maybe God didn't really tell me not to stop and have something to eat. Maybe I misunderstood. Or, maybe God changed His mind and forgot to tell me. I mean, I can't trust that Jeroboam heard from God—he's a wicked sinner. But when I get the same message from someone who's a real man of God, maybe I'd better listen. He can probably hear God better than I can anyway. If I don't listen, God might be angry with me.

When this man of God stopped believing that he had heard from God, and started believing that someone else had a better understanding of God's will for his life than he did, he destroyed himself.

This story used to puzzle me. I always thought it was rottenly unfair for someone to die just because he did something that someone else told him God wanted him to do. But since I've died a few times myself by ignoring what I knew God wanted me to do, listening instead to what other people told me God wanted me to do, I've come to have quite an appreciation for what was going on with this man of God. And I think it has a lot to do with the inner struggles faced by women who are married to men who use pornography.

Listening to Others Instead of Trusting Ourselves

Frequently, before making an important moral decision, we feel a great internal conflict as our minds argue with our consciences and try to explain away the conscience's sense of right or wrong. This is because our minds often do not completely understand what makes something right or wrong. When the mind doesn't understand, it has difficulty submitting to the conscience. Therefore, the leading of our intellects and the leading of our consciences are often quite conflicting. The more we tend to rely on our intellects, the more difficult it can be for us to follow our consciences.

Back to the story. God had spoken to this man and had given him a message for the king. Delivering this message became his God-given task. That task became the property of his conscience. Anything that would interfere with him carrying out his task exactly according to God's instructions would be roundly condemned by his conscience.

But then his mind got involved. He began to reason with his conscience, telling himself that someone else might have a better understanding of God's will than he did. Eventually, his mind got the best of him. He shut off his conscience, went ahead and ate, and shortly thereafter, he died.

⌈A woman who is married to a man who is using pornography will often find that just like in the man of God, there is a battle going on between her conscience and her intellect. The conscience operates on the unseen, whereas the intellect operates on the seen. Our minds tend to deny things that cannot be immediately verified as fact, whereas our consciences "sense" that something is either good or evil apart from any data to confirm the hunch. When our minds overrule our consciences, fear results, because we are brushing aside our God-designed early-warning system.⌉

When our minds overrule our consciences, self-condemnation results, because even though our minds might seek to rationalize our actions, our God-designed guidance system knows we're off track. It's crucial for a woman whose life has been affected by pornography to understand how to recover the proper function of her conscience because living with someone whose sexuality is out of control has an enormous impact on it.

Encountering Static

Have you ever encountered static when listening to your car radio? Looking around, you saw that you were driving by high-tension power lines. High-tension lines put out electromagnetic fields that temporarily overpower the electromagnetic fields of the radio waves. The clash between these two fields produces static, which makes it hard to hear your favorite program clearly.

When we are living with someone who is not listening to his conscience, his behavior creates high-tension waves in our home. Those high-tension waves clash with what our consciences say are standards of right behavior. The resulting static makes it harder to hear our consciences.

For example, because your husband has immersed himself in a world where using others for personal gain receives hearty approval, his conscience is wounded in the area of treating others with respect. It is also wounded in the whole area of property rights. He cannot recognize property rights, because pornography has told him there are no boundaries. Instead, he believes he has the right to take for his own pleasure anything he wants from anyone he wants.

If the husband acts on this belief, others will be hurt. For example, Ann's husband, Bill, felt free to go to friends and family with a hardluck story and borrow money with no thought of paying it back. He would simply take it and never repay it. "After all," he often said, "I don't have to live by the same rules everyone else does."

These acts wounded Ann's conscience. She knew they were wrong. She knew Bill was using others, but she didn't know what to do about it. She couldn't stop it without being controlling, and she couldn't pay others back herself without enabling Bill to continue to be a user. Ann was caught between a rock and a hard place and her conscience suffered greatly.

Ann still struggles with the dilemma today. This is one of the difficulties of living with someone who practices evil. There are no easy solutions to the problems that arise.

Encountering Static in Your Maternal Instincts

When a woman's husband is involved in pornography, her conscience may be wounded in the area of her motherly instincts. Sally watched as her husband, Ben, moved in on their daughter, Joyce. It was so subtle: the compliment that seemed just a little off-base, the look that felt just a little uncomfortable, the touch that lingered just a bit too long, the gifts that were just a little inappropriate.

Sally's intuition flashed a warning, even though she wasn't sure what was going on. When she said something to Ben about it, he told her she was paranoid. There's nothing wrong with a father building up his daughter, he said. Maybe if she wasn't such a nag, he might bring her gifts, too.

Sally's intuition kept flashing that her daughter was in danger, and her conscience urged her to take steps to protect Joyce. But Sally's mind started to be swayed by Ben's argument that she was being paranoid. Perhaps it was outrageous for her to think Ben would have anything on his mind but fatherly love, she told herself. Perhaps she was seeing things that weren't there. Surely, these kinds of things didn't happen in Christian homes.

But they do. And if Sally doesn't start to listen to her conscience, her daughter may very well become an incest statistic, since there is voluminous evidence that pornography promotes incest.

Encountering Static in Our Sexual Boundaries

A woman's conscience may also be wounded in the area of her sexuality, because pornography has schooled her husband in sexual perversion. Say, for example, her husband wants her to perform a specific sex act that he became interested in through pornography. Her conscience flashes a warning—she feels uncomfortable with the whole idea. Her mind doesn't know why she feels uncomfortable. Perhaps she's never even heard of this particular thing before. Her mind has no knowledge on which to judge whether this act is right or wrong, but her conscience immediately feels repelled by it.

Now her husband may take the how-to-win-friends-and-influence-people approach by trying to explain to her why this whole thing will be just great because, after all, the book, magazine, or video told him this was the ultimate experience. His goal is to persuade her mind that this is okay. Or, he may take the beat-her-down-until-she-gives-in approach by comparing her to other women or expressing dissatisfaction with her willingness to experiment. If he's a Christian, he may even remind her of 1 Corinthians 7:4 ("For the wife does not have authority and control over her own body, but the husband . . .") and 1 Peter 3:1 (". . . you married women, be submissive to your own husbands . . .") and tell her that God requires her to submit her body to his desires. His goal is to make her think if she doesn't do this, she's either not much of a woman, or a real dud of a wife, or a failure as a Christian. Whether his approach is persuasive or condemning, the goal is to win her mind over to his way of thinking.

Thus, there's an inner tension. Her mind begins to become convinced and it argues with her conscience. The progression goes like this: First, she begins to lose her ability to trust her own instincts (after all, what does *she* know?). Then, she goes ahead and does what he asks (see the man of God from the Bible story here?).

There's just one little problem. Her conscience was never convinced that this act was okay because the conscience isn't persuaded by logic or cajoled by manipulation.

So, what happens afterward? She feels self-condemnation. The self-condemnation will continue as long as she practices the act, even in the face of massive amounts of mental gymnastics about why this is really okay. However, if she continually tells her conscience to be quiet, it *will* gradually get quieter and quieter. This is not a sign that her conscience has been convinced of the rightness of a certain behavior. It is a sign that her conscience is being mortally wounded.

Becoming Past Feeling

Once the conscience has been mortally wounded, the inner turmoil quiets somewhat because we are now past feeling in this area. When our consciences have been numbed in an area, we lose our ability to have any boundaries in that area. We shove our way past the barricade of the conscience and enter the danger zone of determining good from evil by the power of the intellect alone.

This leaves us vulnerable in two areas. First, the intellect is curious and the flesh is hungry. The hunger and curiosity will pull us in the direction of sampling self-destructive behavior. Second, once we have violated our consciences in a certain area, we are powerless to defend ourselves against having other people trespass on us there. We have removed the boundary ourselves. We cannot shove past the barricade of the conscience without leaving a hole big enough for other people to climb through. They will come in and take advantage of our inability to protect ourselves.

And even though we may tell ourselves we are immune from the consequences, we will begin to reap what we have sown. We begin to experience the devastation of self-destructive behavior and the vulnerability caused by weakened boundaries. We open ourselves to physical or emotional abuse. We watch our children being destroyed. We acquire a sexually transmitted disease. Perhaps we even develop an addiction of our own to keep our consciences quiet.[2]

On the other hand, the wife who has listened to her conscience, and refused to engage in sexual acts that make her feel uncomfortable, experiences no self-condemnation. Instead, she feels inner peace and freedom about her decision.

Learning how to let our consciences be our guides is essential if we're going to be able to love our husbands. It's the only way we can love with integrity. But what if we've already blown it and are struggling under a heavy load of guilt and shame? Fortunately, there's a way out. Let's talk about that next.

Dejunking Your Conscience

*How much more shall the blood of Christ, who through the eternal
Spirit offered himself without blemish to God, purify your conscience
from dead works to serve the living God.*

Hebrews 9:14 (KJV)

Conscience is the most sacred of all properties.

James Madison[1]

I f our consciences aren't clear, we can't really love our husbands because we
will always see them through the filter of our own issues. We will also have
great difficulty hearing God's answers when we approach Him for direction
because our shame distorts our ability to accurately interpret His Word. Hebrews
10:22 says, "Let us all come forward and draw near with true hearts in unquali-
fied assurance and absolute conviction engendered by faith, having our hearts
sprinkled and purified from a guilty conscience and with our bodies cleansed
with pure water." So, in order to get accurate guidance, we must heal our
consciences by dealing with the things that wounded it. In other words, we have
to resolve the issues from the past.

This means we have to deal with a three-letter word that makes most of us
squirm—sin. This is a power word that has been used to beat people over the
head. But looking at sin from God's point of view takes the sting out of it: Sin is
anything that keeps us from being all we can be. When you think of sin that way,

you'd be a fool not to confess and forsake it. Who doesn't want to be all they can be? Who doesn't want to let go of anything that will get in the way of that? Here are some areas where sin might have wounded your conscience.

Sexual Activity Before the Marriage

You may need to deal with inappropriate sexual activity that occurred before you were married. Many young people who came of age in the sixties and after were sexually active before marriage. Even though our generation was told love is "free," the cost of free love is high. Shoving past the barricade of the conscience to allow sex outside marriage leaves a gaping hole in the God-ordained boundary around the marriage bed. In today's permissive society, it becomes quite easy for one or both spouses to justify stepping through that hole by committing adultery.

Past sexual issues become huge boulders in the pathway to resolving the problems pornography raises in a marriage. By violating our consciences in the area of our sexuality, we have failed to cherish ourselves and we have communicated to our husbands and others that they do not have to cherish us either.

The way we repent of our failure to cherish ourselves depends on whether we violated our consciences with our husbands or with others. There is a difference of opinion about whether or not you should tell your spouse about previous sexual partners. If, before you were married, you were intimate with someone other than your husband and your husband doesn't know about it, it may be best to settle this just between you and the Lord.

We are not entitled to clear our consciences at the expense of another's emotional health. That is not love, that is selfishness. Before you tell your spouse about past sexual sins, make sure you have carefully considered the potential damage full disclosure could cause, and proceed only after you have thoroughly dealt with the issue between you and the Lord.

On the other hand, a woman may have given herself only to her future husband. But if she gave herself before marriage, she violated her conscience and she enabled him to violate his. When Marilyn began seeking the Lord about the cause of the problems in her marriage, He pointed out the fact that she had been sexually intimate with her husband before they were married. She didn't know that her husband was involved with pornography, so she had no idea that lust was at the root of her marital problems.

She was puzzled about why the Lord would point out something that happened 15 years earlier, but because she loved God, she decided to ask His forgiveness for not following His plan for her sexuality. When she knelt down to pray, however, He stopped her. He told her that first she needed to ask her husband to forgive her for her part in their sin. Then He told her she needed to ask her husband to pray with her while she confessed her sin to God.

It seemed like such a bitter pill, but she decided to do it. When she approached Lance, he laughed at her and told her he thought it was "cute" that she had wanted him before they were married. But she persevered and asked him to forgive her, which he did with a snicker.

Then she took a deep breath and asked him to pray with her while she asked God to forgive her. He told her she was making a big deal out of nothing.

"I understand that you feel this is not important, but I need to do this. Will you pray with me?" she asked.

When he finally agreed to pray with her, Marilyn got down on her knees and began to confess her sin. Suddenly, she saw it in a whole new light. She saw how she had violated her conscience and how she had encouraged Lance to violate his. She saw how she had encouraged him to disrespect her by making herself available to him without demanding a full commitment from him.

She saw that by encouraging Lance to view her as a sexual plaything, she had damaged any desire he might have to see her as a woman who deserved to be cherished and protected from the baser things of life. She saw how by using time during their courtship for sex that should have been used to develop good communication skills and to plan a life together, she had left herself wide open to the pressures she now was feeling from problems of poor communication and their lack of a life plan.

At this point Marilyn still did not know that her husband was involved with pornography. It would be a number of years before he was willing to face his choices. But when Marilyn confessed her sin to God before Lance, she unwittingly took from him one of the things he was using to justify his choices to commit adultery. By her confession and repentance, she opened the way for God to begin to work on Lance's conscience.

Inappropriate Sexual Activity in the Marriage

If you have participated in a sexual act with your husband that violated your conscience, the only way to get rid of the shame attached to it is to confess this to the Lord. You show true repentance when you draw a firm boundary around that area of your sexuality by refusing to participate in the act again. God is not shocked when we are explicit with Him about our failings. He already knows what we have done, and He is not disgusted with us. It is the enemy of our souls who would make us think we're too defiled to come before the throne of grace. God loves us much more than we can ever comprehend, and in that love, He invites us to boldly approach Him for forgiveness so we can feel the inner freedom that comes from a clear conscience.

If the marriage bed has become defiled, the wife may find she needs to abstain from relations altogether. This is especially true if there is a risk she may contract a sexually transmitted disease. It is not true, as one Christian counselor told me, that God would protect me from contracting an STD. This counselor informed me that if I withheld myself, I could be forcing Jack to visit prostitutes. There was no awareness that her argument lacked logic since trying to be a great sex partner hadn't kept him from soliciting them in the first place.

This argument, in which the counselor used 1 Corinthians 7:4,5 and 1 Peter 3:1, is wrong on two accounts. First, to say that God will protect a wife from getting an STD if she has sex with a husband who is being unfaithful is the same lie that Satan used when he tried to get Jesus to leap from the temple. Satan told Jesus that He didn't have to worry—God would protect Him. Jesus rebuked Satan for his arrogance, saying, "Don't you dare test the Lord your God" (Matt. 4:7). It is the height of arrogance to expect God to save us from foolishness.

The second reason this argument is wrong is that it is based on a faulty assumption about the reasons behind a sexual addiction. Sexual addiction is not about fulfilling normal, healthy sexuality. It is about using sex as an anesthetic for life's pains. Those who specialize in treating sexual addictions often advise recovering couples to practice periods of abstinence as part of a way to recover healthy sexuality.

Dr. Mark Laaser has said,

> Early in recovery, sex addicts will need to observe a period of celibacy in order to reverse their belief that sex is their most important need. They also need to discover that sex is not an indicator of whether their spouse loves them, and their spouses need to learn that sex is not always the way they please their partner. Abstinence takes the sexual pressure off the relationship so that the couple can work on play and communication during this time.
>
> Throughout recovery a couple may want to be celibate in order to center themselves emotionally and spiritually. Other times for celibacy include when a spouse needs to confront his or her childhood abuse. Celibacy contracts can demand that sex happen only under certain safe conditions and in certain ways.[3]

Offenses Against Others

If we have stolen from others either by withholding from them what is rightfully theirs or by outright taking and keeping something that belongs to another, we need to repent of that and do whatever is necessary to make restitution. Some things are obvious—like the money we borrowed and never returned. I've already explained how Jack's failure to pay back some money he had borrowed put such a block in his relationship with the Lord that he couldn't go to Him and ask for help when he was first tempted with pornography.

Other things can be very subtle, but our consciences always know. If we're behind in our bills, our consciences know. If we've stolen someone's good name by gossiping about him or her, our consciences know. If we've cheated a little on our taxes, or taken work supplies home for personal use, our consciences know.

We need to clear our consciences by asking forgiveness and making restitution whenever possible. It doesn't matter if the offense happened a long time ago. If it still bothers us, it needs to be taken care of.

Baggage We Grew Up With

Our consciences do have limitations. After all, they're just as fallen as the rest of us. One of the consequences of being fallen creatures is that we have lost much of our knowledge of God. Another consequence is that as we go through life, we pick up bad knowledge about the way life ought to work. Often, we take this bad knowledge and try to turn it into theology. As a result, we sometimes believe that God requires or allows behaviors from us that are contrary to His true nature.

This is why Scripture says we must be transformed by the renewing of our minds. I love Eugene Peterson's translation of 1 Peter 1:18–19 in *The Message*: "Your life is a journey you must travel with a deep consciousness of God. It cost God plenty to get you out of that dead-end, empty-headed life you grew up in. He paid with Christ's sacred blood, you know."

Some of us who are married to men addicted to pornography came into the marriage with the baggage of dead-end, empty-headed ways of living that we inherited from our families. These traditions included unwritten rules for how life is and how we should relate to others. Sometimes, in the families we grew up in or the churches we've attended, we have learned that it is wrong to stand up for ourselves. We have learned that we must be nice at all costs. This has contributed to our feeling that we must be victims of someone else's bad behavior because we don't know any "nice way" to make them stop mistreating us. When we do set boundaries, because our consciences are operating on limited knowledge, we feel false guilt.

If we came from a family where there was an addiction or dysfunction of some kind, then many of the rules we learned will conspire together to make fruitless our search for a way out of the mess our marriages are in. This is because our damaged consciences will condemn us when we take healthy actions, because we grew up believing these actions are wrong or because someone told us God says they're wrong.

This is especially true if we are victims of childhood sexual abuse. When a trusted family member abused us, our consciences may have felt uncomfortable. If we were then reassured that this was all right, or perhaps even told that it was an obligation on our part, our tender consciences were bent by incorrect information. Thus, as we struggle to achieve healthy boundaries, we may experience false condemnation from damaged consciences.

When I started praying 2 Corinthians 10:5—"Inasmuch as we refute arguments and theories and reasonings and every proud and lofty thing that sets itself up against the knowledge of God; and we lead every thought and purpose away captive into the obedience of Christ, the Messiah"—I didn't realize how fallen my conscience was. But God knew, and fortunately God is in the business of helping us clear our consciences of self-destructive baggage.

God wants to deliver you from the shame an unhealthy conscience dumps on you, but first you have to ask Him. I hope you will, because it feels really good to have a clear conscience.

CHAPTER 20

Finding Peace in the Midst of the Storm

May grace and peace be given you in increasing abundance—that spiritual peace to be realized in and through Christ, freedom from fears, agitating passions and moral conflicts.

⌐1 Peter 1:2b⌐

You'll never have the healing your heart cries for until you've walked through what it's going to take to get you there.

(The Rev. Charlie Guest)

I have a picture on my refrigerator door that someone gave me years ago. It's one of those 2 1/2-by-4-inch cards that's designed to be slipped into a card or letter as a gift of encouragement. That it has been. The card shows a little boy riding bareback on a sturdy horse. Perched behind him is a little girl, her weary head resting on his shoulders and her arms wrapped tightly around him. The couple has just forded a river and now they're entering a dark, spooky forest. The caption reads: "The best way out is always through."

It's so true. Even though we're tempted to go over, under, or around painful circumstances, the best way out of a situation is always through. I've thought a lot about that as I've struggled with Jack's addiction to pornography. I could go over his addiction by pretending that it didn't matter. I could tell myself and others that I was a "with-it, nineties woman." I could say that only a Puritan would be bothered by her husband's preoccupation with other women's naked bodies.

Or, I could go under by joining Jack in his addiction. Many women have.

Desperate to salvage their marriages, they join the swinging scene—sharing their beds with other men and women, taking drugs to numb the shame of it, or having an affair to get even. Women who decide to lick 'em by joining 'em go under themselves.

Then, there was always the temptation to go around. I could take a detour in my life plan and divorce Jack. It would be so simple. I'd just abort my assignment as a wife, declaring it a mission impossible, wipe my hands, and go on.

None of these seemed like good options to me because they all required me to abandon something precious to me. If I went "over" the addiction by abandoning the truth about it, I would have had to pretend that breaking our marriage covenant was no more serious than bouncing a check at the local store. Denying a truth because it's too painful to bear is a form of insanity.

If I went "under" the addiction by joining in, I would be abandoning myself and all I hold dear. I would be living as if my relationship with Jack were more important than my relationship with God and my personal integrity. Even though nothing I can do will separate me from God's love, if I abandon His laws, I abandon my right to intimate relationship with Him. And if I abandon my principles to preserve a relationship, I lose myself.

If I went "around" the addiction by divorcing Jack, I would be abandoning my marriage vows. I knew I had biblical grounds for divorce and I realized that if Jack continued to refuse to seek healing, it might ultimately be necessary. But my heart was crying to go a different way. I longed to see if God would do for us what He had done for others in the Bible. Did He care about Jack and me and our family or did He only care about people who lived thousands of years ago? Was His power for today or was it just for yesterday? I wanted to know.

If I was ever going to find out, I realized "over," "under," and "around" were out for me. I would have to go through. So, I climbed on the back of Jesus' horse, held tightly to Him, and buried my face deep in His back as we entered the haunted woods.

"I don't know what's going to happen, Lord. There are all kinds of bogeymen out there that want to get me," I sobbed. "Help me hold tight and bring me to the other side as fast as you can."

Yes, the going on the road called The Way Through is rough and tough: boulders of hatred to climb over, rivers of tears to ford, fallen branches of self-pity to trip on, an abyss of rejection to carefully skirt around—and always, always, poisonous serpents of gossip hiding in the underbrush, waiting for a tasty bite of flesh. It's enough to make anyone turn and run.

Good News for Fearful Women

Because pornography disempowers women, it engenders fear. Much of it shows the woman in a helpless, subservient position. Only when she is powerless can the object of his fantasy be totally available for whatever a man wants from her.

When a woman feels powerless, fear is the nearest emotion in her heart. It is impossible to be peaceful when fear is gripping your soul, but peace is the thing you long for most. The message of the gospel speaks life to a woman in this situation. We are promised that God wants to give us peace in increasing abundance. We are told that peace is freedom from fears, agitating passions, and moral conflicts (1 Peter 1:2b).

As a woman learns who she is in Christ and who He is in her, she is able to let go of the spirit of fear that has consumed her because she finds security in her relationship with God, rather than in her relationship with her husband. Second Timothy 1:7 tells us that security based on our relationship with God has a powerful impact on our emotional state: "For God did not give us a spirit of timidity . . . but of power and of love and of calm and well-balanced mind."

Notice the progression in the 2 Timothy passage.

$$\text{power} \left(\frac{\text{know who we are}}{\text{know whose we are}} \right) \rightarrow \text{love} \left(\frac{\text{gives out of security}}{\text{knows proper boundaries}} \right) \rightarrow \text{sound mind}$$

You can see from this equation that power comes from knowing who we are by learning *whose* we are. This is very different from the way most of us operate. Usually, we see ourselves in light of what we do. This mind-set puts us on the performance treadmill. Although we may desperately try to act like we've got it all together, inside, there is a gnawing powerlessness that tells us we will never achieve enough to make us worthy of love. Learning that completely apart from any tremendous feat we can accomplish, God sees us as holy, as saints who are the sisters and friends of Jesus, takes off the performance mode. We cease the endless striving and rest in God's unconditional love. We are now able to reach out to others in love.

This is a true love, not a cringing fearful love that does unto others to try and control what they do unto us. True love flows from a deep understanding that as children of God, all men have dignity and worth. The woman who embraces this understanding will respect her boundaries and the boundaries of others. Knowing where the boundaries are allows her to give out of a sense of security. She knows she will not give away something she should keep for herself. She also knows where to draw the line in the way others treat her.

Failure to have proper boundaries or being the victim of someone who doesn't respect our boundaries is one of the primary sources of mental anguish. When boundaries are respected, it leads to a sound mind. A sound mind is a mind free from the fears, disturbing emotions, and endless introspection that come when we see ourselves as powerless victims.

As a woman dwells on what it means for her to have power because she has been reconciled with God, she learns how to "hold her peace." I used to think this meant biting my tongue and holding back my raging feelings. Then, one day, in the midst of feeling overwhelmed by something Jack had done and straining at the bit to react to it, the Lord said to me, *Is it worth losing your peace over?*

Suddenly, I got this picture of a beautiful plant in the midst of a raging storm. The only way I could protect the fragile thing from the gale-force winds was to cup my hands gently around it. I knew then that holding my peace wasn't biting back the storm; it was cherishing the fragile calm by remembering who I am by listening to my conscience, and whose I am by making choices based on what's right and not what's urgent. Why should I let that go to become part of the storm?

Hold My Peace When My Whole World Is Falling Apart? How Do I Do That?

First, you need to know that the presence of peace doesn't mean the absence of feeling. Being peaceful doesn't mean you beat down all your feelings of shame, fear, and anger. Being peaceful doesn't mean being passive. Being peaceful doesn't mean ignoring the battle around you. No general ever ushered in peace by pretending the enemy wasn't occupying his territory. Generals usher in peace by studying where the enemy is attacking and then drawing up a battle plan to retake the land.

Ephesians 6:15 says that for the great battles of life, our feet are to be shod with the preparation of the gospel of peace. Why did God say the presence of peace and the function of the feet are intimately related? Because we obtain peace through action. Feet are for moving. They're for taking us where we want to be or for moving us away from where we don't want to be. To refuse to take action is to frustrate your feet.

While it may look spiritual on the surface, passivity is a violation of the principles of peace. It's false spirituality to pretend that you're unruffled by the devastation of your life. Passivity is one of Satan's greatest tools. Through it, he urges us to accept all manner of evil. We are never to endure evil. Instead, we are to ask God to deliver us from it (Matt. 6:13). We are not to tolerate evil; we are to overcome it (Rom. 12:21). Peace will not come by ignoring the war raging around (and within) you. Peace will come when you make a realistic appraisal of what has caused the present battle and then take appropriate action to alleviate those causes.

Taking a Sighting

Ever been hiking in the woods and suddenly realized you were off the trail? Remember the nasty feeling that started churning in the pit of your stomach? Survivalists tell us that the greatest danger doesn't come from being lost, it comes from the panic that sets in when we can't find our way. Panic wastes our energy by driving us to go faster, but it rarely leads us out of the woods. Instead, it usually drives us to go in circles.

It's not always easy to tell that we're going in circles. That's why we keep going in them. But at some point our exhaustion drives us to pause long enough to ask, "Haven't I seen that bush before?" The panic factor then pushes the pedal to the metal and we run harder and faster, until we're stopped cold by a tree we've been by a half dozen times.

Now it's time to take a sighting. How? By taking a compass reading or orienting yourself by the sun, or by climbing into the nearest tree and seeing where you are in relation to where you want to be.

"Well, I'm not lost in a literal forest," you say. "I don't have any trees I can climb, and there's no compass out there that can help me. I'm hopelessly lost in some unseen world. And since I don't know how I got here, I sure can't figure out how to get out."

Though it may seem as if you're wandering about in some unseeable place, it isn't so. The place seems invisible because your eyes are blind to it. Isn't this the basic problem that Scripture says we all have? Isaiah, when he prophesied about the coming Redeemer, said the reason He was coming to visit Israel was "to give light to them that sit in darkness and in the shadow of death, to guide our feet into the way of peace" (Luke 1:79) The Greek word used here for "darkness" is *skotos*, which means "to restrain." When we are overcome by the darkness of sin and misery, we're stuck. We stop making progress in life. Hopelessly lost, we either go in circles, or we fall off a cliff, or we fall into a ditch.

So, do what the survivalists tell us we must do if we would save ourselves from being lost: Stop, look, and listen. *Stop* the panic and use that part of you He has given you for taking sightings—your ability to know truth. *Look* into His Word for His standard of how life ought to run. And *listen* to Him in prayer so your feet can be guided onto the way of peace.

⚜ Playing the Hand Dealt to You

As we stop, look, and listen, we notice that there are patterns to the craziness of our lives. Once our patterns become apparent, we have to decide to play from the hand life has dealt us rather than the fairy-tale hand we wanted. This means we respond by adapting ourselves to the truth of our situation. And just like any good card player, if we're going to win the game, we have to know when to hold 'em, when to fold 'em, when to walk away, and when to run.

Know When to Hold 'Em

In the beginning, you'll have to hold 'em a lot. That means you'll stop talking. You'll stop saying things like, "We need to sit down and figure out a budget" and "You promised you weren't going to take out another charge card."

If disciplining the children is causing friction, you'll stop saying, "But you told me she couldn't go out, and then when she went behind my back and asked you after I'd already told her no, you told her she could" and "Why are you jumping on him? You didn't tell him what you wanted him to do and then you got all mad because he didn't do it."

If you know your husband is using pornography, you'll stop saying things like, "Why do you buy those trashy magazines anyway?" and "You promised you wouldn't bring them home."

This, of course, will be hard. In the beginning, your tongue will have grooves in it where your teeth have had to come to a skid stop. But stop talking you must. For three reasons.

• *First,* you have to stop talking so you can quietly observe the patterns of behavior in your marriage. You want to see what happens when you don't interfere at all. You want to know what actions he's generating, and the only way you can do that is to refuse to muddy the waters by generating any of your own.

• *Second,* you have to stop talking because your husband has learned that he can use talk as a way to manipulate you. He has learned that if he says he didn't really say that, or if he terrifies you with abusive language, he'll confuse you enough to stop the discussion. He has learned that if he says, "You know, you're right," that you will think that you are finally making headway and you'll calm down so that he can go on and do just as he's always done.

Talk is an effective refuge for those who refuse to change. You want to show goodwill, so you listen eagerly to all he says. You want to believe the best, so you take him at his word. But his words mean nothing. They are a tool he uses to distract you from the real issues.

Remember, he's been steeped in a world where words are not the outward symbol of an inward commitment to action—they're just a tool to get what he wants. He's also been steeped in a world where the woman never means what she says. So what if she says, "Stop! That hurts!" Porn teaches him that what she really means is, "If you keep doing it long enough, I'm going to love it."

(•) *Third,* you have to stop talking because it's not working, and besides, it's making you weird. The decibel level of the voice of frustration will continually shatter the peace inside you. So, cup your hands around that fragile calm and hold your peace.

That Old Submission Thing

Here's where 1 Peter 3:1 comes in: "In like manner you married women, be submissive to your own husbands . . . and adapt yourselves to them. So that even if any do not obey the Word of God, they may be won over *not by discussion* but by the godly lives of their wives" (emphasis added).

At first these seem like hard words, but they're liberating when you grasp what's being said. First, you have to be honest with yourself and say that your husband isn't obeying the Word of God. This is a difficult step for the wife of a man who claims to be a Christian, especially if he's a leader in the church.

We want to believe that our husbands really are the mighty men of God they work so hard to convince people outside the home they are. But the truth is, if your husband is involved in pornography, at the very least, he's committing mental (if not actual physical) adultery (Matt. 5:28). If there are financial problems because his profligacy is causing him to fail to provide for his family, Scripture says he's worse than an infidel (1 Tim. 5:8). If there are discipline problems with the children because he's provoking them to wrath, he's violating Ephesians 6:4. If he's lying, he's put himself under Satan's authority (John 8:44).

Once you've come to grips with the fact that your husband is not obeying Scripture and have identified the patterns of behavior that are flowing from that disobedience, you have to adapt yourself to him, just as 1 Peter 3:1 says. This doesn't mean that you compensate for him or that you enable him. This doesn't mean that you sweetly pretend the problems aren't there. It doesn't mean that you usurp his position as head of the home. It means that you order your feet to take godly action (so that he may be won over by your godly *behavior*). Taking godly action means you do what's right and refuse to cave in to fear (1 Pet. 3:6). Taking godly action means you have to decide when to fold 'em, when to walk away, and when to run.

Know When to Fold 'Em

Knowing when to fold 'em means you know when to say, "This isn't working." Knowing when to fold 'em means you decide to stop doing things the same old way because that way is bringing shame and judgment into your life. A porn addict's wife is intimately familiar with shame and judgment. Though you can't control the shame your husband generates, you can control the shame you allow him to transfer to you.

There is a close connection between the use of pornography and poor financial planning. Perhaps this is a pattern in your home. You go from financial crisis to financial crisis. Bills don't get paid; creditors are calling. You're always feeling under the gun. You're ashamed to go into the store, wondering if the register is going to beep when your credit card is scanned.

You restrained yourself from jumping in immediately with your own solutions. You've given your husband plenty of time and opportunity to get help. You've been supportive; you've tried not to blame. "We'll make it through this," you've said countless times. You've cut back on your personal spending, and you might even be generating income of your own to help out. But it's not getting any better.

At some point, it becomes apparent that although your husband may be talking about wanting to do what is right with your money, he is making no move toward doing it. At some point, you understand that all that's going on is manipulation. This is the time to say, "This is not working," and take godly action of your own. When you take godly action, you use your feet to walk away from shame toward peace.

What Is the Right Thing to Do?

How do you determine what godly action is? Godly action is doing what's right. In any situation where you see a pattern of craziness in your life, ask yourself, "What is the right thing to do?" Godly action is following the counsel of Proverbs 22:3 and Proverbs 27:12: "A prudent man sees evil and hides himself." Ask God to show you what the evil is and how to prudently hide yourself from it.

Taking prudent action is how we wives adapt ourselves to our husbands' behavior—not by passivity, not by blaming, not by reasoning, but by taking a sighting and then doing the prudent thing. Perhaps we have to pay our own bills, file a separate tax return, or take our names off joint charge accounts if money isn't being handled wisely. This is not being controlling. This is being responsible for your own issues.

Think of it as laser surgery. You go in and, after careful consideration, slice off only the things that are directly impacting you. You deal only with *your* responsibility for those things. You don't touch the rest of the situation. You treat your husband with honor when you recognize that he's grown up enough to experience the natural consequences of his choices.

One more thought. When you figure out what you think is the right thing for this situation at this time, and you begin to act on that plan, you may still be filled with doubts about whether you're doing the right thing. The more you love, the more you care about the outcome, the greater will be your doubts. Proceed anyway. After you take action, the peace will come.

The Lord said He'd rather we be hot or cold than lukewarm. Lukewarm people are afraid to move in either direction for fear of being wrong. So, look at it this way. If you do the wrong thing, you're cold. If you do the right thing, you're hot. Either way, it's better than doing nothing out of fear of doing the wrong thing.

A Chapter Out of My Own Book

As I began to do what was right, I no longer felt afraid. I began to find peace. Jack still hadn't changed, but I found that since I was no longer required to pay a price for his irresponsibility, I was freer to love him where he was.

For example, several times we had our auto insurance canceled because Jack hadn't made the payments, even though he told me he had. Once he was stopped for speeding and given a stiff fine for driving with no insurance. This was a troubling incident for me because I thought we were insured, since he had told me he had made the payment. Because he hadn't, I realized that I was also driving without insurance. I decided it was crazy to continue to be upset about this. I told him I would let him pay his own auto insurance and I would pay mine.

He said he was sorry and he wanted to do what was right. Could he have one more chance? I acquiesced. When it was time for the next quarterly payment to be made, he came in one day all excited and said he had just paid the bill. "It feels so good to be responsible," he said. I really wanted him to be able to do it, so I was thrilled. I gave him a hug and we danced around the kitchen. Then, several weeks later, I got a call from our agent saying the payment hadn't been made. It was the same old thing.

When it was time for the next quarterly payment to be made, I told Jack I would make the payment myself. He asked for another opportunity and I told him the only way I would agree to that was if he understood that I was going to call the insurance company two days before the premium's due date to find out if the payment had been made. That way, if it hadn't been paid, I would have the time to drive to the agency and make the payment myself.

Jack was so thrilled about it that he told our pastor I was "allowing" him to make the payment. Because he didn't know the whole story, this man made a faulty judgment about what was going on. He said I was wrong to call the insurance agency because it was controlling. He told me Jack needed to learn to stand up to me. When I asked him what he thought I should do, he offered no solutions, except to say I needed to learn submission. It was a painful interview.

Neal Clement, who, as director of the American Family Association's OutReach Division, has counseled thousands of sex addicts and their wives, said, "In my experience about 60 per cent of the feedback wives get from the pastors is not positive, it's negative. This is because they're not knowledgeable about how to deal with a sex addict. Counseling a woman in this situation to be submissive is a form of spiritual abuse. Submission will not fix this problem."[2]

Although they mean well, pastors who do not understand how addictions work may give counsel that actually enables the addict. The church has much education to do in this area. Those of us who have been through it can help by sharing our experiences with caring pastors and helping them learn how to minister to addicts and their families.

Don't Play the Blame Game

Whatever she decides to do, the wife of a sexually addicted husband risks the disapproval of others. But she can't passively sit in the darkness, hoping things will magically turn out right. If she doesn't take positive action, the only course left open to her is blame. When a wife feels vulnerable because of her husband's failures, she will often use blaming to try and make her husband feel guilty enough to do what's right.

Blame is the awkward weapon of passive people. It accomplishes nothing and is likely to fall backward and bludgeon the one wielding it. When a wife takes godly action, she can leave blaming behind. Once she has taken positive steps to do what she can to change the pressure that's falling on her, she can escape the bitter trap of resentment. When she no longer has to wallow in his mire, she becomes free to love her husband right where he is.

Knowing when to hold 'em and when to fold 'em are essential first steps for a woman who wants to actively pursue peace. But sometimes our situations call for more drastic action. Sometimes we have to walk away, and sometimes we have to run. We'll look at those difficult choices in the next chapter.

Upping the Ante

Anyone who intends to come with me has to let me lead. You're not in the driver's seat; I am. Don't run from suffering; embrace it. Follow me and I'll show you how. Self-help is no help at all. Self-sacrifice is the way, my way, to finding yourself, your true self. What kind of deal is it to get everything you want but lose yourself? What could you ever trade your soul for?

[Matthew 16:24–26]

We lose our confidence when our conscience is murky.

(Watchman Nee[1])

Sometimes a woman whose husband is involved in pornography will find that saying, "This isn't working," isn't enough. Sometimes a woman must walk away from danger.

Know When to Walk Away

A Christian, Dan had been heavily involved in pornography since his early teens. He masturbated several times a day and had exposed himself on several occasions. He thought that once he was married, he'd be okay. He thought that once he could have sex regularly, he would be able to leave his lust behind and get on with living. But the bondage was too great and so secretly, he carried on his other life.

When Dan would come home after stopping off for a peek at a favorite magazine, his sense of shame and guilt would spill over into anger. His language was abusive and Joan and the children were subjected to harsh punishments for minor infractions. Although Joan didn't know about Dan's secret life, she had discerned his pattern of anger and she came to talk with me about it.

So far, life-threatening violence had been avoided, but Dan was tottering on the edge. He spanked the children much too hard and they were terrified of him. Joan told me she had been handling the situation by trying to be submissive. Her understanding of submission was to try and be so good that Dan wouldn't have anything to be angry about when he got home.

I explained to her that her actions were not what was provoking Dan to anger, so her being "good" wasn't going to stop it. I also told her that if she didn't do something quickly to show Dan this behavior was unacceptable, someone was going to get hurt. I showed her Proverbs 22:24–25, "Make no friendships with a man given to anger, and with a wrathful man do not associate, lest you learn his ways and get yourself into a snare."

Her boys were already learning their father's ways, and Joan was alarmed at the anger they showed each other. "They're always fighting," she told me.

Together, we worked out a plan that would allow her to follow the path to peace. She found a friend she could stay with on the spur of the moment and kept an overnight bag for her and the kids in the trunk of her car.

The next time Dan came home angry, before there was any time for confrontations, Joan quickly ushered the children to the car. Then, standing in a safe place, as calmly as she could, she told Dan that his anger made it unsafe for her and the children to be with him, so they would be leaving for the night. And then she left . . . immediately . . . without telling him where she was going. Because Joan didn't know what Dan's reaction would be, it was safer that he not know where Joan and the children had gone.

Joan's courage set Dan free to begin to look at himself, and he didn't like what he saw. Alone in the house that night, he was devastated to realize that his behavior was alienating his family. It would be seven more years before Dan was willing to deal with the cause of his anger—a cause that Joan was still blissfully unaware of. But that night when Joan broke her pattern of going along to get along and instead strapped on her trembling feet the preparation of the gospel of peace, God broke the stranglehold of anger in their home.

Although she kept the overnight bag in her car for many months, Joan never had to leave again. That's because Dan had been confronted with the reality that there were consequences to his behavior. Joan and Dan worked out a plan that if he came home angry, he would work outside for a while until he'd done enough physical activity to burn the anger off. The children were to stay inside until Dan knew all was clear. Once Dan began to get a handle on his anger, the boys started getting along better.

One action of tough love didn't "fix" everything. Real life isn't like that. There were still many problems in their home associated with Dan's covert use of pornography; but as Joan learned to respond to the problems by pursuing peace, she unwittingly began hacking away at the chains that held her husband in denial about his choices. And the fragile flower of peace began to take root in their home.

Know When to Run

This last choice is reserved for the big issues. Don't run if walking will do. It's overkill to use a cannon to fight a battle a .22-caliber gun can handle. And it's downright dangerous to use general anesthesia when over-the-counter analgesics will do the job. So, why waste your energy by overreacting? But sometimes walking away isn't enough. Sometimes, the danger level is so great, a woman has to lace up her track shoes and run.

Karen was a woman who had to run. Tim's preoccupation with pornography affected his ability to be a good father because pornography glorifies incest.[2] It makes it seem as if incest is a responsibility any loving father would undertake. After all, someone has to teach Lucy the facts of life. Who better than her dear old dad, who "cares" more about her than some guy off the street? So Tim took it upon himself to introduce Lucy to the "joys of uninhibited sex."

Only it wasn't so joyous to Lucy, who reported the action to her high school counselor, who contacted the Department of Social and Rehabilitation Services. Lucy was immediately put in foster care, and Karen had a choice to make. Lucy could come home, SRS said, but only if Tim left. Would she choose her daughter, or would she choose her husband?

No woman should be put in such a situation. It rails against all that is natural within her. Being usurped by another woman is a deep assault to a woman's self-esteem; and having her daughter violated is a deep assault to the mother's heart of a woman. But having the man who promised to forsake all others and cleave only to her, the man who by natural instinct should want to protect his daughter from harm, having that man violate her daughter rocks a woman to the core of who she is.

Seeing her child's innocence stolen and trust shattered is incredibly painful.

And what about her own pain? Does she dare feel jealousy and resentment against her daughter? How can she comfort the child, who through no fault of her own, usurped the woman's own place in her husband's heart? Whose pain does she take care of?

Karen made the difficult choice to run. She refused to believe Tim's story that the incest charge was false. Later, when he confessed, she stood firm against Tim's pleas that the incest wasn't his fault. Instead, she submitted herself to the Department of Social and Rehabilitation Services' conditions for the return of her daughter. Her courage showed the SRS that she was a fit parent and avoided having Lucy removed to foster care on a long-term basis.

Karen's courage also put Tim in a position of either admitting his behavior was wrong or totally removing himself from any further contact with his family. Tim came to see how his use of pornography had changed his values from a man who truly loved his family to a man who would use his family in unnatural ways. Then, under SRS guidelines, the family began an incredibly difficult course of counseling and accountability that was designed to assure that Tim had thoroughly dealt with his issues and Lucy had thoroughly dealt with her fears before Tim was even allowed into the house.

It is now four years since the incest, and the SRS still hasn't allowed Tim to move back home. He can visit the house for a certain number of hours per week (a time limit he holds strictly to) and he can spend the night if Lucy is away at friends. Though these measures may seem harsh, incest is a deep violation of trust. Deep violations of trust, especially where children are involved, cannot be excused or negotiated away. They must be dealt with deliberately. The betrayer must be held accountable for his actions and he must, over a long period, show that he is worthy of future trust.

Getting the Wrong Advice from People Who Mean Well

Jeanne didn't fare as well as Karen. When her husband, Sid, incested their daughter, Amy, Jeanne went to her pastor for help.

"As long as he said he's sorry, that has to be the end of it," she was told. Later, Sid was asked to be an elder in the church.

Several years later, because things still weren't resolved in her home, Jeanne went to see another pastor.

"You shouldn't have said anything to Sid about this incident," he told her sternly. "It's up to the Holy Spirit to convict him, not you."

To the wounded daughter, this pastor said, "Well, what were you wearing and how did you act around your dad?" He seemed to imply that somehow Amy had enticed her father.

Because Sid refused to deal with the incident other than to say he'd done it (after being caught red-handed) and he was sorry, Jeanne was told she could do nothing further about the situation. Because Sid said Amy didn't need any counseling, Jeanne was told she would be usurping her husband's place if she obtained counseling for her daughter. Amy was told it was her responsibility to forgive her father (which it was, but forgiveness doesn't mean pretending that an offense never happened or telling the offended that she has no right to feel angry about a violation).

Wives of sex addicts experience this kind of response regularly. There are also sex addicts who go for pastoral help and are either told to "just say no" or who are driven out of the church because "we don't allow that kind of behavior in here." Sometimes this kind of bad advice is given because the pastor doesn't know how to deal with sexual addictions. Sometimes it's given because the pastor himself is involved in some type of inappropriate sexual behavior.

Sometimes, of course, there is a wise, compassionate pastor who understands how to lead those suffering the effects of sexual addiction to wholeness in Jesus Christ. I'm so thankful for our present pastor whose tender heart and keen insight has been such an essential part of our healing.

Sexual addiction is a big problem in this country, and those locked in its grip are desperate for hope. The best that secular counseling can offer is a way to "cope." But God offers a way to be healed. When the church finally learns how to provide that healing, it will find people flooding to its doors.

It's a Lose-Win Situation

All the stories you have read have something in common—loss. In each situation, women had to choose to lose something important to them so they wouldn't lose something more important to them.

A woman who loves her husband wants her name to be associated with his. She wants to feel proud about who her husband is and the way he conducts business. Taking her name off credit cards or filing a separate tax return to avoid enabling financial irresponsibility is an action that makes her feel separate from her husband. She loses the share-and-share-alike that is so important to the heart of a marriage.

A woman who loves her husband wants to spend time with him. She wants her children to delight in their father. Packing her bags and fleeing for a night to avoid possible violence is an action that temporarily separates her from her husband. She loses the companionship that is so important to the essence of a marriage.

A woman who loves her husband wants to be his sexual partner. She wants to trust him with her heart and with her children. Requiring him to leave home so she can protect her child from sexual violation is an action that separates her from him. She recognizes that she can no longer believe in him and accepts the loss of trust that is so important to the spirit of a marriage.

Commonality, companionship, trust—these things weren't lost by the wives' choices, but by their husbands' actions. These basic marriage values were already lost before the women had to decide which course of action to take. But we women are a funny lot—sometimes we think by hanging on to the appearance of a thing, we can have the reality of it. By actually making choices that reflected the reality of their situations, these women let go of making believe everything was all right. They gave up trying to pretend that their marriages were working in the areas of commonality, companionship, and trust.

They gave up trying to walk the way their husbands were walking and took off on a different path. Two cannot walk together if they aren't agreed, the Scripture says. These women decided they couldn't agree with irresponsibility. They decided they couldn't agree with violence. They decided they couldn't agree with breaking trust. Trying to walk in their husbands' ways was causing tremendous inner and outer turmoil. By courageously suffering the loss of their illusions, and turning their feet onto the path of peace, these women cherished the fragile calm within where they knew who they were and whose they were.

Sowing Self-Control and Reaping Peace

As a woman discovers how to "hold her peace," she learns how to be God-controlled rather than other-controlled. Instead of reacting to someone else's values, she can act based on her own. Instead of responding in kind, she can respond in love. Now she can be what Paul referred to 2 Corinthians 5:18, "a minister of reconciliation" to her husband and children, inviting them to come in from the storm.

Peace is that settled conviction in your heart that you are doing what is right. It is that assured understanding that there is a well-fastened anchor holding your ship in the midst of the storm. But just as the ship still bobs up and down when it's battered by the wind and the waves, a woman at peace still experiences swings of emotion. The presence of tears doesn't mean the absence of peace. The presence of anger doesn't mean the absence of peace. Your anchor still holds and because it does, you can experience the emotions in total safety.

Maybe you need to grieve for a while, to drain off some of the pain and disappointment. After you've used up a few hankies, learn to cherish yourself by doing something that's going to give you pleasure. Take a nice walk, luxuriate in a bubble bath, drive to the lake, go star-gazing, take up painting, play the piano—above all, cultivate friendships that are affirming.

Remember, in the midst of the tumult and confusion, your anchor will hold. You are doing what's right. You are safe, so don't be afraid.

Becoming Faith Full

Thy faith hath made thee whole.

[*Matthew 9:22b (KJV)*]

Not the labour of my hands
Can fulfill Thy law's demands;
Could my zeal no respite know,
Could my tears forever flow,
All for sin could not atone;
Thou must save, and Thou alone.

[*Augustus Montague Toplady, "Rock of Ages"*]

U sually, second labors are shorter than first. Our first child, Ian, came after about 10 hours of intense labor. So I thought I had it made in the shade when it was time for our daughter, Sandy, to be born. No such luck. It took us from Friday night to Sunday morning to convince Sandy that she was ready for her debut.

The goal of labor is to dilate or open the cervix (the bottle neck of the womb) and bring the baby far enough down so that you can see a bit of the head at the peak of a contraction. That's called crowning. Once the baby crowns, it's push, push, push, and then it's "Oh wow!" time as you fall in love with your new baby.

Labor lasts as long as it has to. Every contraction is an essential step moving you toward the goal of birth. The length of labor varies for every woman and, as you can see from my example, even for every pregnancy a woman has. Labor is individually designed for the baby's size, head shape, and position and the woman's pelvic diameter, laboring position, and physical strength.

The Hard Labor of Change

There's a reason labor is called labor. It's hard work. You groan and sweat, and sometimes you say, "I don't want to do this anymore." In Galatians 4:19, Paul said waiting for someone to change is a lot like being in labor: "My little children, for whom I labor in birth again until Christ is formed in you" (NKJV). The Greek word used for "labor" here is *odino*. It means "to be in pain." When you're waiting for someone to change, you're in pain. You groan and sweat, and sometimes you say, "I don't want to do this anymore."

I've attended many births, and one thing I've seen repeatedly is a desperation and despair that settle on a woman who's been in pain for hours of hard labor only to find that she's made no progress in dilation since the last time the doctor checked her. That same desperation and despair settle on a woman who's been through incredible amounts of emotional pain while waiting for her husband to work through his addiction to pornography. She tells herself that it's all going to be worth it because progress is being made. He's finally getting a handle on this thing, he tells her. She, desperate for hope, believes him.

Then there's a reality check. She realizes he's been lying all along. She finds out he hasn't really stopped doing the pornography, just cut back a little. She discovers he's stolen money from one of their children to fund his addiction. And the darkness of despair descends as she realizes they're back to square one.

And she sees the light go out of her children's eyes. She sees their shoulders hunch in defeat. She sees the hardness come into their faces, and her heart cries, *Will it ever end? How could he do this again? He promised!* This scenario repeats itself over and over through endless years until her heart isn't just broken, it's crushed and ground into dust and she's made to drink it.

If you've never been involved in pornography, it may be difficult for you to understand the degree of bondage addicts experience; it may also be difficult for you to understand the degree of distress a wife experiences. Porn is more addictive than cocaine or alcohol. Porn sends its tentacles in deep. It wraps itself around a basic physical need (sex), entwines itself in a basic emotional need (to be in control), and enmeshes itself with a basic spiritual need (for intimacy).

Our true selves become hopelessly entangled until we're totally lost to porn's overwhelming power. In order to be set free, each tentacle has to be extracted with enough force to break its stranglehold but enough delicacy to preserve what's left of our selves. Meanwhile, since husband and wife are one flesh, the vile tentacles have full access to the wife's spirit.

Yes, waiting for someone to change is hard labor. It's a fiery trial of faith.

What is faith anyway, and how do we get it? To answer that question, let's start by looking at some common confusions about what constitutes faith.

Faith Isn't the Same as Love

A former pastor told me that Jack was involved with pornography because he didn't feel good about himself. "Jack suffers from low self-esteem. He needs you to have some faith in him," the pastor said. "A wife's job is to build up her husband and make him feel good about himself, then he doesn't need to find it anywhere else."

TRANSLATION: He wouldn't be in this fix if you were the loving, supportive wife he needs.

As well-intentioned as he was, this pastor has it backward. We don't do bad things because we feel bad about ourselves; we feel bad about ourselves because we do bad things. He's also confused faith with love. It's a common mistake. We think if we just love someone enough that we can impart to them the faith they need to overcome whatever difficulty they're facing. And it's true. Sometimes the unconditional love of just one person can empower another so much that he is able to leap tall buildings with a single bound.

For many years, I thought if I believed in Jack enough, if I helped him believe in himself enough, if I reached out to him time and time again with forgiveness, he would be empowered to let go of his addiction to pornography. That might work for some men—especially men who haven't been involved with pornography for very long. But I don't think it works for most men, at least not according to the wives I've talked with who tried the "I'm just going to love him through this" approach.

Mere human love is not enough to break the stranglehold of pornography. Lust creates a bottomless pit of need in a man. The more you pour into him, the more he demands from you. Pornography has already taught him that you exist only to fulfill his needs. So if you comply with that fantasy by trying to meet his needs so he'll feel loved, the lie he's believing has been validated before his very eyes. No matter how much we love our husbands, our love cannot give them the faith to change if they refuse to see that what they're doing is wrong.

⟩ Faith Isn't Believing Hard Enough to Make It Happen

"We're just going to believe Jesus for healing in this," my counselor said to me. Then she quoted Matthew 21:22: "And whatever you ask for in prayer, having faith and believing, you will receive."

TRANSLATION: This sounds very spiritual. But as the course of counseling developed, it became apparent that what the counselor meant was I was to be entirely passive in my actions. The only action that was considered to be one of "faith" was praying and believing that God would heal Jack. I was encouraged to will myself and Jack to the level of faith that would allow God to do the necessary healing.

Faith has also sometimes been confused with an act of our will, as if we could make something happen just by willing ourselves to believe hard enough. Can you fix the broken place in your heart by an act of your will? Can your husband be healed of pornography and your home and marriage restored if you just believe hard enough? Let me save you some time on this one. I spent many years checking this out and I can say with absolute surety, not only do you not have enough belief and will to bring about the necessary changes, you have no right to impose your will on another—even though that will might be noble and good in your own eyes.

Rather than being an act of faith, "willing" a person to behave in a certain way is actually an attempt to usurp his control of his life. He may be making a rotten choice, but it is his rotten choice to make. You can say you won't participate in the rotten choice, you can say you won't allow the rotten choice to be acted out under your roof, but you can't force the other person to stop making his rotten choices by an act of your will.

Controlling others by acts of your will is a form of manipulation. Manipulation seeks to force the will of others to be in subjection to our wills. We become usurpers, seizing and holding by force that which isn't our right to have. There is only one who seeks to usurp the will of man, and it is not God. God seeks to conform our wills to His, but He does not usurp them.

God clearly states what type of behavior is acceptable if we want to remain in fellowship with Him, but He does not force us to behave that way. Instead, if we continue to make self-destructive choices, He withdraws His fellowship from us. He doesn't withdraw His love, and He doesn't divorce us from being His children; but He does say, "I can't be with you anymore. I'll have to love you from a distance" (see Exod. 33). This is the approach the wife of an addict must take. She must set clear boundaries.

There's another reason why "willing" a person free of pornography doesn't work. Pornography is basically an issue of the will. Pornography seeks to force the will of another to be in subjection to your will by inflaming the imagination. In the imagination, the one desired has her will totally surrendered to the imaginer so that the object of the fantasy will do whatever you desire her to do. She has no will but your will. She exists only to do what you want. This is total control.

If you use "will" to get people to stop doing something they have been using their wills to do, you may change some of their outer behaviors, but you haven't begun to address the brokenness that drives them to use their wills in controlling ways. Instead, by using will to control will, you have reinforced will. You now have someone who is more controlled than ever by his will. That's what Jesus was talking about when He said the Pharisees' way of changing people by having them use their wills to follow the rules made them twice as controlled by hell as the Pharisees themselves (see Matt. 23:15).

God says our wills are totally incapable of saving us. God's way isn't to fix the will so it can do better. God's way is to have our wills surrender to His love. Only then, by grace, through faith, can we find freedom from the tyranny of self-will.

Faith Isn't Blind

"You need to make positive confessions," the counselor told me. "Every day pray, 'I thank You, Lord, that Jack is a godly man who loves me as Christ loved the church.' Then, receive your positive confession by faith until God gives it to you in reality."

TRANSLATION: Do not tell yourself the truth about your situation; tell yourself what you want the truth to be.

Not only is faith not forcing our wills on someone else, it's also not creating our own reality. Faith isn't saying, "If I believe it, it will be." Believing something hard enough doesn't make it happen. That type of thinking is a form of self-deception that, if unchecked, leads to insanity. I believe that creating our own reality is also similar to witchcraft. Witchcraft designs its own reality and attempts to bring it about by mesmerizing the mind with illusions. Witchcraft casts a spell on the mind so that the one afflicted will believe something different from what is true, prompting him to act in a way that will bring harm to himself or others.

Jesus said the natural condition of man is to lie to himself. When we refuse to see the truth, we pluck out our eyes and plunge ourselves into darkness. In this darkness, we thrash about, wounding ourselves and others on unseen reality. The only way out, Jesus said, is to tell ourselves the truth. The truth is what sets us free. (See John 3:19–21; John 8:32; Matt. 6:22–23; Luke 11:34–36.)

Because the truth about where we really are and what is really happening to us often strikes fear into our hearts, it takes a tremendous amount of faith to open ourselves to it. This faith doesn't come from any reality we manufacture but from a conviction of the truthfulness of God that when we see the truth, we won't perish from the pain of it, but rather, we'll be freed from our darkness by embracing the reality of it.

In Ephesians 6:16 Paul compared our faith to the shield Roman soldiers took into battle. When the soldier wasn't using his shield, he rested it on a small clip on his loinbelt. In our armor, Paul said, the loinbelt represents truth. This means that our faith rests on that which is true, not on that which we would like to be true. If we rest our faith on anything else, it will come crashing down.

Faith Is Persevering in the Course of Action Based on the Truth of the Situation

In chapter 19, we talked about how peace also rests on truth. Peace isn't obtained by telling ourselves, "It's not hot, and I'm not here." Peace is obtained by a three-step process:

1. Making an assessment of the reasons why it's hot (telling yourself the truth about your situation).
2. Determining whether you should turn down the thermostat, open the window, or get the fire extinguisher (determining what is the right thing to do).
3. Doing it (moving your feet to action).

Faith is believing that the principles behind the thermostat, open window, and fire extinguisher will eventually make the room cooler.

Imagine what would happen if you kept fiddling with the thermostat or opening and closing the window because the room wasn't cooling down fast enough. Worse yet, imagine what would happen if you used the fire extinguisher only long enough to reduce the flames and then abandoned your effort because the room temperature was still sizzling. Faith perseveres in the required course of action until the room reaches a comfortable temperature, even if it takes a long time.

Faith overarches all the other principles. That's why Paul called it a "covering shield." It rests on truth, acts on righteousness, and moves toward peace. Without faith, we grow weary in the labor and stop the work we're doing.

Faith Is Letting Go of the Results

Faith realizes that while our actions can facilitate change, our actions don't actually cause change. In a warm room, when we open the window, we facilitate the change in temperature by making a way for cooler air to enter and warmer air to escape. It is the exchange of air that causes the room temperature to drop, not the simple act of opening the window. Likewise, we facilitate putting out a fire when we activate a fire extinguisher, but it is the chemicals inside the fire extinguisher that actually cause the fire to be quenched. Our actions of opening the window and activating the fire extinguisher are important, but only because they open up the possibilities for another power (wind or chemical) to come in and cool the room down. Another power is doing the work while we employ the instrument that allows the work to happen.

When you begin to tell yourself the truth about your situation, when you determine to do what's right, and when you start taking appropriate actions, you don't effect change; rather, you open up the possibility for God to come in and effect change. If your actions only facilitate change rather than cause it, *you* are not responsible for making the change happen. You are laboring together with God, but He is the One responsible for making changes happen. Letting that truth sink in sure took the burden off my shoulders!

A Little Mop-
Up Action

Some Final Skirmishes and

What to Do with All the Rubble

CHAPTER 23

Those Flaming Arrows

For we do not have a High Priest Who is unable to understand and sympathize and have a fellow feeling with our weaknesses and infirmities . . . , but One Who has been tempted in every respect as we are, yet without sinning. Let us then fearlessly and confidently and boldly draw near to the throne of grace . . . and find grace to help in good time for every need—appropriate help and well-timed help, coming just when we need it.

[Hebrews 4:15,16]

When an old family friend heard that Jack and I were separated because he'd been involved with pornography and hookers, she sought to give me some grandmotherly advice.

"I didn't always like sex either, dear," she said, patting my knee. "But I'd pray and ask God to help me and He always would."

There it was. What I just knew people were thinking—*Jack got involved in a sexual addiction because she is a failure in bed.* Earlier, a pastor had asked Jack if I had "driven him to it" by withholding myself sexually. This pastor and woman couldn't imagine that "a fine Christian man" would make such choices unless he was driven to it. They couldn't imagine that a husband would sexually abuse his wife. They couldn't imagine that a husband would reject his wife sexually.

Later, this same woman gave me a tape on forgiveness and hummed a chorus about how sweet it is to forgive each other. She told me how God hates divorce and implied that if there was a divorce, the fault would be largely mine because

I was too hardhearted to forgive. Her implication was that if I would just forgive Jack, everything would magically be all right.

She meant to be helpful, but her helpfulness left me feeling pummeled. She never in any way acknowledged the hurt I was feeling. She never said, "God hates adultery and what's happened to you is wrong." She never dealt with the fact that despite repeated "repentance," Jack had continued in his addiction. No, I was simply counseled to "forgive" and be a better bed partner. Every time I thought about what she'd said, it felt like a burning in my soul.

She was a kind woman, really, a simple saint who had been a missionary for over 30 years. Married to a wonderful man, she'd never had to worry about infidelity. She'd had her ups and downs, but she'd never suffered deep injustice and so she had a simplistic answer to my pain.

Neal Clement, director of the American Family Association's OutReach Division, has counseled thousands of sex addicts and their wives. He said, "You can't imagine how many times I've heard from a wife that she was told, 'You need to perform sexually for him.' This kind of advice is abusive. It makes women feel like the answer to his problem lies in her ability to bring him sexual gratification. This is just setting her up for a lot of hurt. It doesn't work and she's left feeling more shame and guilt because she couldn't do it for him."[1]

What You See Isn't What You Get

Once you know the truth about your situation and determine to use unchanging principles to guide your response to the nightmare pornography has brought into your home, once you clear your conscience and learn how to build your faith in God, who is able to heal you, you still have another hurdle to overcome—the giant hurdle of other people's judgments of you. Some of these people are genuinely trying to be helpful. Others are genuinely trying to be superior. Either way, when you're hanging by your fingertips to the edge of the abyss of despair, gossip and cutting remarks feel like someone is stomping all over your hands.

Part of the difficulty people have in understanding the devastation of sexual addiction comes from a misunderstanding of what a sex addict looks like and how he behaves in public. At least in the beginning, sex addicts are good at their public persona. I have talked to women whose husbands had a public life as pastors, deacons, lawyers, choir members, youth workers, and other pillars in their community. But privately these men were involved in pornography, and that involvement led them to prostitution, strip shows, homosexuality, and bestiality. Their wives were living in a hell that few people could believe or understand.

We think that someone who is involved in a degenerate lifestyle would have something immediately recognizable about him, like hair growing on his teeth. But police can tell you that the friends and families of serial rapists (81 percent of whom admitted to regular use of pornography[2]) are often completely incredulous that their loved ones could have done such a thing. And it's not because their friends and families are stupid; it's because pornography so dulls the conscience that their loved ones can act like two different people at will.

Because her husband often seems so "normal," the wife of a man with a sexual addiction will have a difficult time finding understanding from others. They are quite sure that the problem can't be as described. So, those passing by her suffering will make judgments. She's too strong for him. She's too weak for him. She's too controlling. She's too passive. She's a dud in bed. She's too demanding in bed. She's stupid for staying in the marriage. She's hardhearted for divorcing him. Everyone will have a different opinion about what she should do and why she finds herself in this situation, and most of the opinions will be whispered behind her back, but not so far behind that she's out of earshot.

Most hurtful of all are the things her husband says in the privacy of their own home: "You drove me to it." "With a wife like you, who wouldn't . . ." "If you would only . . . , I wouldn't have to . . ." "You're too fat." "You're too flat." "You're too old." "Why can't you look like the girl in the picture?" "If you would just dress up a little bit more . . ." "If you weren't so hung up . . ."

A husband will work hard at convincing his wife and others that the addiction is her fault. This is because God designed human nature to be uncomfortable with guilt. If we're feeling guilty about something, but we don't want to repent of having done it, the only way we can deal with the guilt is to shift the blame.

Guilt: The Gift That Keeps on Giving

No matter whether the source is "helpful" comments made by others or put-downs made by her husband, accusations are like flaming arrows that pierce to the depths of a woman's being. The hurtful comments and disdainful looks feel like they're burning a hole right through her. I think accusation was the most painful part of my ordeal—more painful than the actual betrayal of adultery, more painful than the physical and emotional abuse.

And that's because I knew I hadn't done everything right. I tried to be the perfect wife. I did the notes in the lunch box; the smile, hug, and cold drink when he came through the door at the end of the day; the sexy nighties, clean house, clean clothes, and homecooked meals; the forgiving over and over. I worked hard at honoring him even when he wasn't honorable.

But I still didn't do everything right. I still wasn't the perfect wife. Sometimes it was because I couldn't figure out what the right thing was, and sometimes it was because I knew what the right thing was, but I couldn't get up the will to do it. So, every time those accusations would come, I would say, "Well, yes, I could have done better there." And I'd work harder at being a better wife because I had a dream. And the dream was a home filled with love, laughter, and happy, secure kids. I told myself that if only I could be all I should be, Jack would be all he should be, and my dreams would come true. (And isn't that what those accusations implied?) But it wasn't quite working out like that.

When, despite your best efforts, your dreams are dying before your very eyes, Satan will attack you through thoughts of false guilt and through the judgmental comments of others. People don't even have to say a thing. Their body language can hurl their opinions against you just as easily as their words can. They roll their eyes, they purse their lips, they shake their heads, they cross their arms, they deliberately avoid you. They may not be saying anything, but we know how they feel about us. The disapproval, the condescension, oozes out. You know you've been judged and found wanting. The eyes of flesh see the faults. The eyes of love see the needs.

One of Satan's names is *diabolos*, which means "one who falsely accuses." False accusations act like curses on your spirit. Cursing someone is the opposite of blessing her. A blessing brings life, hope, and purpose. A curse takes our strengths and makes them weaknesses. Cursing takes our weaknesses and cunningly exposes them, to shame us into compliance. Cursing is designed to rob us of power, dignity, and vitality. Curses must be dealt with carefully because they have tremendous potential to harm us.

Those Flaming Arrows

In Ephesians 6:16, Paul compared false accusations to flaming arrows. I think that's a great analogy because when I got hit by a judgmental comment, it felt like a burning in my soul. The kind of arrow Paul had in mind was first used by the Greeks. The Romans knew a good thing when they saw it, and they added it to their arrow arsenal. Flaming arrows were the greatest military terror of Paul's day. Soldiers would pour combustible fluids designed to explode on impact into the slender canes that formed the shaft of the arrow.

Once these arrows were filled to the brim, they were sealed and disguised to look like normal, minimally dangerous arrows. Only after impact, after a great fire had begun, could one know for certain whether or not these arrows had been equipped with the potential of fire and disaster.[3] Then, as the troops scrambled to put out the fire, the enemy would send arrow after arrow into the camp until the whole place was an inferno.

Notice the parallels. False accusations are often disguised to look minimally dangerous. "I only want to help." "I just want you to think about *your* part in all this." "We were talking the other day and we think you should . . ." The arrow is launched, and when it hits, the fiery poison spreads throughout your heart.

No wonder James 3:6 says, "The tongue is a fire . . . a world of wickedness set among our members, contaminating and depraving the whole body and setting on fire . . . the cycle of man's nature, being itself ignited by hell."

Flaming arrows weren't used in normal combat situations. If enemy soldiers were where the Romans could get to them easily, they used regular arrows. But if they were in a fortified place, a secure place, the flaming arrows were the weapon of choice. These arrows were designed to keep enemy soldiers so busy putting out fires that they left their walls unguarded, or better yet, were driven out of their encampment into the open, where they could be easily slaughtered.

Out of the Oven into the Frying Pan

When we've been falsely accused, the most natural thing to do is to try and defend ourselves. It's also one of the most counterproductive things we can do. We open ourselves up to greater vulnerability and waste a lot of energy if we try to defend ourselves by explaining why we aren't guilty of a false accusation. Now we're out of the oven into the frying pan. While we're out there defending ourselves, instead of the comfort we'd hoped for, we receive further wounding. So, we design a new "safe place" to shield our shame and nakedness. There are a variety of ways we "defend" ourselves.

- We might adopt the part our husbands want us to play, appearing hard and seductive.
- We might act as if we don't care that our husbands are doing such things, telling others the abuse isn't really abuse.
- We might become overly assertive, making sure that none of our rights are trampled on again.
- We might hide behind anger, because it's a great way to cover the fear inside.
- We might become defensive, immediately denying any wrongdoing on our part. We know how long it took us to convince ourselves that we weren't to blame for what's going on, and we're not about to let anyone try and put the blame back on us.

I've known women who have hidden behind laughter, chuckling in situations where the appropriate response would have been tears or anger. Sometimes we adopt several defense mechanisms, whipping them on and off as we think the situation demands.

Falling into the Ground and Dying

Let's think about seeds for a moment, because there's an important parallel between seeds and defense mechanisms. Seeds consist of three parts: (1) the embryo, (2) the food storage tissue (also called the endosperm), and (3) the seed coat. The seed coat covers the embryo and food storage tissue and protects them from injury, insects, and loss of water. Seed coats range from thin, delicate layers of tissue to thick, tough coverings.[4]

Without the seed coat, the food storage tissue and the embryo would be destroyed by the normal hazards of everyday life; but for the seed to bear fruit, the seed coat has to go.

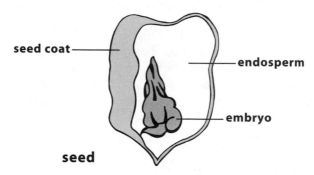

During germination, as the embryo absorbs and digests food from the endosperm, the lower part of the embryo forms a primary root that breaks through the seed coat and starts to grow into the soil. Then the upper part of the embryo develops a stem and leaves and pushes through the top of the seed coat toward the sun. For a while, the seed coat remains, but as the plant grows and all the endosperm is used up, the seed coat sloughs off. Now the plant is finally ready to begin bearing fruit.

Jesus compared us to seeds. He said, "Unless a grain of wheat falls into the earth and dies, it remains by itself alone. But if it dies, it produces many others and yields a rich harvest. Any one who loves his life loses it. But any one who hates his life in this world will keep it to life eternal" (John 12:24b–25a).

Jesus is talking about the principle of germination. Each of us has a tender embryo inside, a hidden person God has filled with potential. Each of us has an endosperm to help the embryo grow. Each of us also has a seed coat, something we use to "shield" our tender parts from the harshness of life. This protection is essential—without it, we would wither and die. But there are a couple of problems with defense mechanisms.

- You're not being you. Underneath that hard outer shell is a woman who's denying her real self to try and protect herself.
- The shield may make you such an uncomfortable person to be with that others will begin to form judgments about you that are true. Now you *are* a difficult person to live with. By trying to protect yourself, you have ended up proving the false accusations true. (Wasn't that their goal?)

Still, the protective outer shell is necessary until it's time to grow and bear fruit. Then it must come off. But you can't peel it off. To do so would be to expose your softness to the elements before you're ready. Instead, follow the principle of germination: The shell will naturally come off as the fruit within grows and bursts through it.

There will be some places that the shell comes off quickly and completely; but there are others where, for a time, it will remain stuck fast. These are your most tender spots (you know where they are).

In the beginning, when the flaming arrows come against your most fragile places, you'll have a tendency to whip out your old shield of defensiveness, overassertiveness, denial, anger, or whatever, to protect yourself, and it will seem as if you're hiding in the same old way. Don't despair. Instead, concentrate on the fruit growing within you, and those stuck places will take care of themselves.

Our Teflon-Coated Stainless Steel Shield

As the fruit comes forth and the old shell sloughs off, you'll find you still need protection from hurtful comments (they aren't going to go away).

Paul said the shield of faith is the only weapon that can quench the flaming arrows. The Roman shield was made out of wood, covered by many layers of leather. That means something had to die before a soldier could defend himself from the enemy's flaming arrows. A tree had to die, a cow had to die; and from their carcasses came a shield capable of keeping the soldier safe as he advanced in battle.

Something also had to die to defend us from the flaming arrows of false accusations—actually, Someone: Jesus. He took the false accusations for us. This is what He said to us: "The reproaches and abuses of those who reproached and abused you fell on Me" (Rom. 15:3b). As He hung on the cross, the crowd heaped shame and rejection upon Him.

"Failure!"

"So, you think you're king of the Jews, huh? Some king!"

"If you're such a great big god, why don't you save yourself?"

I used to think that Jesus didn't feel the shame of these insults and jeers, that as He hung there, He was thinking about heaven, not caring what people said to or about Him. But one day when I was trying to work through forgiving some false accusations, a phrase from Hebrews 12:2 came to mind: "[He] endured the cross, despising the shame . . ." (KJV). That means He felt it—He felt it and hated it. He didn't hate the rejecters or the shamers, but He experienced the full range of shame and rejection they were sending His way, and He despised it. But He ignored the shame and persevered in what He knew was the right thing to do.

Has your heart been pierced by other people's judgments of you? Jesus has been there before you. He's a high priest who knows what it's like to suffer shame, rejection, and false accusation. From His resurrected body arose a shield capable of keeping you safe enough to advance in battle. And this is the name of His shield: "There is therefore now no condemnation to them who are in Christ Jesus" (Rom. 8:1a, KJV, emphasis added).

But here's the catch. You can't pick up His shield until you've laid down yours by finally agreeing with God that there's nothing you can do to justify yourself. You can't justify yourself in the eyes of others; you can't even justify yourself in your own eyes. As long as you believe there's something you can do to prove to others that you're not the reason your husband is a sex addict, you will continue to experience condemnation when the false accusations that you are somehow to blame are hurled at you.

You can't pick up His shield until you've laid down yours by finally agreeing with God that there's nothing you can do to save your husband. You're not responsible for his salvation—God is. But as long as you believe you can save your husband, you will continue to experience condemnation when that false accusation is hurled at you.

When we lay down our shields by finally letting go of the responsibility to save ourselves and others, we can embrace with joy the truth that we are justified by grace—marvelous, free-flowing grace that comes to us apart from anything we can do. We don't earn this grace, it is a gift. But we cannot receive this gift until we finally acknowledge by faith that we are accepted unconditionally by the One who loves us and gave Himself for us.

Truly, faith is the only shield that can protect us from the flaming arrows of false accusations. If we try to cover ourselves with anything else, we're going to go up in flames.

CHAPTER 24

Help! I've Been Robbed

Sin then, is the breaking of the trust of another person.
One cannot sin in the abstract. Sin is not the failure to accomplish
a certain action. Sin is personal, and sin is relational.

(*Keith Intrater*[1])

God is kind, but He's not soft.

(*Eugene Peterson*[2])

How does a wife get past the fact that, through a series of extramarital romps, her husband has possibly exposed her to a sexually transmitted disease, maybe even AIDS? How does a mother pick up the shredded pieces of her heart when she discovers her husband left their precious five-year-old daughter locked in his truck in the middle of the red-light district while he went off and did his thing with another woman? How does a woman who sold out on her values by allowing her husband to bring other men and women into her marital bed, let go of the shame that hangs all over her like a cheap coat?

"I Can't" Is a Good Place to Start

In the Garden of Gethsemane, on that dark night between treachery and violence, while Jesus was waiting for His betrayer to turn Him over to the inquisition of small minds, He made no secret of His need. He didn't try to hide from the terror, and He didn't deny the pain.

215

He said to His disciples, "I'm so eaten up with grief that it's almost killing Me. I need My friends. Come and watch with Me."

Deeply troubled, He went a ways from them and threw Himself on the ground. Pressing His face into the very earth from which He'd created the beings He was getting ready to die for, He cried out, "Father, can't You come up with another way? I don't want to do this."

Pulling Himself to His feet, He went back to His friends for comfort, but Peter, James, and John were asleep.

"Wake up," He said, shaking Peter. "I need you tonight. And you need to pray because hard times are coming."

Sleepy eyes looked at Him. There was no comfort there.

Prostrate with grief, Jesus stumbled away and prayed again, saying over and over, "Daddy, You can do anything! Take this cup from Me. Don't make Me drink it. But I will, if that's what You want Me to do."

He returned again and found His friends sleeping.

"Why are you sleeping?" He cried.

"We don't know what to say, Jesus," the three friends mumbled, looking at Him through heavy eyes. "We'll try harder to stay awake."

A third time Jesus went off and prayed.

"I don't want to do this, Daddy. I really don't want to do this. Yet, not what I will, but what You will."

In His agony, rivers of blood flowed from Him, soaking the ground where He lay. And while His friends slept, the angels came and ministered to Him. (See Matt. 26:38–46; Mark 14:32–42; Luke 22:39–46.)

Forgiveness Is the Key

Jesus is our model for how to forgive. He forgave perfectly—He forgave the way the Father forgives. After all, Jesus is the Father come down from heaven to show us how to live our lives. So, what can a woman who has had her heart and home broken by pornography learn about forgiveness from the story of what transpired in the Garden of Gethsemane?

Jesus started by saying, "I don't want to." Adultery is treachery. Abuse is devastating. Watching your children wither and die before your eyes ravages you. If you think you can easily forgive such travesties, you are sadly mistaken. So, "I can't" is a good place to start.

The gut-wrenching struggle Jesus went through that night was just the jump-ing-off place for forgiveness. He had not yet bought our forgiveness; He had only agreed to pay the price for it. It takes a serious internal struggle and a lot of bloodletting to come to the place where you're willing to even consider the possibility of forgiving your husband for the pain he brought into your home through his use of pornography. The decision to forgive is only the beginning of a process. It is simply your agreement to examine what this whole betrayal has cost you.

In order to complete our forgiveness, Jesus still had to endure the agony of the cross, and then He had to experience three days in hell. Forgiveness is tough. It is a violent wrench of body, soul, and spirit. Considering the possibility of forgive-ness is excruciating, but the real agony doesn't begin until you start feeling what this horror show has cost you. That's when you begin to feel false accusations burning you alive; that's when you begin to feel the cruel spikes of treachery piercing through your strength as they are pounded in by repeated betrayal; that's when you feel your heart bursting into a million pieces of shattered dreams.

Some people get confused about this. They think the pain should end as soon as you've agreed to forgive. Forgiveness is not a cheap trinket that we put on as a spiritual decoration. Forgiveness costs, and it costs plenty. It cost Jesus everything He had; and should you choose to forgive your husband, it will cost you every-thing you have, too.

Forgiveness is lonely. Although Jesus asked His friends for support, they didn't really understand what He was going through, so no one was able to be of real comfort to Him. He struggled alone, on His face, before His Father. That's the way it is when we're struggling to be forgivers. No one really understands the depth of our pain. Not our best friend. Not our pastor. Not our mother. And certainly not the one who wounded us. We feel lonely, cut off from the comfort we so desperately long for.

What a comfort to know that we have a heavenly Father who is able to under-stand and sympathize with our weaknesses and infirmities because He spent His own time on His face, alone, as He struggled to choose to forgive us. Because of this, we can fearlessly and confidently and boldly draw near to the throne of grace so we can find the grace to get past the pain (Heb. 4:15,16).

Jesus was free to choose the process of forgiveness. There are some people who demand that we become forgivers. They quote Scripture to us: "Forgive us our trespasses as we forgive those who've trespassed against us," and either hint or outright say that we risk hellfire and damnation if we withhold forgiveness from our wayward spouses. They work on our feelings of guilt and worthlessness by telling us that only the hardness of our own hearts keeps us from letting go of the debt that's been accumulated against us.

That's an outrage. God did not require Jesus to forgive us. It was something Jesus freely chose to do because He considered the agony of being separated from us more ferocious than the agony of dying on the cross and enduring three days in hell so that He could be reunited with us. Jesus was not obligated to forgive us. Our forgiveness is a gift of His love.

Love does not obligate. If you feel obligated to forgive, it's not forgiveness and it's certainly not love. There are a number of reasons why forgiveness is a good choice to make, but to make it an obligation is to destroy its power and beauty. To reduce forgiveness to a mere obligation is to reduce the battering of Christ at His trial to a mere inconvenience. To reduce forgiveness to a duty is to walk by the writhing Form on the cross and sneer in disdainful condescension. To reduce forgiveness to an act we "ought" to do is to make the heartbroken cry of abandonment—"My God, My God, why hast Thou forsaken Me?"—a mere whimper of divine love.

Forgiveness is a free-flowing generosity of the spirit. Forgiveness is ferocious love dripping with freshly spilled blood. Forgiveness is a heartbreaking choice to love the sinner more than you hate the sin.

What Forgiveness Isn't

So, what are we choosing to do? Let's start by looking at what forgiveness isn't.

⌐ Forgiveness Isn't Putting a Positive Spin on Things

In spite of Jesus' admonitions to weep with those who weep, the church has frequently been quick to tell us why we shouldn't be weeping.

"God works all things together for good," the devastated are told.

"In everything give thanks for this is the will of God for you," the shattered are advised.

"God is more interested in your attitude than He is in what you're going through," the ravaged are admonished.

Jesus didn't practice spin control in Gethsemane. He told Himself the truth about the awfulness of what our sin was going to cost Him. If a wife is going to be able to forgive her husband for his infidelities, she will have to tell herself the awful truth about what his sin has cost her.

True, God is a redeeming God. He does bring good out of evil. But He never calls evil *good* simply because there will be a redemption. Before He gives back the years the locusts have eaten, we must first face the horror of what those ransacking buggers have consumed. To focus on the redemption before fully examining the loss is to deprive the redemption of its power to thrill. Only when we've fully felt the loss can we revel in the gain.

Forgiveness Isn't Reconciliation

When Christ died on the cross for our sins, He opened up the possibility of reconciliation, but He required something from us first—repentance. Our forgiveness is based on His unconditional love, but our reconciliation is based on our unconditional agreement that we have wronged Him, and wronged Him badly.

Forgiving your husband for the wreckage he has made of your home through his use of pornography and the adulterous liaisons that resulted from it doesn't mean that you are *required* to reconcile with him. Forgiveness opens up the *possibility* of reconciliation, but whether or not that reconciliation happens depends on your husband's willingness to repent for breaking his wedding vows. Repentence opens the way for him to be totally freed from the destructive behaviors that have bound him by restoring him to a proper relationship with God (see 1 John 1:9).

What Forgiveness Is

If we're going to be forgivers, we have to know what forgiveness is.

* Forgiveness Is About Letting Go of the Results

One of the hardest parts of forgiveness is allowing the other person to make his own choices, even if those choices are going to destroy the marriage. This is where forgiveness often fails because we begin to recognize how costly this whole thing will be. Forgiveness costs us everything, because in forgiveness, we let go of the right to make things work out the way we so desperately want them to. We accept that there may be no reconciliation because we cannot make the other person choose the behavior that will bring about the reconciliation.

In order for the marriage to be reconciled, your husband must understand that he has wronged the marriage, himself, God, and you. You cannot force your husband come to this understanding. That is a choice he has to make.

Forgiveness Is About Repentance

According to the law of covenant, if your husband has committed adultery, he has brought curses upon his head by breaking the vows he made to you before

God and "these witnesses." In the Old Testament, death was the penalty for adultery. We no longer stone wayward spouses, but we do divorce them, resulting in the death of the marriage. Although your husband can choose to plead "not guilty," he will have to be convicted of the crimes he has committed against the marriage before you can release him from the penalty he deserves.(That's because there can be no mercy without judgment.)

In order for him to position himself to receive mercy, your husband will have to come to grips with how destructive his behavior has been. Theologically, we call that repentance. Repentance is not groveling. It is expressing deep regret over what we've done and making firm resolves to live more wisely in the future. You can't reconcile your marriage if your husband is unwilling to repent of the things he did to destroy it. To do so, would negate the power of forgiveness to save by making us come face-to-face with who we are and what we've done. Although your heart may long for reconciliation, if you place your desire to be in relationship with him before concern for his eternal soul, you will end up enabling him to continue in his sin.

Just as forgiveness isn't cheap, repentance isn't cheap. Repentance isn't just being sorry we got caught. Repentance is grieving over the fact that we did it in the first place. Repentance is learning from our mistakes. Repentance is walking a mile in the shoes of the one we've wounded. Repentance demands that we lie for a time in the bed we have made. In real repentance, we *feel* the pain we have caused others and ourselves. If we haven't felt the wounding we've caused, we can't possibly appreciate the forgiveness we're offered.

Repentance may come quickly, but most often, it ripens slowly. Before real repentance comes, there will probably be a lot of self-pity that tries to mask itself as repentance. This false repentance simply adds to the load of shame, since in it we are always seeing ourselves as bad. This conception contributes to feelings of victimization, and victims feel they have no power to change. False repentance can become an unending cycle of self-flagellation.

False repentance can also be a clever way to manipulate others. Watching someone "feel bad" about himself makes most people feel uncomfortable, so sometimes they rush in to reassure the repenter that what he did was really not that awful.

"Lots of guys have done the same thing."

"Well, at least you didn't rape, kill, incest [fill in the blank] anyone."

"Look, you're really a good guy in all these other areas."

Such "comfort" destroys the purpose of repentance, which is to lead us to reconcile with the one we have offended by allowing us to see and feel how our actions have caused a breech in the relationship. When we have truly repented, we have lost our taste for the grievous thing we have done because we've eaten of the vile mess we've made of our lives.

Some people may put not-so-subtle pressure on the wife to reconcile with her husband. "Can't you see that he's sincere?" they ask. "A good Christian is required to forgive 70 times seven," they tell her.

But she's lived with him a long time and she's seen this act over and over. In her spirit, the wife senses that it's all theatrics. She feels fairly certain that if she reconciles, he will continue with his behavior, just as he has in the past, once the crisis was over.

Well-intentioned people who attempt to comfort the grieving couple by covering over their pain can actually destroy the possibility of reconciliation by letting the husband off the hook prematurely and forcing the wife to accept what she knows is incomplete repentance. Because the husband has been relieved of dealing with the root causes of his addiction, he will return to his old habits. This adds to the wife's sense of outrage and betrayal. The best way others can encourage forgiveness and reconciliation is to allow the offender to fully feel his offense, and allow the offended to fully grieve her loss. The offended wife knows when her husband's repentance has ripened—she can feel it in her spirit.

Forgiveness Means Risking Additional Pain by Doing What You Can to Mend Your Part of the Breech

God was the innocent party in the breech that led to our separation from Him. Yet, from the beginning of our sin against Him, He devised a plan whereby He would offer Himself to mend the breech. In the fullness of time, He risked and experienced additional insults to His love by coming to earth to fulfill that plan. He was despised and rejected of men for all His efforts at reconciliation. Yet, our rejection did not stop Him from loving us. His love for us is a reflection of His divine character. He is steadfast and stubborn in it.

Although the wife is the innocent party in the breech that pornography has caused in her marriage, if she has a heart to love, she will risk additional rejection by keeping open the possibility of reconciliation. Love is greater than rejection. That doesn't mean love is not wounded by rejection. It means that love overcomes rejection to once more stand in the breech, by offering an open hand to the one who has sinned against us.

Forgiveness Means Accepting That You Have Been Robbed

The hardest part of forgiveness is accepting the loss of something precious to you. I once heard someone say that forgiveness was *consenting to a loss*. For someone who has struggled with proper boundaries, this teaching could be disastrous. *Consenting to a loss* could imply that you are giving permission for the loss. It almost suggests that you are required to consent to future losses(We are not to consent to evil; we are to overcome evil.)

I am more comfortable saying that forgiveness is accepting that you have sustained a loss. To me, there is a world of difference. Accepting that a loss has occurred doesn't set you up to be robbed in the future. It simply recognizes what has happened without implying that you agreed to allow it to happen.

❦ Forgiveness Means Presenting the Case You Have Against Your Offender

In order to accept your loss, you have to know what it is. That necessitates an itemization of the crimes committed. That calls for a detailed examination of the charges. Does that sound vindictive? It's not. Throughout the Old Testament, God made it clear what He had against His wife, Israel. He used the prophets to list her crimes in vivid color. And the number one crime He charged her with was adultery.

Read Ezekiel 23, Jeremiah 4, and the book of Hosea. All contain a detailed listing in raw language of the ways Israel had violated her covenant with God. God clearly spelled out what He had against His wife, not to shame her into compliance, but to provoke her to remember the love she once had for Him. He refused to abandon her without giving her the opportunity to face the fact that she had first abandoned Him.

Just as God was honest with His spouse about how she had broken their covenant, so a wife will have to be honest with her husband about how he has broken his marriage vows. This is much bigger than simply saying, "You committed adultery." Presenting the case you have against your husband is about revealing your sufferings. You lay bare the pain of his abandonment. You unmask the agony of his betrayal. You refuse to hide the torment of his cruelty.

You become tremendously vulnerable when you expose your anguish to someone who may not care at all that he has hurt you. But this vulnerability is absolutely essential for forgiveness, and it is crucial for reconciliation. I constantly marvel when I think about how Jesus revealed His sufferings on the cross. He cried out, "I thirst!" He openly agonized: "My God, My God, why hast Thou forsaken Me?" We might be tempted to say about our unfaithful husbands, "I won't give him the satisfaction of knowing how much he hurt me." But that's not what Jesus did. He expressed His pain to the very ones who caused it. If you're going to forgive your husband, you will have to find the courage to do the same thing.

Presenting your case is not just about revealing your sufferings. The main purpose behind this exercise is to confront your husband with the truth of his choices. He has lived a long time lying to himself about what he has done. He cannot be healed until he tells himself the truth about who he is and how he's behaved. Because of this, presenting your case is a redemptive act. The hope is that your humility will bring him to his senses, because in your brokenness, you have confronted him with the truth of his brokenness.

Forgiving Is Grieving the Loss

Forgiveness Is Not Tidy

Some people want forgiveness to be surgical, as if you could go in and neatly excise the pain and then quickly sew up the wound. But if your forgiveness is surgical, it will also be sterile. The sterilizing process kills every living thing—the good with the bad. If you forgive surgically, you render the marriage barren. If your forgiveness is sterile, you make impotent the passion behind your love.

Forgiveness is a great gushing wound with raw, suppurating edges of ragged pain. It has to be that way to get past the first stage of grief, which is denial. In denial, we are numb to the pain we have experienced. Although our heads may tell us a trauma has occurred, the feelings of that trauma have not registered in our souls, so we are numb. "It's not hot, and I'm not here," we tell ourselves. Leprosy is a disease of numbness. Because the leper cannot feel, he is unaware that he is exposing his body to peril. As a consequence, the leper is continually traumatizing himself.

God compares sin to leprosy. The danger of sin is that we become numb to the trauma that is occurring in our souls. In addition to losing our ability to know that we're being hurt, when we're "past feeling," we can even open ourselves to the possibility of becoming involved in sexual sin of our own (see Eph. 4:19).

Waking Up Is Hard to Do

Denial produces numbness; getting past denial is a lot like waking up a limb that has become numb through frostbite. When your limb is experiencing frostbite, you are unaware of the damage that is occurring because you simply cannot feel it. But if you are going to save the limb, you have to restore circulation, and when the blood begins to breathe life into the dying limb, the first feeling you experience is pain—excruciating, gut-wrenching pain. The degree of pain you feel as your emotional numbness wears off is directly proportional to the length of time you have stuffed that pain. Do not be afraid of the pain—it is a sign that the blood of life is stirring in your soul.

Waking Up Means You Put on Your Mourning Clothes

Mourning is coming to terms with a loss by experiencing the full range of emotions associated with it. Again, God's relationship with Israel is a good example of appropriate emotions for the sin of adultery. If you read through the prophets, you will find God expressing sadness, jealousy, rage, desire, hope, resignation, yearning, bargaining, and a whole host of other emotions as He seeks to restore His wayward wife.

Grieving over the losses pornography has brought into your home is much like peeling an onion: You do it one layer at a time and you cry a lot. You may cry until your eyes swell shut and your bones ache. You will think you are doing okay one day, only to be completely devastated the next.

It's like having your house burn down. You know the major losses right away—the clothes, the refrigerator, the stove, your bed. But in the days and weeks to come, you suddenly remember that scrapbook filled with love letters or the memento from your grandmother. These are the things that can't be replaced. These losses are the most devastating.

Similarly, when your marriage has been devastated by porn, you know your immediate losses—the sanctity of your marriage bed, the ability to trust, the blow to your pride. But then you see a father reading to his children or a couple looking at each other with quiet enjoyment, or you watch a family plan a happy holiday, and the sudden recognition that you have lost more than you realized, makes you catch a ragged breath of pain.

Waking Up Means You Learn When to Get Angry and How Angry to Get

1 Peter 3:4 says that wives are to have meek spirits. *Meekness* comes from the Greek word *prautēs*. Aristotle said this about *prautēs*: "*Prautēs* is the middle course in being angry, standing between two extremes, getting angry without reason, and not getting angry at all. Therefore, *prautēs* is getting angry at the right time, in the right measure, and for the right reason."[3]

The thought that it is okay to be angry may be new and frightening to you. Perhaps you learned it wasn't "nice" to be angry. Perhaps you have always told yourself you must pretend that "it doesn't really matter." If so, you may be finding that your relationship lacks honesty and true intimacy. Proper expression of anger opens the door for true intimacy. It helps us to be honest with ourselves and with each other about the depth of our pain.

Be careful, however, that when you express your anger, you direct it toward the destructive behavior. Meekness is strength under control. You have to remember that your issue is with the choices your husband made. It is all right to tell him that he's made bad choices, but raising up in self-righteous indignation to tell him he is a bad person is not meekness—it's vindictiveness. If you use your anger as an excuse to destroy your husband, you will not be pursuing forgiveness; you will be marinating in the poison of bitterness.

When expressing anger, stay away from "you" statements such as "You make me so angry." That kind of thinking passes the responsibility for the anger to the other person. Instead, use "I" statements to show ownership of your anger—for example, "*I* feel angry when you do that" (be explicit about what "that" is). You can't let go of what you don't own. I was amazed at how quickly my anger dissipated when I took ownership of it by saying, "I am feeling angry about this."

Meekness isn't for cowards. In meekness, we know what is a big deal and what isn't. When something isn't a big deal, the meek have the maturity to overlook offenses. When something is a big deal, the meek feel the full rage of God toward the sin while simultaneously experiencing God's heart of reconciliation toward the sinner. Meekness is always a choice, never a compulsion; and its motivation is always justice and mercy, not fear and guilt.

Who Needs Forgiveness?

If we're going to be forgivers, we have to know who needs forgiveness.

We Are First in Line

In order to forgive those who have hurt us, we have to know that we ourselves have been forgiven. Knowing that we've been forgiven presupposes that we know that we need forgiveness. We begin to embrace the fact that we are imperfect beings with all the frailties and weaknesses common to humanity. We accept that we have made wrong decisions and have done foolish things. We begin to trust that God loves us anyway. We begin to see that the key to our survival is not the love and approval of others, but the love and approval of God.

We find it in our hearts to forgive ourselves for not being "perfect" enough to make our marriages work the way we wanted them to. We find it in our hearts to forgive ourselves for marrying our husbands in the first place. That alone will cause a few self-flagellation sessions. We need to be able to forgive ourselves for choosing as fathers to our children, men who would devastate them with their selfishness.

We Need to Let Go of Our Anger Toward God

Many of us are terrified to admit that we are ferociously angry with God. But being angry with God is actually an act of faith. Being angry with God means we believe He is who He says He is. God says He is love, and yet He has allowed us to experience hate. God says He is good, and yet He has allowed us to experience evil. God says He is all-powerful, and yet He has allowed us to experience powerlessness. So we're confused.

This confusion is repeated throughout the book of Psalms. David repeatedly says, "I don't get it, God. How could You do this to me?" When things aren't turning out according to our understanding of who God is, it feels as if God has lost control of the universe. That makes us fearful, and fear is at the root of most anger.

God is the only One big enough to receive the full fury of our anger. He invites us to come to Him with the confusion and despair. He invites us to use our disappointment in Him as a means of coming to know Him in a deeper way. This step is crucial. We are unable to love those who have offended us until we've wrestled through our feelings of anger, betrayal, and fear with the Lord.

We Need to Forgive Those Who Have Hurt Us

Whether it's the other women in your husband's life, or those who wounded you through their self-righteous posturing and bad advice, you'll need to forgive them before you'll be able to grow beyond your pain. 1 Peter 2:15 says they are only ignorant and foolish people. We need to let go of our "right" to hate them.

It helped me to realize that often people judged me as a way to protect themselves from experiencing the same pain. If we think we have figured out why someone deserves his or her suffering, we can make a formula for ourselves so that we won't have to experience the same pain. We simply tell ourselves that we will never do the things we are sure they are guilty of. Thus, we comfort ourselves by the lie that we can control other people's ability to hurt us. Of course, those of us who have been hurt know this is not true.

We Need to Forgive Our Husbands

After we have gone through the exercise of forgiving ourselves, forgiving God, and forgiving those who have hurt us, we gain a different perspective. We begin to be able to see our husbands as God sees them. We begin to learn how to separate them from the things they have done. As we do, we are able to mourn for their fears and their losses. Though we in no way excuse their behavior, we do feel grief over their self-inflicted wounds. We begin to yearn for them to be restored to wholeness. Now, with our boundaries firmly in place, we can extend forgiveness to them out of hearts that wish them well.

You may find some of these observations on forgiveness disturbing. I certainly did. They didn't fit with some of the theology I had been taught. But they certainly fit with what Scripture says about how God calls us back into a love relationship with Himself. By making forgiveness the act of wimps, we have pared the claws of the Lion of the Tribe of Judah.[4] God is ferocious in His love for us. We dare be no less ferocious in our love for our husbands.

Clearing Out the Rubble to Make Room for the Joy

If all must be right with the world before I may have a fling with joy, I shall be somber forever.

(*Lewis Smedes*)

May the God of your hope so fill you with all joy and peace in believing—through the experience of your faith—that by the power of the Holy Spirit you may abound and be overflowing, bubbling over, with hope.

[*Romans 15:13*]

Forgiveness is a long process of emptying ourselves of the anger, hate, sorrow, disappointment, and fear associated with our grief. Sometimes it feels like a never-ending ride on a merry-go-round of pain. We go down as we feel the anguish. As we come to grips with the loss, we go up. As we round a familiar bend, we congratulate ourselves for moving ahead. Then, out of nowhere, we're lassoed by an unexpected grief, and before we know it, we're flat on our backs in despair.

At such times, it is common to feel bewildered that the pain still has enough strength to overwhelm us. It is also common to feel a bit disappointed in ourselves—we were hoping to be further along in our recovery. It is best to be gentle with ourselves at these times.

Grieving takes a long time. And the greater the loss, the longer it takes us to empty ourselves of the pain. Eventually, the merry-go-round slows down a bit.

There is more time between the ups and downs. We don't get quite so dizzy. We enjoy the ride more. We are feeling better, but there is something missing.

As I began to work through my own process of forgiveness, I found that the churning in my gut had stopped. I found that the heaviness of the grief became more bearable and the hot burning of the shame began to cool. But instead of the bubbling up of joy that I expected, I felt nothing but flatness. It was as if the life had been sucked out of me and my soul had imploded on itself. And I didn't know what to do about it.

There are two parts to forgiveness. The first part is about letting go of the loss. The second part is about learning to fill up the void the loss created. Once we have moved past the outrage, we start to feel the emptiness. Nothing will replace the loss—it's gone forever. And that's the problem, because now we are barren.

We've been cleaned out. It's as if someone came into our home and removed every stick of furniture and every piece of clothing and then cleaned out the cupboards and refrigerator, too. We can forgive them all day long, but we still have nothing to wear, no place to sit or sleep, and nothing to eat.

Getting Paid Back

One day, as I was struggling to make sense of my barrenness, the Lord reminded me of two verses that I had never before put together. First, He brought to mind Romans 12:19: "Beloved, never avenge yourselves, but leave the way open for God's wrath; for it is written, Vengeance is Mine, I will repay, says the Lord."

I thought about that for a while. Much earlier, I had let go of my right to revenge, giving it to the Lord in agonizing prayer. But I had only concentrated on the "Vengeance is Mine" part of that verse. I hadn't thought much about the "I will repay, says the Lord," other than to think that it meant I was to let go of revenge because God was the One who was going to deal with the people who had hurt me and my children.

But I began to see the "I will repay" in a different light when the Lord brought to mind 2 Corinthians 8:9: "For you are coming progressively to be acquainted with and to recognize more strongly and clearly the grace of our Lord Jesus Christ—His kindness, His gracious generosity, His undeserved favor and spiritual blessing; in that though He was so very rich, yet for your sakes He became so very poor, in order that by His poverty you might become enriched—abundantly supplied."

I began to think about how even if I had retained my right to revenge, no one could ever pay me back for what I'd lost. Even if someone determined to work the rest of his life to make things up to our family, our children were grown and no one could ever give them a childhood free of the fears and shame that came from Jack's addiction to pornography. For myself, I had lived with the abuse for 20 years and my youth was gone, along with my hopes of creating a home where love and laughter mingled with the normal tears and frustrations of life. I could have the future, but no one could give me back what I'd lost in the past.

Yet, "though He was so very rich, yet for your sakes He became so very poor, in order that by His poverty you might become enriched—abundantly supplied." I began to see that repayment is a two-edged sword. The Lord deals with the robber, but He also pays back the robbed. He is willing to dip into His great treasury and beggar Himself so that we don't suffer unrequited loss.

I went out behind the barn and found some nice rocks and made myself an altar, and I laid on that altar all the things I'd lost. My home. My youth. My ability to trust. My reputation. My sexuality. Talents and abilities that had gone undeveloped because I was spending so much energy just surviving. The holidays and birthdays that had had the joy sucked out of them by the selfishness of lust, who knows not how to give. My children's losses were the hardest to put on the altar. I wept a long time as I laid them down. I named them all out loud—one by one.

Then I told the Lord that all these things belonged to Him. They never had really belonged to me anyway. They were all just possible gifts. It seemed like a travesty to return the boxes empty, but empty was all I had to give.

"These are all the things that were stolen from me," I told Him. "They all belong to You now. I give up my right to have anyone pay me back. I know that those who've hurt me are utterly incapable of it anyway. I know that You are able to pay me back, if that's what You know is best. If You should choose to give any of these things back to me, I will accept Your gift with a grateful heart. If You should choose not to give any of these things back to me, I will accept Your no with a trusting heart. I know that You are all I really need."

After that, I felt so much better. And every now and then, something would happen, and the Lord would whisper, *Payback!* For example, the gossip that destroyed my reputation had deeply wounded me. I felt like everyone knew all the sordid details of my life and had made a prejudgment of me.

Shortly after I had laid everything I'd lost on the altar, a woman whom I'd only met briefly came up to my daughter and said, "I've always admired your mother." Although this woman had known my daughter for years through mutual time at a Christian camp, I'd spent only a few minutes in conversation with her before that time. How had she formed a good opinion of me? I don't know, but when my daughter related the incident to me, it was as if God were saying, "See, I can pay you back for the vicious things that have been said about you."

Even so, some of the things that left the greatest holes in my heart are still empty boxes on the altar. Sometimes, when I see them there, the sacrifices seem to rise up with a life of their own and try to run off. If I don't put them back quickly, my heart loses its peace and my spirit loses its gratitude.

Making Room for the Joy

When we find ways to cherish ourselves in the midst of the pain, we make room for joy. We look for the gifts amid the disappointments; we find the laughter amid the tears. I was slow to catch on to this, but I'm getting quite good at it now. And I get a lot of practice, because healing from an addiction to pornography is painfully slow. It's one-and-a-half steps forward and one step back.

When the inevitable step backward comes and things seem to be out of control, I ask myself, "What can I do to cherish myself?"

In deciding what to do, I have a few criteria. It has to be something that is edifying—self-destructive behavior such as uncontrolled eating, spending more money than I can afford, or relying on mood-altering substances is not allowed. It also has to be something I can do by myself for myself. If I am asking someone else to be responsible for comforting me, I am placing an unbearable burden on him or her. This doesn't mean I can't call a friend. It is a wonderful thing to have friends comfort you, but no one is responsible for my happiness. Happiness is a gift I give myself. Finally, it needs to be something I can do right away with a minimum of fuss and fanfare.

Here are some of my favorite things.
- I sip a cup of tea on the porch swing.
- I take a bubble bath by candlelight.
- I go for a massage.
- I talk with a friend.
- I blow bubbles.
- I take myself out to lunch.
- I put on one of my favorite tapes and sing my heart out.
- I wrap myself in a blanket, climb to the top of a hill, and watch the stars fall.
- I watch one of my favorite British comedies.

On days when the sadness is overwhelming, I cry as much as I need to and then, because I've found that laughter really is the best medicine, I pull out my *Far Side* collection and laugh until tears of joy begin to fall.

When things get really crazy, instead of staying and toughing it out like I used to, I have healing places I go so I can regroup. One place is a quiet valley just down the road. I go there frequently. My favorite place is a beautiful lake that takes a little over an hour to get to. I save it for the times when I really need healing.

And I have a special friend. His name is Woopy. He's kind of a surprise to me. I never thought I'd have a teddy bear at age 44; I certainly never had one as a child. But there he was, sitting on the shelf in the gift shop with a sign under him that said, "Hold Me." I laughed and picked him up, thinking my girlfriend and I could have a good chuckle. But the joke was on me.

As soon as I picked him up, his arms wrapped around my neck and his legs wrapped around my chest. And I started sobbing, right there in the gift shop.

"I have to have this bear," I said, leaving a hastily scribbled check with the cashier.

Woopy and I have been together ever since. I don't know if he holds me or I hold him. Maybe we just hold each other. But he is there when I need to cry, and I find him so comforting.

Letting Go

Forgiveness means "to let go." It means making courageous choices to rise above our pain. We do that by taking positive action rather than passively saying, "Oh, well."

I leave you with this. I don't know who wrote it, but it was given to me about four years ago. I had been feeling the Lord telling me to "let go," but I didn't know what that meant.

"I don't have a picture for it, Lord," I said. "I can't just pretend I don't care because I do. You'll have to explain it to me."

The next day, I went to see my doctor as part of follow-up care for an automobile accident I'd been in. While I was waiting for my appointment, the receptionist said, "I just have a feeling I'm supposed to give this to you." And she handed me a plain piece of paper with the following written on it:

LET GO . . .

To "let go" does not mean to stop caring; it means I can't do it for someone else.

To "let go" is not to cut myself off; it's the realization that I can't control another.

To "let go" is not to enable, but to allow learning from natural consequences.

To "let go" is to admit powerlessness, which means the outcome is not in my hands.

To "let go" is not to try and change or blame another; it's to make the best of myself.

To "let go" is not to fix, but to be supportive.
To "let go" is not to care for, but to care about.
To "let go" is not to judge, but to let another be a human being.
To "let go" is not to be in the middle arranging all the outcomes, but to allow others to effect their own destinies.
To "let go" is not to be protective; it's to permit another to face reality.
To "let go" is not to deny, but to accept.
To "let go" is not to nag, scold, or argue, but instead to search out my own shortcomings and correct them.
To "let go" is not to adjust everything to my desires, but to take each day as it comes and cherish myself in it.
To "let go" is not to criticize and regulate anybody, but to try to become what I dream I can be.
To "let go" is not to regret the past, but to grow and live for the future.
To "let go" is to fear less and love more.
To "let go" is to let God.[2]

Once again, as He had so many years before, the Lord had come with a rainbow in the night. Once again, as He had in the beginning of this adventure, the Lord was assuring me He was my Immanuel. Once again, as He had so often when I stumbled in the darkness, the Lord was showing me the way. What more do I need?

Pushing Past the Pain

We know that the whole creation has been moaning together in the pains of labor until now.

[Romans 8:22]

I am prepared for battle when my desire to love is simply stronger (even by one molecule) than my desire to snuff out the flame of mercy that God has graciously intruded into my heart. I am prepared for battle, if I cannot do anything but go.

(Dan Allender and Tremper Longman III¹)

I n several places in this book, I've written about how going through the process of healing is similar to what a woman goes through in labor. I've attended many births, and one thing I've noticed is that when a woman is ready to deliver, she often pushes up to the point at which she feels pain and then she stops. It just hurts too much to go on. The pain is real, but stopping keeps the baby from coming.

I think a woman in a marriage that's been damaged by pornography tends to do the same thing. The first pain she encounters is the pain of having to accept what's happening. It's easy for her to stop at that point and go into denial. The second pain she encounters is the pain of being misunderstood and judged, and it's easy for her to stop and become hard and defensive. The third pain she encounters is the pain of working through to forgiveness. She can stay here and become bitter—it hurts too much to go on. Stretching our hearts enough to come to terms with the betrayal can be excruciating. But stopping the work keeps the healing from coming.

When I'm serving as a midwife, I help the woman in labor to get into a position that is going to be easier on the perineum, use massage, remind her to stay open, and keep saying, "Push past the pain." I ask her to visualize her baby and keep focused on the place outside herself where the baby is going. These tools help the woman to overcome her natural tendency to stop pushing.

By sharing my own labor with my husband's addiction, I hope I've helped women get into a position that will make things a bit easier on their hearts. I hope I've helped them find comfort measures and encouraged them to keep open to the direction of the Lord. Women in this situation need to visualize what God is going to bring forth and keep focused on the place outside their present pain where the healing will come. My hope is that these tools will help other women in situations like mine overcome their natural tendencies to give up.

Job's Comforters

In my own labor with my husband's sexual addiction, there were so many times when I was tempted to give up because the pain was just so overwhelming. A large part of this pain came from not being able to find real help. In fact, I found that much of the advice actually created behavior problems because it either denied me the right to be upset about what was going on or told me that loving my husband was a sign there was something wrong with me.

A recent survey by Promise Keepers of those who attend their conferences revealed that more than 50 percent of the men who attend a Promise Keepers event have been exposed to pornography within the week before that event. This fact only demonstrates how pervasive the problem is within the Christian world.

The good news is, we have the Answer. There is hope. The church that can offer this life-giving message will find sufferers pounding down its door. Truly, the fields are white unto harvest. Now is the time for laborers to get the training they need so they don't break the bruised reed or quench the smoking flax.

So, How Are Things Going?

To answer that question, I return to the introduction and my experience going for the AIDS test. That day was the most hopeless day of my life. I sat in my car in my driveway for interminable minutes, awash with the reality of what having to go for this test meant. Everything was useless, I told myself. My life was a waste. Nothing I had done amounted to anything. In spite of my best efforts, circumstances beyond my control had robbed me of the thing I wanted most—a happy home. My children had been robbed and I couldn't stop the robber. Nothing mattered. Nothing at all.

As I sat there, arguing with myself about going, the mailman pulled up.

"Might as well get the mail. At least it delays the departure for a few minutes," I said.

In the mail was a letter from a writing school. I had always wanted to be a writer, but except for some short stories that I had written when I was a child (everyone was tall, slim, and good-looking), collaborating on a book about childbirth, and putting together a family cookbook, I had never penned anything but college research papers. Several months earlier, I had subscribed to a writing magazine and discovered a correspondence course that promised to teach me how to write. When I inquired about it, they sent me a diagnostic test to see what my writing skills were. The test looked at five areas of writing: screenplay, poetry, nonfiction, fiction, and newswriting. I had sent it back about six weeks earlier and had promptly forgotten about it.

Now, here in my mailbox, were the results. I tore open the envelope.

"You have the ability to write in all five genres. This is very unusual," the evaluation read. The letter went on to say some amazing things about my writing potential.

"I bet they say that to all the girls," I said.

Then, the Lord impressed this on me.

I'm going to use what you're going through right now and I'm going to use it in writing. I want you to write a book about what pornography has done to your marriage.

Shaking all over, I began to sob. Maybe the suffering wouldn't be a waste after all. Maybe there would be a redemption.

Jamming the letter in my purse, I roared out of the driveway to face the test. As I sat in that community health clinic terrified of what was to come, I kept fingering the letter, remembering that there was a reason to go on. When I came home, I immediately enrolled in the course.

Almost exactly five years to the day when I had gone for that AIDS test, Jack and I sat at the breakfast table. It was not a happy morning. In recent months, the children had been expressing their pain, and though Jack had been sexually sober for almost three years, he hadn't come to terms with what had happened in our home. He couldn't understand or feel what the children were going through. He was still telling himself, "What I did was personal. It didn't have any effect on anyone else." He spent a lot of time feeling sorry for himself that anyone would

be upset with him. This particular morning, he descended into the silent funk he
had spent most of our married life in.

*I don't know how much more of this I can take, Lord. When is the healing ever going
to come?* I thought.

Before me sat the edited copy of the first part of this manuscript. Gwen Ellis,
then managing editor for Focus on the Family book publishing, had sent it back
to me for my finishing touches. Ten months earlier, I had given Jack the first two
chapters to read. He read them and silently gave them back to me.

"What do you think?" I asked.

"It's nice," he said.

"Nice?"

"The writing's good."

"That's it?"

"Yes, it's nice and the writing's good."

"This is not a nice story. It's a story about how our family almost died. How can
that be nice?"

After I had peeled myself off the ceiling, the Lord showed me that Jack couldn't
afford to let himself see the depth of the pain his addiction had cost. It was just
too risky. I had a real need for him to identify with the story, but the Lord encouraged me that Jack could see it only a little bit at a time.

*For now, it will have to be enough that I know. You will have to trust Me that at the
right time, I will help Jack see what he needs to see.*

So, I kept writing the book. Jack prayed for me daily as I wrote, but he never
asked to see any more of the manuscript. Now here I was 10 months later,
putting on the finishing touches.

"Would you like to see this?" I asked.

"I wouldn't like to, but I think I need to," Jack replied.

Once again, I gave him the first two chapters to read and kept on working.
About 15 minutes later, I heard a heart-wrenching wail. I looked up and Jack had
collapsed, weeping.

"I've been such a jerk," he sobbed. "I'm so sorry. I'm so sorry. I'm so sorry."

And then it all spilled out of him. For the first time, I heard him speak from his
heart about what all this had cost us. For the first time, he was owning responsibility for his behavior. For the first time, he was surveying the devastation and
seeing beyond his pain to the pain of his family. Then we held each other, and
for the first time, we were able to cry *together* about what had happened to our
family. And it was so healing.

In the months since then, there have been some major ups and downs, but there is a resurrection occurring. On that night so many years ago, when I was ready to walk out of my marriage and God graciously intervened by showing me the passage in 1 Peter 1:3, He reminded me that He specializes in resurrections. In the years since then, I have had to believe that He could raise my marriage from the dead by faith. There was nothing my eyes could see that would prove it. But, lately, I've heard the rustling of grave clothes, and my eyes have actually seen some movement in the tomb. God is reminding me once more that He gives an ever-living hope. That fragile hope will continue to grow as long as Jack and I continue to tell ourselves the truth about who we are, how we are, and whose we are.

I plan to keep doing just that—one day at a time.

A Word from
the Battlefront

He who hath begun a good work in you will be faithful to complete it.
Philippians 1:6

G od is so faithful. I've seen it over and over as He's brought me out of my sexual addiction. Throughout the healing process, I've begun to see how He really loves us in a personal way. The God who designed and built the universe loves me, a mere speck in the universe! He loves me the way I am, but too much to allow me to stay that way.

If you have casual interest or a compulsion for any kind of pornography, please find help. Casual interest in "soft" porn can, and most often will, pull you under before you realize what's happened. It occurs slowly enough, making you unaware of the damage. You lose your self-respect, ability to reason well, ability to tell the truth, ability to give, ability to love, and ability to live a godly life.

I don't want you and your family to experience our nightmare. My casual interest in porn led to neglect, unfaithfulness, broken promises, stealing, manipulation, fear, emotional abuse, broken dreams, humiliation, embarrassment, and broken trust. It ripped our family apart. Yes, God has begun to heal us, but He never intended my wife and children to go through the pain caused by my addiction.

My wife has been writing this book for over two years now. She has gone through hell both during my addiction to porn and after, reliving it again and again by putting it into print. She has suffered more than I'll ever understand. I pray that God will show me the suffering and pain she and the children have endured. It's essential to have a strong idea of what your family has gone through in order for the addict to take responsibility, start giving back, and start healing.

My wife and children have shed many, many tears over this addiction. I pray that this book will help you heal, whether you're an addict or a victim of an addict.

I'd like to talk about my recovery—what made me want to recover and what gave me the courage to go through it.

When I experienced loneliness as a teenager, I made it worse by isolating myself. I found that looking at porn magazines was an anesthetic for loneliness. The woman smiling at me in the picture was all mine. She cared, I thought. Porn was a comfort to me because it provided a way out and was reassuring to a loner.

I wasn't willing to admit I had a problem until my wife asked for a separation. That was a wake-up call that I'll never forget. Then, while we were separated, the Lord began to show me how I'd hurt my family and how I was destroying myself, too.

Just as Nehemiah and the children of Israel needed to see the damage to Jerusalem before they could start to rebuild the wall, when I began to see how hurtful I'd been to everyone, the healing began to take place. The Lord gave me courage to go through this difficult process by showing me how much He loves me, something I'd never understood before. He gave me a vision of Jesus on the cross, and His eyes were looking directly into mine. The look on His face said, "I love you enough to die for you, yet you're not allowing Me to love you. If you will let Me, I will heal you of your past hurts so you can live freely and I can finish the good work I started in you." In the past, whenever my wife would ask me to get help, I would tell her, "I have my pride, you know." When I saw the look of love in Jesus' eyes, I saw the awfulness of my pride. I finally saw that my pride was spitting in the face of His love, and it broke me.

You might ask whether it's worth the pain and struggle to recover from sexual addiction. Why not just get along? Well, I no longer want to just get along! I want Christ to finish that good work He started in me, the work I helped put on hold. The Lord didn't put us here to just get along. We exist to give others hope and live a victorious and fruitful life. Some of the fruits have been so sweet and wonderful—for example, a pure mind. It's still going through the cleaning process, but my mind is already much better. A clear conscience is also in the works, freeing me more and more as I ask for forgiveness and make wrongs right. (Being able to problem-solve more quickly is also encouraging. I've often felt "frozen," trying to figure things out.) The guilt that I tried to carry is now in the

Lord's hands. It is freeing to be able to come to Him when I sin and ask Him to carry that guilt. Being able to talk to the Lord as He walks beside me is the best relationship I can think of. Yes, it is worth the struggle to come out of a frozen state of lust and self-centeredness.[1]

Appendixes

Characteristics of an Adult Child from a Dysfunctional Home

Write out a family tree. If you're able to, go back to your great-grand-parents on both sides. Put down your aunts, uncles, cousins, and brothers and sisters. Put down all the people who married into your family, too. Then circle anyone who was an alcoholic or used alcohol regularly; used drugs; was physically or emotionally abusive; was a homosexual, lesbian, or promiscuous; or anyone who came from a family with these kinds of behaviors. If you have several circles on your family tree, see if any of the following characteristics apply to you.

The following characteristics are those most commonly found in adult children of alcoholics and other dysfunctional families. You may find that few or many of these characteristics are present in your life, even though you have no conscious recollection of alcoholism or other dysfunction in your childhood. These characteristics are referred to in the ACA Program as *THE PROBLEM*. Read through them and circle all that apply.

1. We are isolated and afraid of authority figures.

2. We are approval seekers and lose our identity in the process.

3. We are frightened by angry people and any personal criticism.

4. We either become alcoholics, marry them, or both—or we find another compulsive personality, such as a workaholic, to fulfill our need for abandonment.

5. We live life from the viewpoint of helping and seeking victims, and we are attracted by the weakness in our love and friendship relationships.

6. We have an overdeveloped sense of responsibility, and it is easier for us to be concerned with others rather than with ourselves. This enables us to avoid looking closely at ourselves.

7. We feel guilty when we stand up for ourselves; instead, we give in to others.

8. We are addicted to excitement.

9. We confuse love with pity and tend to "love" people we can pity and rescue.

10. We stuff back our feelings from our traumatic childhoods and lose the ability to feel or to express our feelings. It hurts too much (denial).

11. We judge ourselves harshly and have a very low sense of self-esteem, sometimes compensated for by trying to appear superior.

12. We are dependent personalities who are terrified of abandonment. We will do anything to hold on to a relationship in order to avoid experiencing the pain of abandonment. We are conditioned to these types of relationships.

13. Alcoholism is a family disease, and we become para-alcoholics. We take on the characteristics of that disease even though we do not pick up the drink.

14. Para-alcoholics are reactors rather than actors.

From Friends in Recovery, *The Twelve Steps for Adult Children of Alcoholics and Other Dysfunctional Families* (San Diego: Recovery Publications, 1988).

Annotated Bibliography

Working Through Life's Difficulties

Backus, William. *Telling Each Other the Truth.* Minneapolis: Bethany House, 1985.

We all want to learn what to say, how to say it, and when to say it. This book changed my life by showing me just that. Highly recommended.

Groom, Nancy. *Married Without Masks.* Colorado Springs, Colo.: Navpress, 1989.

This book will help you understand how masking your real feelings keeps you from experiencing true intimacy in your marriage. A great resource to help you understand why things aren't working.

Intrater, Keith. *Covenant Relationships.* Shippensburg, Pa.: Destiny Image, 1989.

Although this book doesn't deal with marriage, it still helps you understand how a covenant works.

Johnson, Barbara. *Pack Up Your Gloomees in a Great Big Box.* Dallas: Word, 1993.
_____. *So, Stick a Geranium in Your Hat and Be Happy!* (Dallas: Word, 1990.

As usual, Johnson shares how to survive grief by learning to find the joy that keeps us sane.

Lerner, Harriet. *The Dance of Anger.* New York: Harper and Row, 1985.

Attempting to change another person's behavior is a self-defeating move. In this book, Lerner shows you how to take responsibility for your own behavior. She also helps you understand how anger often protects rather than challenges existing relationship dynamics. This book needs to be read with discernment since it's not written from a Christian perspective. Enjoy the meat, but make sure you spit out the bones.

Smalley, Gary, and John Trent. *The Blessing*. Nashville: Thomas Nelson, 1986.

Living with someone who's caught up in himself or herself keeps us from experiencing the affirmation we all long for. This book shows how to work through that so you can give affirmation to others.

Working Through Bondages

Allender, Dan B., and Tremper Longman III. *Bold Love*. Colorado Springs, Colo.: Navpress, 1992.

I wept when I read this book. Finally, someone was talking about what I had been trying to do for so many years. Allender and Longman help you understand the difference between dealing with a fool, an ordinary sinner, and an evil person. Essential reading.

Anderson, Neil T. *Bondage Breaker*. Eugene, Ore.: Harvest House, 1990.

How to overcome negative thoughts, irrational feelings, and habitual sins. Highly recommended.

_____. *Victory Over the Darkness*. Ventura, Calif.: Regal Books, 1990.

An excellent book about realizing the power of your identity in Christ. Highly recommended.

Friends in Recovery, *The Twelve Steps for Adult Children of Alcoholics and Other Dysfunctional Families*. San Diego: Recovery Publications, 1988.

An excellent book that shows how those living with an addict are affected.

Jakes, T. D. *Woman, Thou Art Loosed!* Shippensburg, Pa.: Destiny Image, 1993.

Jakes's book is a special comfort to abused women.

Littauer, Florence. *Your Personality Tree*. Dallas: Word, 1986.

Littauer shows how family relationships and circumstances can affect your personality.

Littauer, Fred, and Florence Littauer. *Freeing Your Mind from the Memories That Bind*. Nashville: Thomas Nelson, 1988.

The Littauers identify the symptoms of childhood trauma and offer biblical steps toward restoration through Jesus Christ.

Seamands, David A. *Healing for Damaged Emotions*. Wheaton, Ill.: Victor Books, 1988.

This was the first book that gave me some understanding of what was going on inside me. Highly recommended.

Smedes, Lewis B. *Forgive and Forget*. New York: Simon and Schuster, 1984.

Smedes shows you how to move from hurting to healing. Highly recommended.

_____. *Shame and Grace: Healing the Shame We Don't Deserve*. San Francisco: Zondervan, 1993.

This book helps you work through the undeserved shame that comes when others hurt you.

Working Through Sexual Issues

Carothers, Merlin. *What's on Your Mind?* Escondido, Calif.: Merlin R. Carothers, 1984.

Carothers discusses our thought life and gives some powerful ways to gain control of it.

Hession, Roy. *Forgotten Factors*. Fort Washington, Pa.: Christian Literature Crusade, 1976.

An aid to deeper repentance of the forgotten factors of sexual misbehavior.

Laaser, Mark R. *Faithful and True: Sexual Integrity in a Fallen World* [formerly titled *The Secret Sin*]. Grand Rapids: Zondervan, 1992.

Highly recommended reading.

Payne, Leanne. *The Broken Image*. Wheaton, Ill.: Crossway, 1981.

In this excellent book, Payne explains the root of most sexual addictions. She then shows how to invite Christ in to minister healing to the sex addict. Highly recommended.

White, John. *Eros Defiled*. Downer's Grove, Ill.: InterVarsity Press, 1977.

In this frank book, White looks at how God's plan for sex is defiled by premarital sex, extramarital sex, masturbation, homosexuality, and various forms of perverted sex.

_____. *Eros Redeemed*. Downer's Grove, Ill.: InterVarsity Press, 1993.

This book offers a way to receive God's grace to free one from the stranglehold of sexual sin.

Christian Growth

Covey, Stephen R. *The Seven Habits of Highly Effective People*. New York: Simon and Schuster, 1989.

Next to the Bible, this is the most transformational book I've ever read. Step by step, Covey explains how to change from the inside out. His thoughts are simple, but the results are powerful. This is a secular book, but it is profoundly biblical in its understanding of how we work. Essential reading.

Greig, Gary S., and Kevin N. Springer, eds. *The Kingdom and the Power*. Ventura, Calif.: Regal Books, 1993.

In this book, noted scholars such as Dr. Jeffrey Niehaus, Dr. J. I. Packer, Dr. Wayne Grudem, and Dr. John White take an in-depth look at the healing power of the cross.

Sherrer, Quin, and Ruthanne Garlock. *A Woman's Guide to Spiritual Warfare and the Spiritual Warrior's Prayer Guide*. Ann Arbor, Mich.: Servant, 1991.

This book reinforces the importance of the power of prayer. Recommended reading.

Stanley, Charles. *How to Listen to God*. Nashville: Thomas Nelson, 1985.

Wagner, Peter C. *Warfare Prayer*. Ventura, Calif.: Regal Books, 1992.

Although this book deals with praying for regions, there are some excellent insights into the nature and struggle of prayer. Highly recommended.

Wallis, Arthur. *God's Chosen Fast*. Fort Washington, Pa.: Christian Literature Crusade, 1968.

This is the "thin" volume on fasting that helped me learn about this forgotten discipline.

Learning More About Pornography

Books

Kirk, Jerry R. *The Mind Polluters.* Nashville: Thomas Nelson, 1985.

Dr. Kirk is the president of the National Coalition Against Pornography. In this book, he explains the problem and provides a step-by-step plan to combat pornography in your community.

Minnery, Tom, ed. *Pornography: A Human Tragedy.* Wheaton, Ill.: Tyndale House, 1987.

Charles Colson, James Dobson, and C. Everett Koop are contributors to this book that shows how pornography hurts real people.

Schlafly, Phyllis, ed. *Pornography's Victims: Excerpts from the Official Transcript of Proceedings of the Attorney General's Commission on Pornography.* Westchester, Ill.: Crossway, 1987.

Organizations

The American Family Association
107 Parkgate
P.O. Drawer 2440
Tupelo, Mississippi 38803
1-800-FAMILIES

This excellent organization is the premier place to get good research on pornography. They have also recently started an OutReach division to help those with sexual addictions.

Enough Is Enough
P.O. Box 888
Fairfax, Virginia 22030
(703) 278-8343

Dee Jepsen heads this organization that helps women take action against child pornography, hard-core pornography, and other illegal pornography in their local communities.

Morality in Media
Robert W. Peters, President
475 Riverside Drive
New York, NY 10115
(212) 870-3222
   The purpose of this organization is to protect children and teenagers from pornography in the media. It sponsors the "Real Men Don't Use Porn" billboard campaign.

National Coalition Against Pornography
Dr. Jerry Kirk, President
800 Compton Road, Suite 9224
Cincinnati, Ohio 45231
(513) 521-6227
   This organization offers training resources, videos, organizational materials, audiocassettes, and research reports for use in the battle against pornography.

National Family Legal Foundation
11000 N. Scottsdale Road, Suite 144
Scottsdale, AZ 85254
(602) 922-9731
   This organization is available for help dealing with obscenity and child pornography.

New Creation Ministries
2513 W. Shaw, No. 102A
Fresno, CA 93711
(209) 227-1066
   This organization reaches out to the homosexual community and those involved in infidelity and sexual or pornography addictions.

Music

Music has the amazing ability to minister to the deepest parts of our beings. The tapes below were life-giving for me. When I didn't have the strength to pray, I'd put on one of them and sing my heart out. They always reestablished my connection with God by reminding me that God was in control and He cared about how much I was hurting.

Steve Green

I used Steve Green's tapes extensively. I found their scriptural soundness kept me grounded when I was tempted to cave in to my circumstances. Try singing along and then pausing the tape after each song to thank God for the character qualities that song celebrated. This simple exercise will lift your personal worship time to a new level and remind you in a way that nothing else can that God is *able* to deliver you.

He Holds the Keys
For God and God Alone
Hymns: A Portrait of Christ
A Mighty Fortress

David Meese

David Meese sings about the struggle of living with an addict. His music will help you get in touch with some of the hidden pain.

Learning to Trust
Odyssey

Twila Paris

Twila Paris's honesty about the struggles of life helped give me courage to go on.

Cry for the Desert
Sanctuary

Good for General Praise and Worship

All Hail King Jesus—Integrity Music
Psalms Alive!—Maranatha Music
Psalms Alive! 2—Maranatha Music
Rejoice, Sing Praise—Brentwood Records
Sing Praise—Brentwood Records
Vineyard Psalms, Vol. 1—Vineyard Music Group

Notes

Chapter 2

1. Testimony before the Attorney General's Commission on Pornography, cited in Tom Minnery, ed., *Pornography: A Human Tragedy* (Wheaton, Ill.: Tyndale House, 1987), p. 165.

2. Eugene H. Peterson, *The Message* (Colorado Springs, Colo.: Navpress, 1995).

3. Sex-addict therapist Patrick Carnes in an interview on National Public Radio's program *Voices in the Family,* Jan. 30, 1996.

4. *Lowell* (Mass.) *Sun,* Jan. 29, 1995, p. 1.

5. Keith Stone, *Los Angeles Daily News,* reprinted in Jan. 29, 1995, *Lowell Sun,* p. 46.

Chapter 3

1. Dan B. Allender and Tremper Longman III, *Bold Love* (Colorado Springs, Colo.: Navpress, 1992), p. 30.

2. Conclusion of a study by Prof. James Weaver, University of Kentucky. Weaver said, "Men who watched sex scenes from selected R-rated movies—especially scenes between consenting adults or sex initiated by women—developed a loss of respect for women and believed women to be more sexually permissive or promiscuous than they had imagined before the viewings. Both men and women who watched the sex scenes from the movies favored lighter penalties against a convicted rapist." Cited in *Pornography: A Report* (Tupelo, Miss.: American Family Association, 1989), p. 2.

257

Chapter 4

1. The Rev. Dr. Craig Bensen said this in a personal conversation with me in October 1995.

2. Eugene H. Peterson, *The Message* (Colorado Springs, Colo.: Navpress, 1995).

3. Actually, I was right. God was casting down the strongholds. It's just that He has to use a battering ram sometimes, and it takes repeated blows to even make a crack in a fortress that has been as carefully constructed as the stronghold Jack was hiding in. The Lord gave me a picture. He showed me that the first time Jack lied or looked at pornography, it was as if a thin thread of bondage wrapped itself around him. If he'd simply confessed what he'd done, he could have easily broken that thread. But each time he repeated the lies and viewing the pornography, a thicker rope of bondage wrapped itself around him. Even so, with a bit of a struggle, he probably could have broken free. But his lies and porn viewing were repeated so many times that the bondage became like a great thick chain that bound him from head to toe. Eventually, he was totally incapable of breaking free. Now someone skilled in using a welding torch had to be called in to cut him free. Soon sparks were flying and chunks of chain were whizzing through the air.

I hope you noticed the progression of the answer to my prayers from 2 Corinthians 10:3–7. First God dealt with anything that I was doing that was getting in the way of His ability to work in Jack's life. Then He went to work by uncovering the things Jack was doing that were secretive. If a wife doesn't understand that uncovering is a vital part to the answer to her prayers, she can find it unnerving. This is because suddenly you are aware of things you never knew before. You wish you had never known them because the knowing can cause greater initial anxiety than the ignorance (as the old saying goes, "Ignorance is bliss").

Uncovering will probably happen in stages. It starts with only one or two people becoming aware of the problem. This is God's grace. He doesn't reveal our failures to a broader audience who doesn't care about us until He has given us an opportunity to repent in a smaller circle of people who really love us. For a long time, I was the only one aware that there were problems. For example, Larry never knew that Jack lied to me about the car. When Jack refused to deal with things, the Lord began uncovering him to others. His boss caught him in lies; other people became aware that he was no longer able to think clearly. The consequences of Jack's lies and behavior were big. He was fired. That's how much God loved Jack. It's not easy to be loved like that.

You know that phrase "All hell broke loose"? There is a lot of truth in that statement. The Lord showed me that when He uncovers something that has been hidden, all hell literally breaks loose. It's like this: Suppose you have a nice carpet on your living room floor, but there are all these lumps in it. Over the years, you've learned where each one is and you've gotten so skillful at navigating your way through them that you're barely aware they're there. But they are, and one day you realize you're tired of the extra effort those lumps require. You know you've got to get rid of them, so you pull back the carpet. Your immediate reaction is to gasp and say, "I had no idea *that* was under there."

You bring someone in to pry up the crud that has welded itself to your floor because it's been under the rug for so many years. As he pries, stuff starts flying around. Some of it might even hit you. Things now look a whole lot worse than they did before you pulled back the carpet. They are certainly more dangerous. But they are also moving in the right direction. The hold that hell has had on your life is breaking loose. If you focus on the chunks that are hitting you, it's easy to feel you're under assault. But if you look at the place on the floor where the lumps have been and notice that they're breaking up, you realize you're under deliverance. If you know this, you can hold fast when the trials come—you see that they are a necessary part of the answer to your prayers.

Chapter 5

1. Neil T. Anderson, *Victory Over the Darkness* (Ventura, Calif.: Regal Books, 1990), pp. 71–72.

2. Appeals are made on the basis of Matthew 18:15–20. I had already gone to Jack one-on-one; now I was bringing in the additional witnesses. I purposely chose Jack's dad because he had witnessed our covenant vows. I was calling on the authority of covenant (see chapter 8).

Chapter 6

1. Dan B. Allender and Tremper Longman III, *Bold Love* (Colorado Springs, Colo: Navpress, 1992), p. 242.

Chapter 7

1. Harold M. Voth, M.D., "The Psychological and Social Effects of Pornography," in *Pornography: A Report* (Tupelo, Miss.: American Family Association, 1989), p. 8.

2. *The Report of the Commission on Obscenity and Pornography* (Toronto: Bantam, 1970), p. 159.

3. Research on memory done by psychologist James L. McGaugh at the University of California suggests that experiences that occurred at times of emotional arousal (which could include sexual arousal) get "locked into the brain by an adrenal gland hormone, epinephrine, and are difficult to erase." Cited in Victor B. Cline, *Pornography's Effects on Adults and Children* (New York: Morality in Media, n.d.), p. 7.

4. There is much research that shows that pornography addiction is both progressive in nature and destructive of our mental capacities. Among the researchers who have discussed this are Dr. Victor Cline, professor of psychology at University of Utah, and Dr. Harold M. Voth, on the faculty at Karl Menninger School of Psychiatry, Topeka.

   Dr. Cline has said, "It is difficult for non-addicts to comprehend the totally driven nature of a sex addict. When the 'wave' hits them, these men are consumed by their appetite, regardless of the costs or consequences. Their addiction virtually rules their lives."

   For more information, see Cline, *Pornography's Effects,* which includes an in-depth discussion of Dr. Cline's views on pornography; or Tom Minnery, ed., *Pornography: A Human Tragedy* (Wheaton, Ill.: Tyndale House, 1987), which looks at studies by preeminent social scientists on the destructive power of pornography.

5. Voth, "Psychological and Social Effects of Pornography," p. 9.

Chapter 8

1. Keith Intrater, *Covenant Relationships* (Shippensburg, Pa.: Destiny Image, 1989), p. 13.

2. Ibid., p. 19.

3. Ibid., p. 20.

4. Numbers 35:30; Deuteronomy 17:6,7; Deuteronomy 19:15; Ruth 4:9–11; Isaiah 43:9; Jeremiah 32:10,12,25,44; Matthew 18:16; and 1 Timothy 5:19 are among the many passages that talk about the importance of having at least two witnesses to testify about what happened before someone can be judged guilty.

5. The lines of inheritance in Great Britain's royal family are important to the nation's sense of identity. Every man and woman who sits on the throne must be able to prove royal lineage. So even today, it is against the law in Great Britain to sleep with the wife of the heir to the throne, lest a bastard be conceived and usurp it. Unfortunately, the British have not held their kings to the same standard they expect of their queens.

6. Tom Minnery, ed., *Pornography: A Human Tragedy* (Wheaton, Ill.: Tyndale House, 1987), p. 137.

7. *Pornography: A Report* (Tupelo, Miss.: American Family Association, 1989), p. 2.

Chapter 9

1. Tom Minnery, ed., *Pornography: A Human Tragedy* (Wheaton, Ill.: Tyndale House, 1987), p. 137.

2. *Pornography: A Report* (Tupelo, Miss.: American Family Association, 1989), p. 3. This statistic shows a difference in the Canadian market and the U.S. market. As mentioned earlier, the President's Commission on Obscenity and Pornography found that the primary market for pornography in the United States were white, middle-class married men.

3. David Larson, Mary Ann Mayo, Joseph Mayo, and Paul Meier, "Behind Closed Doors," unpublished manuscript.

4. "Redbook Survey on Female Sexuality," *Redbook* 145 (Sept. 1975): 54. See also Michael Newcomb, "Sexual Behavior of Cohabitors: A Comparison of Three Independent Samples," *The Journal of Sex Research* 22 (Nov. 1986): 492–513; and "Sex: The Ultimate Survey—2,400 Women and Men Go All the Way," *Mademoiselle* (June 1993):132.

5. Karl Menninger, *Love Against Hate* (New York: Harcourt, Brace, 1942), pp. 72–73.

6. Joseph C. Dillow, *Solomon on Sex* (New York: Thomas Nelson, 1977), p. 162.

7. Clifford Penner and Joyce Penner, *The Gift of Sex* (Waco, Tex.: Word, 1981), p. 270. This quote is a paraphrase of two sentences.

8. Minnery, ed., *Pornography: A Human Tragedy*, p. 325.

9. Phyllis Schlafly, ed., *Pornography's Victims: Excerpts from the Official Transcript of Proceedings of the Attorney General's Commission on Pornography* (Westchester, Ill.: Crossway, 1987), p. 50.

10. Minnery, ed., *Pornography: A Human Tragedy*, p. 325.

11. *Family Policy* 6 (Feb. 1994). Published by Family Research Council, Washington, D.C.

12. Penner and Penner, *Gift of Sex*, p. 79.

13. Ibid.

14. Deborah Wilson, "Study Shows the Harmful Effects of Non-violent Pornography," in *Pornography: A Report*, p. 2.

15. "Study Finds Strong Correlation Between Pornography and Rape," in *Pornography: A Report*, p. 3.

16. Ibid.

17. Minnery, ed., *Pornography: A Human Tragedy*, p. 72.

18. Ibid., p. 134.

19. Ibid.

20. Ibid., p. 135.

21. Wilson, "Study Shows Harmful Effects," in *Pornography: A Report*, p. 2.

22. Alan Combs Show, "Interview with Hugh Hefner," Oct. 2, 1994.

23. Schlafly, *Pornography's Victims*, pp. 91–96. Brenda's extensive testimony has been summarized.

24. Ibid., pp. 39–49. Sara's extensive testimony has been summarized.

25. Victor B. Cline, *Pornography's Effects on Adults and Children* (New York: Morality in Media, n.d.), p. 13.

Chapter 10

1. Thomas Moore, *Care of the Soul* (New York: Harper Perennial, 1992), p. 12.

2. Mark R. Laaser, *Faithful and True: Sexual Integrity in a Fallen World* [formerly titled *The Secret Sin*] (Grand Rapids: Zondervan, 1992), p. 26.

Chapter 11

1. Victor B. Cline, *Pornography's Effects on Adults and Children* (New York: Morality in Media, n.d.), p. 12.

2. Tom Minnery, ed., *Pornography: A Human Tragedy* (Wheaton, Ill.: Tyndale House, 1987), p. 338.

3. "I would say that about 80 to 90 percent of the models delve into cocaine, and definitely use pot and alcohol. I have seen producers, directors, and photographers hand out coke on the set to relax the girls—to entice them into doing scenes they don't really want to do. And many of the models themselves bring drugs for relaxation between scenes." George, a former porn film star, testifying before the Attorney General's Commission on Pornography. Cited in Minnery, ed., *Pornography: A Human Tragedy,* pp. 181–182.

4. Amy Harmon, "The 'Seedy' Side of CD-ROMS," *Los Angeles Times,* Nov. 29, 1993.

5. Patrick J. Buchanan and J. Gordon Muir, "Gay Times and Diseases," *The American Spectator* (Aug. 1984):15–18. Cited in Minnery, ed., *Pornography: A Human Tragedy,* p. 65.

6. *Pornography: A Report* (Tupelo, Miss.: American Family Association, 1989), pp. 3–4.

7. Because this job was repetitive in nature and because the repetitions had to occur quickly, doing these simple tasks worked almost like "physical therapy" for Jack's mind. He would come home literally dripping with sweat because it had been so hard for him to concentrate. But as the weeks passed, his mind started to function better. At the same time he was working at this job, he was spending a lot of time meditating on Scripture. Every morning, he would spend about 20 minutes "visualizing" a Bible passage, such as John 5:2–9 or John 8:2–11. He would think about those passages until they became as real and riveting to him as the fantasies that had previously gripped his mind. These two activities began to heal him. Recently, he was offered a job as an assistant to the engineer in this same chocolate factory. It's a position far lower in pay and status than the one he left, but it is far higher than assembly-line work and he has the opportunity to move up. Although Jack still has periods when his mind is terribly confused, he is steadily regaining skills in problem solving. It's wonderful to see him restored.

8. Minnery, ed., *Pornography: A Human Tragedy,* p. 139.

Chapter 12

1. Leanne Payne, *The Broken Image* (Wheaton, Ill.: Crossway, 1981), p. 89.

2. Ed Murphy, *The Handbook for Spiritual Warfare* (Nashville: Thomas Nelson, 1992), p. 123.

3. "Reading Penthouse Linked to High-Hostile and Sex Fantasies," in *Pornography: A Report* (Tupelo, Miss.: American Family Association, 1989), p. 3.

4. Dr. Ron Miller made this comment during a counseling session Jack and I had with him. His wife, Ardyce Miller, who became the executive director of Freedom Ministries after Ron died, agrees with the statement.

5. Victor B. Cline, "The Current Status of Research on Pornography's Effects on Human Behavior," in *Pornography: A Report*, p. 11. Emphasis added.

6. Murphy, *Spiritual Warfare*, p. 122.

7. William S. Banowsky, *It's a Playboy World* (Old Tappan, N.J.: Fleming H. Revell, 1969), p. 78. Cited in Tom Minnery, ed., *Pornography: A Human Tragedy* (Wheaton, Ill.: Tyndale House, 1987), pp. 63–64. Emphasis added.

8. Payne, *Broken Image*, p. 89.

9. Thomas C. Oden, *Game Free: A Guide to the Meaning of Intimacy* (New York: Harper and Row, 1974), p. 23. Cited in Minnery, ed., *Pornography: A Human Tragedy*, p. 65.

10. Payne, *Broken Image*, p. 55.

11. Ibid., p. 59.

12. *Pornography: A Report*, p. 11.

13. Victor B. Cline, *Pornography's Effects on Adults and Children* (New York: Morality in Media, n.d.), p. 13.

14. Mark R. Laaser, *Faithful and True: Sexual Integrity in a Fallen World* [formerly titled *The Secret Sin*] (Grand Rapids: Zondervan, 1992), pp. 28–29.

15. C. S. Lewis to a Mr. Masson, Mar. 6, 1956, Wade Collection, Wheaton College, Wheaton, Ill. Cited in Payne, *Broken Image,* pp. 91–92.

Chapter 13

1. *The New Dictionary of Thoughts,* originally compiled by Tryon Edwards, revised and enlarged by C. N. Catrevas and Jonathan Edwards (New York: Standard Book Company, 1955), p. 120.

2. Eugene H. Peterson, *The Message* (Colorado Springs, Colo.: Navpress, 1995).

3. Roy Hession, *Forgotten Factors in Adultery* (Fort Washington, Pa.: Christian Literature Crusade, 1976), p. 36.

4. Ibid.

5. Ed Murphy, *The Handbook for Spiritual Warfare* (Nashville: Thomas Nelson, 1992), pp. 151–152. This quote has been abridged.

6. See 1 Corinthians 15:45–46, John 6:48–51, and Romans 1:20.

7. Dr. Durham related this information in personal correspondence with me after I sent him this chapter for evaluation.

8. Dr. Gary Durham and Dr. Ronald Miller, *Principles of Restoration* (Hyde Park, Vt.: Entrust Media for Freedom Ministries. 1994). This quote was on a handout distributed during a seminar sponsored by Freedom Ministries.

9. Ronald Miller, *Personality Traits of the Carnal Mind* (Hyde Park, Vt.: Entrust Media for Freedom Ministries, n.d.), p. 53.

10. Peterson, *The Message.*

Chapter 14

1. Stephen R. Covey, *The Seven Habits of Highly Effective People* (New York: Simon and Schuster, 1989), p. 70.

2. I don't know to whom to attribute these definitions. I had them copied in my notes, and they were so transformational that they stuck with me.

3. Keith Intrater, *Covenant Relationships* (Shippensburg, Pa.: Destiny Image, 1989), p. 79.

Chapter 15

1. Keith Intrater, *Covenant Relationships* (Shippensburg, Pa.: Destiny Image, 1989), p. 28.

2. Ibid.

Chapter 16

1. Noah Webster, *1828 Dictionary of the English Language* (San Francisco: Foundation for American Christian Education, 1987), n.p.

2. "Venereal Disease," *World Book Encyclopedia* (Chicago: World Book, 1983), 20:239.

3. Alan Combs Show, "Interview with Hugh Hefner," Oct. 2, 1994.

Chapter 17

1. Tryon Edwards, *The New Dictionary of Thoughts* (New York: Standard Book, 1955), p. 501.

Chapter 18

1. Watchman Nee, *The Spiritual Man* (New York: Christian Fellowship, 1977), p. 111.

2. Some wives have resorted to drugs to numb the self-condemnation. In *Sexual Idolatry,* recovering sex addict Steve Gallagher told how his wife began using amphetamines to deal with the anguish she was experiencing. "The more I became obsessed with sex, the more she reverted to drugs," he wrote. In Gallagher, *Sexual Idolatry* (Crittenden, Ky.: Pure Life Press, 1986), p. 136.

Chapter 19

1. Rosalie J. Slater, *Teaching and Learning America's Christian History* (San Francisco: Foundation for American Christian Education, 1987), p. 225.

2. Eugene H. Peterson, *The Message* (Colorado Springs, Colo.: Navpress, 1995).

3. Mark R. Laaser, *Faithful and True: Sexual Integrity in a Fallen World* [formerly titled *The Secret Sin]* (Grand Rapids: Zondervan, 1992), p. 170.

Chapter 20

1. The Rev. Charlie Guest made this statement in a seminar on spiritual warfare held at Cambridge United Church, Cambridge, Vt., in the summer of 1995.

2. Neal Clement said this in a personal conversation with me in November 1995.

Chapter 21

1. Watchman Nee, *The Spiritual Man* (New York: Christian Fellowship, 1977), p. 115.

2. In her testimony before the Attorney General's Commission on Pornography, Dorchan Leidnoldt said, "Pornographers promote and sexualize the abuse of little girls. They don't have to actually use real little girls to do this. What they can do is find young-looking adult women and dress them up as children. The message is the same. The little girls are sex objects who delight in sex with adult men, who seduce the adult men, who, most important of all, aren't harmed by sex with adults. This is the connection between sexual abuse of children and pornography.

   "This is child pornography [she said, referring to a picture she showed the panel]. We have seen a lot of this. It's made to look as authentic as possible, perhaps because this is real documentation of the abuse of real children in their bedrooms. This is how magazines like *Playboy* and *Penthouse* and *Hustler* eroticize little girls, turn little girls into targets of sexual abuse. The caption reads: 'You call that being molested?' The idea is, this middle-aged man couldn't satisfy this sexually voracious child."

   Judith Reisman, a researcher at American University, analyzed the extent to which children were sexualized in every issue of *Playboy, Penthouse,* and *Hustler* from 1954 to 1984 (683 issues in all). Reisman found an average of 8.2 times in each issue of *Playboy,* 6.4 times in each issue of *Penthouse,* and 14.1 times in each issue of *Hustler.* Cited in Tom Minnery, ed., *Pornography: A Human Tragedy* (Wheaton, Ill.: Tyndale House, 1987), pp. 59, 136.

Chapter 23

1. Neal Clement related these comments in a personal conversation with me about this issue.

2. "Porn-Sex Crime Connection Shown in Additional Studies," in *Pornography: A Report* (Tupelo, Miss.: American Family Association, n.d.), p. 4.

3. Paraphrased from Rick Renner, *Dressed to Kill* (Tulsa: Pillar Books, 1991), p. 229.

4. *World Book Encyclopedia* (Chicago: World Book, 1983), 17:225.

Chapter 24

1. Keith Intrater, *Covenant Relationships* (Shippensburg, Pa.: Destiny Image, 1989), p. 16.

2. Eugene H. Peterson, *The Message* (Colorado Springs, Colo.: Navpress, 1995), p. 362.

3. Spiro Zodhiates, *The Greek-Hebrew Key Study Bible* (Grand Rapids: Baker Book House, 1984), p. 1723.

4. Dorothy Sayers coined this phrase.

Chapter 25

1. Lewis B. Smedes, *Shame and Grace: Healing the Shame We Don't Deserve* (San Francisco: Zondervan, 1993), p. 164.

2. When my doctor's assistant handed me this sheet, it had no source notation on it. I've tried unsuccessfully to find out who wrote it. I regret that I'm not able to give him or her proper recognition because his or her thoughts have been so helpful to me.

Epilogue

1. Dan B. Allender and Tremper Longman III, *Bold Love* (Colorado Springs, Colo.: Navpress, 1992), p. 156.

Jack's Story

1. I am so grateful for the prayers and love of my wife, children, parents, siblings, and a buddy named Fred, as well as many others. They have been so faithful, and I can't thank them enough. Prayer does work!